Architecture and Systems Ecology

Modern buildings are both wasteful machines that can be made more efficient and instruments of the massive, metropolitan system engendered by the power of high-quality fuels. A comprehensive method of environmental design must reconcile the techniques of efficient building design with the radical urban and economic reorganization that we face. Over the coming century, we will be challenged to return to the renewable resource base of the eighteenth-century city with the knowledge, technologies, and expectations of the twenty-first-century metropolis.

This book explores the architectural implications of systems ecology, which extends the principles of thermodynamics from the nineteenth-century focus on more efficient machinery to the contemporary concern with the resilient self-organization of ecosystems.

Written with enough technical material to explain the methods, it does not include in-text equations or calculations, relying instead on the energy system diagrams to convey the argument. *Architecture and Systems Ecology* has minimal technical jargon and an emphasis on intelligible design conclusions, making it suitable for architecture students and professionals who are engaged with the fundamental issues faced by sustainable design.

The energy systems language provides a holistic context for the many kinds of performance already evaluated in architecture—from energy use to material selection and even the choice of building style. It establishes the foundation for environmental principles of design that embrace the full complexity of our current situation. Architecture succeeds best when it helps shape, accommodate, and represent new ways of living together.

William W. Braham FAIA is a Professor of Architecture at the University of Pennsylvania, where he is Director of the Master of Environmental Building Design. He received an engineering degree from Princeton University and an M.Arch. and Ph.D.Arch. from the University of Pennsylvania. Braham is Director of the TC Chan Center, a faculty research unit on energy and environment in the built environment. Recent projects include the Sustainability Plan, Carbon Footprint, and Carbon Reduction Action Plan for the university. His publications include *Rethinking Technology* (2006), *Energy and Architecture* (2013), and *Energy Accounts* (2016).

"In a context in which energy efficiency inexplicably and erroneously remains the sole architectural consideration of energy, *Architecture and Systems Ecology* is a superb, and necessary, contribution towards advancing the design and discourse of energy systems in architecture. From salient principles to their application, Braham provides a cogent explication of the latent power of the thermodynamics of building. These principles have yet to transform our collective modes of reasoning and imagination for energy systems, but soon will."

Kiel Moe, Harvard University Graduate School of Design, USA

"Comprehensive and accessible, *Architecture and Systems Ecology* presents environmental building design as both a technical and a social challenge. With solid scientific foundations in thermodynamics and ecology, and understanding buildings as physical shelters, life settings and urban sites, this important book goes beyond energy efficiency to propose principles of sustainable construction for contemporary cities. If Vitruvius established *firmitas, utilitas* and *venustas* as the basis of sound architecture, Braham offers a new triad for the twenty-first century: shelter, setting and site."

Luis Fernández-Galiano, Int FRIBA, Professor of Architecture, Universidad Politécnica de Madrid, Spain

"*Architecture and Systems Ecology* presents a new and challenging perspective on the relationship of architecture and environment in the twenty-first century. The book skillfully embraces themes from the theory of thermodynamics, systems ecology and the humanities to construct a comprehensive strategy for action."

Dean Hawkes, Darwin College, University of Cambridge, UK

"William Braham has produced a rare work of exceptional imaginative and scholarly integration. He effortlessly bridges the concepts of thermodynamics, systems ecology, building science, envelope performance, water supply, waste and waste water treatment and reuse, building material selection, transportation, environmental economics and urban spatial theory; giving a history of their formative principles by seminal authors. He has developed an ecological system for the built environment, using the concept of e(m)ergy (embodied energy) from systems ecology, as a more realistic form of environmental accounting to evaluate building performance across three scales of operation: shelter, setting and site. He has created, no less, a comprehensive framework for evaluating architectural design ideas that takes into account the full complexity of designing a more sustainable, self-organizing future. This is a must read for all serious environmentalists."

Harrison Fraker, Dean Emeritus and Professor of Architecture and Urban Design, College of Environmental Design, UC Berkeley, USA

Architecture and Systems Ecology
Thermodynamic principles of environmental building design, in three parts

William W. Braham

LONDON AND NEW YORK

First published 2016
by Routledge
2 Park Square, Milton Park, Abingdon, Oxon OX14 4RN

and by Routledge
711 Third Avenue, New York, NY 10017

Routledge is an imprint of the Taylor & Francis Group, an informa business

© 2016 William W. Braham

The right of William W. Braham to be identified as author of this work has been asserted by him in accordance with sections 77 and 78 of the Copyright, Designs and Patents Act 1988.

All rights reserved. No part of this book may be reprinted or reproduced or utilized in any form or by any electronic, mechanical, or other means, now known or hereafter invented, including photocopying and recording, or in any information storage or retrieval system, without permission in writing from the publishers.

Trademark notice: Product or corporate names may be trademarks or registered trademarks, and are used only for identification and explanation without intent to infringe.

British Library Cataloguing-in-Publication Data
A catalogue record for this book is available from the British Library

Library of Congress Cataloging-in-Publication Data
[CIP data]

ISBN: 978-1-138-84605-0 (hbk)
ISBN: 978-1-138-84607-4 (pbk)
ISBN: 978-1-315-72772-1 (ebk)

Typeset in Bembo
by Keystroke, Station Road, Codsall, Wolverhampton

Contents

	List of figures	ix
	List of tables	xvii
	Preface	xix
	INTRODUCTION	**3**
	Wealth and power	4
	Synergy and correalism	5
	Glass walls	8
	Ecotopia	16
1	**Environments of maximum power**	**21**
	Accounting for a living, self-organizing environment	22
	Thermodynamics of living systems	24
	Limitations of efficiency: the roles of entropy and exergy	26
	Bioenergetics	31
	Maximum power	39
	Hierarchies of production and e[m]ergy	41
	Material cycles and the pulsing of systems	49
	System principles in the built environment	54
	Self-organization	54

Contents

2		**Buildings in three parts**	**61**
		Three aspects of buildings: site, shelter, setting	62
		The Ellis House	66
3		**Building-as-shelter**	**69**
		Building construction	70
		Accounting	72
		Disposal and recycling	76
		Layers and longevities of construction	79
		Climate modification	80
		Bioclimatic approach	82
		Mechanical approach	90
		Ventilation and waste processing	98
		Illumination: windows and lamps	104
		Wasting waste heat	110
		A thermodynamic minimum	115
4		**Building-as-setting for the work of living**	**125**
		Material services	127
		Water supply	130
		Wastewater treatment	132
		Food supply	135
		Supplies and solid waste	136
		Concentrated power	139
		Fuels	141
		Electricity	145
		Information	147
		Currency	150
		The work of living	152

Contents

5	**Building-as-site in urban and economic locations**	**161**
	Spatial hierarchies: urban self-organization	163
	Evaluating location	179
	Design for location	183
	Social and economic hierarchies	183
	Cultural evolution	186
	The common good	192
	The slow and the fast of location	192
6	**Design of thermodynamic narratives**	**199**
	Design methods at multiple (or at least three) scales	204
	Shelter	206
	Setting	207
	Site	208
	Thermodynamic principles for environmental building design: a conclusion	210
	Three points of leverage	211
	Building well	212
	Appendix A: Energy systems language	**215**
	Appendix B: E[m]ergy synthesis of the Ellis House	**219**
	Index	**247**

List of figures

I.1 The all-glass wall exemplifies the almost magical capabilities of the materials and conditioning systems that were developed through the twentieth century and allow us to experience the climate of our cities as a kind of visual backdrop to contemporary life   2
Hancock Observatory, © 2014 Tribune News Service.
All rights reserved Distributed by Tribune Content Agency, LLC

I.2 Diagram of correalism showing the continuous evolution between human (H), technological (T), and natural (N) environments   7
Frederick Kiesler, *Architectural Record*, 1939

I.3 Active glass wall: Le Corbusier, heating pipes between two layers of glass to "neutralize" the wall, Maison Citrohan, Stuttgart, 1927   10
© F.L.C./ADAGP, Paris/Artists Rights Society (ARS), New York

I.4 Active glass wall: William Lescaze, double-envelope construction to moderate climate and control condensation   11
Alfred L. Loomis House, Tuxedo Park, NY, 1937

I.5 Active glass wall: Cannon Design, responsive horizontal shades in ventilated zone between layers of glass   12
Occidental Chemical, Niagara Falls, NY, 1981

I.6 Active glass wall: Foster Associates, double box window adjustable for ventilation, viewed from plant-filled atrium, Commerzbank, Frankfurt, 1997
Photo: Danijela Weißgraeber   13

List of figures

I.7 François Dallegret, The Environment-Bubble: Transparent Plastic Bubble Dome Inflated by Air-Conditioning Output showing architecture as a "fit environment for human activities," from Reyner Banham, "A Home Is Not a House," *Art in America*, April 1965   15
© 1965 François Dallegret

1.1 Two scales of environmental self-organization, weather, and urban settlements. A nighttime view of Tropical Storm Isaac and the cities near the Gulf Coast of the United States, August 28, 2012   20
NASA, Visible Infrared Imaging Radiometer Suite (VIIRS) image from Suomi-NPP satellite

1.2 Sunlight converted into three different qualities of energy: into daylight through windows, hot water through vertical solar-thermal collectors, and electricity through photovoltaic panels   28
Solar Decathlon, University of Cincinnati, 2007

1.3 Four boundaries of analysis for evaluating the upstream costs of materials, products, and services, with general scope of LEED and LBC indicated as overlay, after Buranakarn   29

1.4 "The trophic–dynamic viewpoint [...] emphasizes the relationship of trophic or 'energy-availing' relationships within the community unit to the process of succession"
R. Lindeman, *Ecology*, © 1942 Ecological Society of America   38

1.5 "A characteristic web of converging energy transformations and feedback of interaction control loops found in self-organizing systems"   40
H. T. Odum, *Systems Ecology*, © 1983 John Wiley & Sons

1.6 "The four ecosystem functions and the flow of events between them"   50
C. S. Holling, *Ecological Monographs*, © 1992 Ecological Society of America

1.7 "Hypothetical counterpart for Holling's diagram, created by plotting the biomass of the system against the mutual information inherent in the flow structure"
From R. E. Ulanowicz, *Ecology: The Ascendent Perspective*, © 1997 Columbia University Press. Reprinted with permission of the publisher   51

List of figures

2.1 Axonometric of the "Ellis House," a mid-century house designed on a nine-square grid around a central, skylit atrium with front and back porches cantilevered on steel beams. Every room in the house has at least two doors (including bathrooms), and there are seven doors to the outside 60
Mather Lippincott, Architect

2.2 An updated version of Kiesler's correalism diagram, showing the biophysical interactions among the three coevolving environments: natural, human, and technological 63

2.3 Diagram of the three, nested scales of purpose for the construction and use of buildings: intensification of a site, shelter from the climate, and setting for work and living 64

3.1 "Two basic methods of exploiting the environmental potential of that timber exist: either it may be used to construct a wind-break or rain-shed—the structural solution—or it may be used to build a fire—the power-operated solution" (Banham 1969) 68
Photo: Robert Kerton, CSIRO

3.2 Thermodynamic diagram of building construction and operation. Resources invested in the substance of the building regulated the flows of environmental and purchased resources 71

3.3 One of the early *bürolandschaft* (office landscape) experiments by the Quickborner consulting group in the 1950s, including one of the earliest office plants 74
© 1968 O. Gottschalk

3.4 Thermodynamic diagram of seven layers of building construction based on longevity and purpose: site, envelope, structure, interiors, FF&E, systems, and software 74

3.5 System boundaries for four life cycle inventory and impact assessment methods used to evaluate the built environment 77
Srinivasan 2014

3.6 Materials of building structure and envelope plotted by weight and annual e[m]ergy cost: the Ellis House, normative version 80

3.7 Thermodynamic diagram of basic thermal regulation of a building 84

3.8 (a) Temperature simulation of the original, normative, unconditioned version of the Ellis House, full-year, hour-by-hour;

List of figures

	(b) Temperature simulation of the improved, insulated, unconditioned version of the Ellis House, full-year, hour-by-hour; (c) Temperature simulation of the responsive, unconditioned, *Passivhaus* version of the Ellis House, full-year, hour-by-hour	85
3.9	Thermodynamic diagram of the building-as-shelter, the Ellis House, original, normative version	92
3.10	Thermodynamic diagram of the building-as-shelter, the Ellis House, *Passivhaus* net zero energy version	94
3.11	Tree-filled atrium of the Ford Foundation used for biofiltration of conditioned return air © 1968 Roche Dinkeloo Associates	101
3.12	A biofilter living wall combining biofiltration and phytoremediation in a hydroponic plant wall, Nedlaw Living Walls	102
3.13	Thermodynamic diagram of ventilation with biofilter	103
3.14	Luxfer prism glass redirects incident daylight into the interior, extending the effect depth of the building, 1909	107
3.15	(a) Temperature simulation of climate-dominated building. Original, normative version of the Ellis House with normative internal gains; (b) Temperature simulation of internal load-dominated building. Improved version of the Ellis House with normative internal gains; (c) Temperature simulation of balanced loads and gains. Responsively managed, *Passivhaus* version of the Ellis House with reduced internal gains	112
3.16	Detail, heat gains and losses in the Ellis House, original version	114
3.17	(a) Energy–e[m]ergy intensity chart of thermal exchanges in the Ellis House, original, normative version; (b) Energy–E[m]ergy intensity chart of thermal exchanges in the Ellis House, *Passivhaus* net zero energy version	116
3.18	Illustration of energy–e[m]ergy intensity spectra for different energy regimes After Tilley	119
4.1	Fred McNabb's visionary *House of the Future* (1956) predicted almost everything available in the contemporary US household, from microwave ovens to video phones (Skype), although personal helicopters are not yet common and he did not anticipate the mobile, handheld "screens"	124

4.2 Water supply and wastewater treatment, distinguishing ecosystem
work from work of economy 131
After Buenfil (2001)
4.3 Time analysis and taxonomy of food delivery near Meyerson
Hall, comparing calories per minute 136
Blomeier, Evans, Feigon, Johnson, and McDonald (2009)
4.4 Thermodynamic diagram of production and consumption
showing linked cycle of environmental and extracted resources 141
After Odum
4.5 "Benefits of North African Solar" demonstrating the land area
required to capture sufficient renewable resources to supply a
contemporary economy 143
OMA/AMO Roadmap 2050, European Climate Foundation
4.6 "Three-arm diagram" of renewable, non-renewable, and
purchased resources 144
4.7 Thermodynamic diagram of the building-as-setting, the Ellis
House, original, normative version 153
5.1 A high-density city in a rural county, illustrating the land use
patterns of twenty-first-century renewable economy 160
Butcher and Kurtz (2014)
5.2 The occupations and locations depicted in Patrick Geddes'
"valley section" emerged organically over the millennia of
human development, and those pre-industrial relationships
are still frequently offered as an antidote to the patterns of
industrial and post-industrial growth 164
5.3 "'Habitat' is concerned with the particular house in the
particular type of community. Communities are the same
everywhere. (1) Detached house-farm. (2) Village. (3) Towns
of various sorts (industrial/admin./special). (4) Cities
(multifunctional). They can be shown in relationship to their
environment (habitat) in the Geddes' "valley section" 165
Smithson and Smithson (1954/1962)
5.4 "Central Place Theory," showing the hierarchical self-organization
of market towns and administrative centers in a largely agricultural
economy 167
Christaller (1933)

List of figures

5.5 A logarithmic "rank-order" chart of US communities over 2,500 from 1790–1930, showing a power series distribution 169
Zipf (1949)

5.6 (a) Thermodynamic land use diagram of Chautauqua County, showing existing land use and e[m]ergy intensities; (b) Chart of land use and e[m]ergy intensity for four scenarios: existing, efficient, renewable, and changed county 176
Butcher and Kurtz (2014)

5.7 "A changed county," showing land use distribution in Chautauqua County after the redistribution of land uses to accommodate a renewable economy, with thermodynamic diagram of resources and flows 177–178
Butcher and Kurtz (2014)

5.8 Thermodynamic diagram of the building-as-site, the Ellis House, original, normative version 182

5.9 Socioeconomic hierarchy of households 188
After Abel

5.10 Socioeconomic web, Bonaire, 1950–1995. In 1950 Bonaire's future changed as the result of a new constitution, which redefined its relationship with the Kingdom of the Netherlands. Dutch financial aid began to flow in and was invested in building infrastructure such as a port, an airport, and roads. By the 1970s several export industries had moved to Bonaire. Construction industries were emerging in support. A new water and electric plant was built. From 1950 to 1985 Bonaire's population doubled, and much of the population was working for wages. Tourism was about to take off, encouraged from within and without 189
Abel (2004)

5.11 Spatial hierarchy of Taiwan within its world system context, showing regional spatial hierarchies. Flows differ at each location in this spatial hierarchy of convergence and feedback. Each area has its unique environmental inputs, which are represented by the four distinct "production" symbols, and flows from sun, wind, rain, tide, and uplift to each. Only some areas receive direct inputs from international markets, which are selectively fed back as needed. Households (and

	the businesses they may control) attract different resources related to their different roles in the production, Abel 2013	190
6.1	The Ark, Prince Edward Island, New Alchemy Institute © 1977, John Todd	198
A.1	Symbols of the energy systems language	216–218

List of tables

B.1	Materials of construction	222
B.2	E[m]ergy synthesis summary	226
B.3	E[m]ergy synthesis summary, organized by site, shelter, and setting	228
B.4	Automobile composition, weight, and sej	234
B.5	Transformity of electricity based on 2010 EIA Annual Energy Report	239

Preface

The genesis of this book was in a conversation with an architecture student over 10 years ago, when she asked how to focus her studies on environmental topics. The notes from that conversation were the beginning of a certificate program in ecological architecture (EARC) for students in the professional degree like herself, and then of a new post-professional program, the master of environmental building design (MEBD). While preparing the foundation course for those programs, I rediscovered H. T. Odum's *Environment, Power, and Society*, which I had read in the 1970s and which had conveniently been updated and republished in 2007. The graphic nature of the energy systems language seemed the perfect introduction to environmental thinking for designers, but as I read the updated text 30 years later, I realized that the system diagrams and net energy accounting I recalled only scratched the surface of a much deeper body of work. His thinking about self-organization resonated with ideas that had become popular in architecture schools in those years, but systems ecology was connected to topics much deeper than the generation of novel form that has become the obsession of the profession.

Somewhat paradoxically, the thermodynamic basis of systems ecology helped me reconcile my education at Princeton in the 1970s with Daniel Nall, Robert Socolow, Ted Taylor, Doug Kelbaugh, and Harrison Fraker, based on systems thinking and energy calculations, with the humanistic orientation of my architectural education with Joseph Rykwert, Marco Frascari, David Leatherbarrow, Ivan Illich, and the remarkable circle at Penn in the early 1990s. Odum's bold propositions about the selection principles of self-organization undermined the

Preface

easy determinism of engineering calculations and the apparent autonomy of architecture and culture, forcing them together in the restless exploration of arrangements for enhancing power in all its forms. It provided a social and cultural context for interpreting building performance simulation and revealed the environmental basis of social and cultural hierarchies.

I was fortunate through those years to have many students and colleagues help me understand how systems ecology might apply to architecture. Each class of EARC and MEBD students has pushed the research further, and continues to question its premises. Many of their projects have become examples or topics in this book. I will always be grateful to Ravi Srinivasan for not only risking his dissertation on such a new topic, but for seeking out the current generation of e[m]ergy researchers. I owe a particular debt to that remarkable community of former students and colleagues of H. T. Odum, who continue to advance the research he initiated, refining the techniques, expanding the scope, and tackling their own new topics: Daniel Campbell, Mark T. Brown, Sergio Ulgiati, David Tilley, and Thomas Abel have been especially generous, although the misinterpretations are all mine. There is also a growing body of architects for whom systems ecology and e[m]ergy accounting have become a point of reference. Luis Fernandez-Galiano was among the first to explore the full potential of thermodynamics in architecture in *El fuego y la memoria* (1981), and many other colleagues and interlocutors have contributed to the conversation: Daniel Barber, David Leatherbarrow, Mark Alan Hughes, Franca Trubiano, Richard Wesley, Yun Kyu Yi, Ali Malkawi, Dan Willis, Kevin Pratt, Dana Cupkova, Kiel Moe, Iñaki Ábalos, Renata Sentkiewicz, Dean Hawkes, Simos Yannas, Rania Ghosn, David Orr, Vivian Loftness, Billie Faircloth, Christoph Reinhart, Jason McLennan, David Owen, Stephen Kieran, Philip Steadman, Daniel Williams, and Rob Fleming.

For concrete help with the preparation of this book, I must thank Alex Waegel for preparing and checking the calculations, Jill Sornson Kurtz and Chris Colgan for drawing the diagrams, and Shai Gerner, Hwang Yi, Luke Butcher, and Gera Feigon contributed images. My editor, M. O. Kirk, connected many loose, narrative threads.

And to my family, Persephone and Hugh Leander, who patiently made it all possible.

Chautauqua, NY
2014

Figure I.1: The all-glass wall exemplifies the almost magical capabilities of the materials and conditioning systems that were developed through the twentieth century and allow us to experience the climate of our cities as a kind of visual backdrop to contemporary life

Hancock Observatory, © 2014 Tribune News Service. All rights reserved.
Distributed by Tribune Content Agency, LLC

Introduction

Modern buildings are both wasteful machines that can be made more efficient and instruments of the massive, metropolitan system engendered by the power of high-quality fuels. A comprehensive method of environmental design must reconcile the techniques of efficient building design with the radical urban and economic reorganization that we face. Over the coming century, we will be challenged to return to the renewable resource base of the eighteenth-century city with the knowledge, technologies, and expectations of the twenty-first-century metropolis.

This book, *Architecture and Systems Ecology: Thermodynamic principles of environmental building design*, recognizes this looming design dilemma and explores three key topics—environment, buildings, and design—using concepts developed in systems ecology. In the following chapters, we review the architectural implications of the energy systems language developed by H. T. Odum, an American ecologist known for his pioneering work on ecosystem ecology. Odum and his collaborators extended the principles of thermodynamics from the nineteenth-century focus on more efficient machinery to the contemporary concern with the resilient self-organization of ecosystems (Odum 1983). Odum's energy systems language provides a holistic context for the many kinds of performance already evaluated in architecture—from energy use to material selection and even to the choice of building style. It establishes the foundation for environmental principles of design that embrace the full complexity of our current situation. Architecture, we would argue, succeeds best when it helps shape, accommodate, and represent new ways of living together.

Introduction

The first section in the book introduces the thermodynamic principles of self-organization as they occur in the natural and built environments. The second and central section on buildings applies these principles in three parts—shelter, setting, and site—to explain building performance at three nested scales of activity: the thermodynamic characteristics of the building as a shelter from the climate; the demands of the building as a setting for work and living; and the building as an intensification of its location in urban and economic production hierarchies. The book's third and final section on design explores how the thermodynamic narratives of wealth and power, waste and efficiency contribute to the design of buildings.

Wealth and power

This account was made possible by the many benefits—the food, education, time, and well-conditioned buildings—of one of the wealthiest civilizations yet to emerge on the planet. Wealth conditions every proposal we might make for environmental building design in the twenty-first century. The unprecedented growth in human population, the ever expanding "throughput" of energy and materials, and the accumulation of pollution effects have combined to create the need for specifically environmental design practices. The pace of that growth has overturned almost every point of reference we might have used to guide our designs for the future. We have been altering the environment to suit our purposes for hundreds of thousands of years, since at least the first fire or shelter. We have been making cities for nearly 10,000 years, and we have produced 2,000 years of architectural treatises and manuals to guide our work. But the magnitude of our current growth and environmental condition simply demands new ways of living and working.

It is not enough to imagine buildings that are more efficient or solar powered, although such designs are urgently needed. Neither can we simply turn back to previous patterns of settlement and construction, although they have much to teach us. With over 7 billion people, the planet is now too crowded for older, agricultural solutions, and the momentum is too great for incremental ones. We are steadily being pushed into an unfamiliar future that demands new ways of living together, ones based on the realities of our situation instead of technological dreams or nostalgic desires. Strategies developed in a less populous world will no longer work, as environmental effects have become systemic and global.

Previously negligible, local activities interact and accumulate in unexpected ways. Environmental buildings can only be conceived as part of a sustainable, global enterprise.

There are now so many environmental claims, simulation tools, and metrics that architects need to develop a context within which to evaluate them. Our current approach to design is largely based on economic determinations of value, in which environmental contributions and renewable resources are almost entirely discounted or even considered free. This has been a remarkably effective system for the last two centuries of growth, but it is ill suited to long-term planning or encounters with precipitous changes in the biosphere. Although ecological economists have long argued for the internalization of environmental costs and have developed new techniques of accounting for ecosystem services, environmental building design requires a comprehensive approach that puts natural, technological, and social values on an equal footing.

The basic premise of this approach is that real wealth is determined by the work it takes to make or accomplish things, whether we are considering materials, products, services, or information. The exchange values of a market system provide a powerful mechanism for allocating scarce resources, but the fluctuating price of a house, for example, doesn't alter the work and skill required to build it or the services that it can provide. Even more precisely, it is power—or the rate at which useful work can be accomplished—that underlies wealth. This claim is fundamentally thermodynamic, and rests on both the equivalence between energy and different forms of work (first law), and the severe restrictions on the diminishing amounts of useful work actually available (second law). The scarcity required for economic value is linked to the amounts of energy actually available, but this grim second law alone cannot explain the emergence of ever wealthier and more powerful ecosystems or societies. R. Buckminster Fuller addressed this question when he demanded a "whole new synergistic assessment of wealth" in the *Operating Manual for Spaceship Earth*, which requires an assessment of self-organization itself (1969, 112).

Synergy and correalism

From the eighteenth-century writings of the Scottish Enlightenment, with Bernard Mandeville's bees and Adam Smith's "invisible hand," to the flowering of cybernetics and systems theory in the late twentieth century, we increasingly recognize that aggregate, cumulative behaviors have their own kind of logic (Hamowy 1987). Complex phenomena such as weather, ecosystems, and financial markets can only be understood holistically and historically as events that unfold over time. Fuller was thoroughly optimistic about the potential of technocratic planning, but he recognized that the "world engulfing industrial evolution" was both a cause and an effect of contemporary wealth (1969, 128). In other words, wealth is self-perpetuating until it encounters limits it cannot overcome. Fuller adopted the term *synergy* to mean the "behavior of wholes unpredicted by the behavior of their parts," specifically to alert designers and planners to the unintended consequences of their proposals (78).

Contemporary, high-powered buildings are sophisticated industrial products that support highly specialized human activities, and so exemplify the many dimensions of synergistic self-perpetuation. As physical artifacts, contemporary buildings can only exist within a vast network of infrastructures, from the electric grid to transportation and information networks, which, in turn, require buildings (and people) of a certain capacity. Buildings are also commissioned by social and economic entities highly differentiated by wealth, which establishes the need for the many different types and sizes of building. But those differentiated, high-powered buildings also alter the expectations of those who use them, as the luxuries of one generation become the necessities of the next. Central heating, for example, was an innovation introduced to save labor and increase productivity, but it quickly became a regular service and is now mandated by law (in cold climates). Lastly, buildings mirror the spatial and economic geography of cities, where their placement both confirms and alters the value of the land on which they stand.

The architect Frederick Kiesler, who collaborated with Fuller in the 1930s, prepared one of the simplest illustrations of the synergies influencing building design (see Figure I.2). Kiesler coined his own term *correalism* to describe "the dynamics of continual interaction between man and his natural and technological environments," and his diagram depicts the interacting coevolution of three different environments: natural, technological, and human (Kiesler 1939, 30). He explained that "just as living organisms are generated through their own species from a long chain of generations," technologies develop by iterated refinements over time (63). Living creatures evolve as their genetic potential is shaped by their ecosystems, but man alone has developed a third, technological capacity that liberates information about design from the slow pace of genetic adaptation.

Introduction

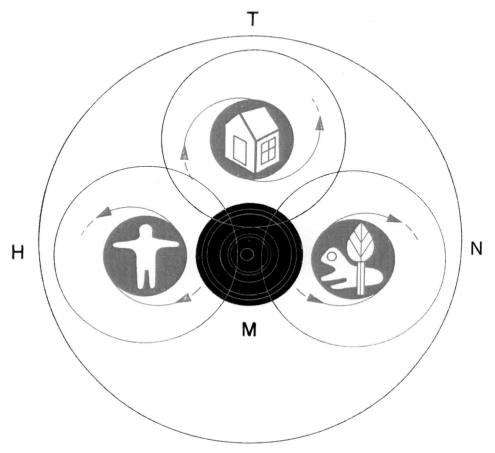

Figure I.2: Diagram of correalism showing the continuous evolution between human (H), technological (T), and natural (N) environments

Frederick Kiesler, *Architectural Record*, 1939

In the *Operating Manual*, Fuller called for a "realistic economic accounting system" that would include the coevolving infrastructure of people and their technologies, as well as the energetic resources from which their wealth is derived (112). With that appeal, Fuller effectively outlined the task of this book: to identify the principles for a realistic form of environmental accounting necessary to develop and evaluate building proposals, including all the kinds of resources and work required for their construction and use. It must also account

Introduction

for the way in which people, buildings, and societies coevolve in the landscape, understanding not just individual performances but the roles they play in social and urban self-organization.

Glass walls

Let's begin with the all-glass wall, the remarkable form of construction around which so many aspirations and challenges of contemporary design revolve. Picture the citizen of almost any major city in the world—Chicago, Dubai, Beijing—walking into an all-glass building, riding to an upper floor, and standing next to the nearly invisible barrier that separates conditioned from unconditioned space (see Figure I.1). That boundary exemplifies the almost magical capabilities of the materials and conditioning systems that were developed through the twentieth century and allow us to experience the climate of our cities as a kind of visual backdrop to contemporary life.

The all-glass wall represents a blind spot for environmental performance standards, which seek to regulate the amounts of glass in walls, on the grounds of energy efficiency. Although they are extravagant, glass walls are not really a matter of waste but a demonstration of wealth. The all-glass wall can rightly be considered one of the symbols of the technological civilization criticized by environmental activists, but when viewed only from the perspective of efficiency, little about our contemporary buildings or cities makes sense. If we cannot understand why people build with glass, how can we hope to design their buildings, environmental or otherwise?

It requires tremendous power to condition those transparently enclosed spaces, just as it requires substantial power to manufacture, transport, and install large glass panels. From the beginning of the glass revolution, the fascination with large areas of transparency has been tempered by their cost and the negative environmental effects they can produce: heat loss in cold weather, heat gain from sunlight, and excessive glare. These problems were recognized by the glazing pioneers of the nineteenth century, and in the 1840s Jean-Baptiste Jobard already wondered about making glass walls "active," heating (or cooling) the air between the layers of glass to modify the negative effects of large glazed walls (Jobard 1857). In 1914 Paul Scheerbart, the visionary author of *Glasarchitektur*, cautioned against this practice, arguing that "convectors and radiant heaters should not be put between the two skins because too much of their output will be lost to the

Introduction

outside air" (Sharp 1972, 14). Thus began over a century of experimentation and dispute about the practice of conditioning the air between the layers. Active glass walls exemplify the tension between efficiency and power, between the urge to control costs and the fantastic attraction of total transparency.

In recent decades, increasing numbers and varieties of active glass wall have been built, initially in northern Europe but increasingly in Asia and the Americas as well. According to the simplest definition, an active glass wall consists of "two transparent surfaces separated by a cavity, which is used as an air-channel" (Saelens 2002, 5). Despite the apparent objectivity of the definition, active glass walls are understood and selected according to very different architectural narratives and performance claims. The complex nature of environmental design becomes evident in the successive and competing arguments for their use.

The modern history of active glass walls begins with Le Corbusier's Villa Schwob of 1916, built in the extreme environment of the Swiss Alps. He inserted heating pipes between the layers of large windows to reduce their chill and subsequently proposed many variations, in solid as well as glass walls. He quickly recognized the transformative effect of this simple technique, which he designated as the neutral or neutralizing wall (*mur neutralisant*). In a description of one variation in the "Maison Citrohan" at the *Weissenhof Siedlung* in Stuttgart in 1927, he explained the concept (1991) (see Figure I.3):

> How, you ask, does your air keep its temperature as it diffuses through the rooms, if it is 40 degrees above or below zero outside? Reply: there are murs neutralisants (our invention) to stop the air at 18°C undergoing any external influence. These walls are envisaged in glass, stone, or mixed forms, consisting of a double membrane with a space of a few centimeters between them ... a space that surrounds the building underneath, up the walls, over the roof terrace.... In the narrow space between the membranes is blown scorching hot air, if in Moscow, iced air if in Dakar. Result, we control things so that the surface of the interior membrane holds 18°C. And there you are.
>
> (Le Corbusier 1991, 64)

The publication of those early projects inspired numerous imitators, and Le Corbusier even arranged with the St. Gobain glass company to build a test cell of the configuration in 1931. Like Scheerbart, the glass company experts concluded that although "warming the air between the panes increases the sensation of

Introduction

Figure I.3: Active glass wall: Le Corbusier, heating pipes between two layers of glass to "neutralize" the wall, Maison Citrohan, Stuttgart, 1927

© F.L.C./ADAGP, Paris/Artists Rights Society (ARS), New York

comfort," it also increases energy loss. Neutralization was a technique for managing glass buildings, not for increasing their energy efficiency (Banham 1969, 161).

In 1937, Swiss-American architect William Lescaze built an elaborate, double-envelope house in the Catskills for Alfred Loomis, one of the developers of radar (see Figure I.4). As Lescaze described it at the time, "the fundamental scheme of the house was dictated by the owner's desire to experiment with a novel system of heating and air-conditioning in an effort to approximate the temperature and humidity conditions of his South Carolina home" (Lescaze 1939, 36). The 0.6-m-wide air space was conditioned by a system separate from the house itself, and the conditioned buffer space allowed the inner house to maintain higher humidity levels without condensation on the inner glass. In

Introduction

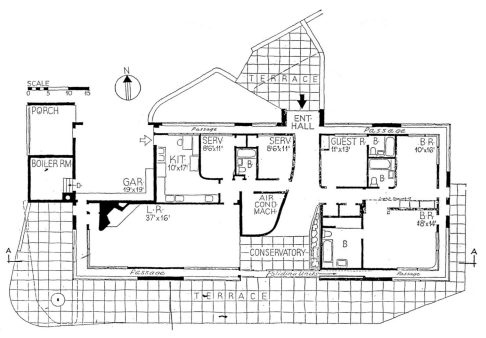

Figure I.4: Active glass wall: William Lescaze, double-envelope construction to moderate climate and control condensation

Alfred L. Loomis House, Tuxedo Park, NY, 1937

effect, the activated double wall was a technique for moving the inner building to a different climate.

During the 1950s an integrated mechanical configuration was developed in Scandinavia to improve the thermal experience of large glass areas in their extreme climate conditions. It was variously known as the air-extract window, air-curtain window, or climate window. By connecting the return air duct to the window, the already heated room air is drawn between the panes of double or triple glass, so the inner glass layer reaches a temperature close to that of the room, reducing the radiant discomfort produced by large areas of glass in winter. By using insulated glass for the outer layer it became more efficient, but like Le Corbusier's original neutral wall, its purpose was to facilitate the use of larger glass panels in cold climates.

The energy supply crises of the 1970s shifted the focus of active glass walls to the reduction in the operating energy used to heat and cool buildings.

Introduction

A variety of new and modified forms were developed as solar collectors, either to provide additional heat to the building or to drive the movement of the air between the layers. Two early US examples were the Occidental Chemical Company building in Niagara Falls and the Prudential Enerplex in Princeton (Rush 1986). In order to capture solar gain and control glare, the Occidental building employed a system of automated louvers situated in the air space, while the Prudential building expanded the southern air channel into a tree-filled atrium. Both features have become characteristic elements of contemporary active glass walls, and the tree-filled atrium, in particular, adds air filtration and biophilia to the conditioning power of the moving air (see Figure I.5).

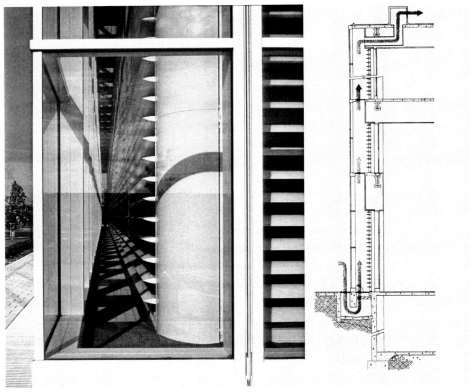

Figure I.5: Active glass wall: Cannon Design, responsive horizontal shades in ventilated zone between layers of glass

Occidental Chemical, Niagara Falls, NY, 1981

Introduction

As active glass walls proliferated across northern Europe through the 1990s, designers developed adaptable configurations that could change the flows of air according to climatic conditions, collecting, rejecting, or redistributing heat as needed. Among the best known of these buildings is the Commerzbank in Frankfurt, which is also frequently cited as the first explicitly "green" high-rise (Oldfield et al. 2009). The increased efficiency of the multiple layers and their careful integration with mechanical conditioning are used to give occupants individual control of natural ventilation, daylight, and views of greenery (see Figure I.6). The mature form of the active glass wall combines energy efficiency with techniques for improved health and productivity.

Contemporary active glass assemblies are lauded for their efficiency, but, make no mistake, these buildings have added an increasing array of environmental services through the century of development, from the first stage of neutralization to the responsive, green devices they have become. They are literally more powerful buildings, with increased capabilities for lowering their operating costs.

Figure I.6: Active glass wall: Foster Associates, double box window adjustable for ventilation, viewed from plant-filled atrium, Commerzbank, Frankfurt, 1997

Photo: Danijela Weißgraeber

Introduction

This enhanced performance is achieved with more layers of glass and aluminum, and with an increased complexity of assembly and operation. A more complete account of their performance has to weigh the savings in operations against the costs of construction, and one of the significant contributions of the energy systems language is to provide common terms for these kinds of comparison. The value of achievements like fresher air or increased comfort cannot be evaluated at the level of operations alone and has to be considered at multiple scales.

The successive refinements of active glass walls help reveal the many different environmental goals of buildings—comfort, health, efficiency, views, and control—and the importance of the narratives that explain those goals. One of the fundamental arguments of this book is that those narratives are thermodynamic, that they represent social and political negotiations about real wealth, which translate to narratives about power. One of the most pervasive of contemporary environmental narratives is about efficiency itself, which is offered as a method for reducing consumption. However, in periods of abundant resources and growth such as the last 200 years, efficiency has largely been a technique for increasing power, population, and overall consumption. It is odd that economists call this a "paradox" when the urge to enhance power seems evident everywhere, ranging from the budgets of households and companies to the implicit goals of ecosystems and civilizations.

The narrative connection between power and active glass walls was made explicit in Reyner Banham's 1965 proposal for a double-layered, transparent bubble, which was supported and conditioned by the pressurized flow of air between its layers that allowed it to dispense altogether with the opaque, enclosing elements of architecture (Banham 1965). It represents the final refinement of the active glass wall before its dematerialization into an architecture of pure power (see Figure I.7) In the *Architecture of the Well-tempered Environment*, Banham traced the evolution of "full control" in the crudely conditioned buildings of the mid-twentieth century and the steady transformation of the traditional, "structural" elements of architecture—walls, windows, roofs, etc.— into power-operated elements of that conditioning (1969, 171). Active glass walls exemplify that transformation, combining the selective transparency of glass with the invisible transport of thermal conditioning in the air stream. Along with rooftop solar panels and green roofs, they have become a contemporary symbol of a green architecture, leveraging environmental energies to reduce costs and maximize their power.

Introduction

Figure I.7: François Dallegret, The Environment-Bubble: Transparent Plastic Bubble Dome Inflated by Air-Conditioning Output showing architecture as a "fit environment for human activities," from Reyner Banham, "A Home Is Not a House," *Art in America*, April 1965

© 1965 François Dallegret

The successive refinements of the active glass wall over the last century illustrate the process of natural selection in buildings, which evolve both by purposeful design and according to unintentional choices and systemic effects. The cycles of architectural fashion, real estate sales, financial markets, and even weather operate

Introduction

at multiple scales to channel and constrain the inventiveness of designers. It is fascinating to sort out the various stages and innovations of a configuration like the active glass wall, with its dead ends, breakthroughs, and consolidations, but it is equally important to consider the larger historical events from which these walls have emerged, what Siegfried Giedion called their "anonymous history" (Giedion 1948). A central aspect of that history involves the vast infrastructures of power collection and concentration that have engendered the modern metropolis, and with which contemporary buildings have coevolved. A fully environmental explanation requires an account of the mechanisms of self-organization that make historical processes anonymous, that drive natural evolution, ecosystem succession, and the growth of human civilization.

Ecotopia

The formulation of environmental building design is not complete without considering ecotopia, the ecological utopia toward which sustainable development points. And we cannot understand ecotopia without the alluring concept of the climax forest, characterized by the great temperate forests of Europe and North America, and also now by the even more complex tropical rain forests. The idea of a climax state for a particular region, a "climatic climax," began with observations about the succession of species that occur in ecological communities over time. On volcanic rock, after a fire, or when a plot of farmland is abandoned, for example, the sequence of plant life is predictable and relentless. Kevin Kelly described the process on a "worn-out, 100-acre farm in Michigan":

> The first weeds on the Michigan plot are annual flowering plants, followed by the tougher perennials like crabgrass and ragweed. Woodier shrubs will shade and suppress the followers, followed by pines, which suppress the shrubs. But the shade of the pine trees protects hardwood seedlings of beech and maple, which in turn steadily elbow out the pines. One hundred years later the land is almost completely owned by a typical northern hardwood forest.
> (Kelly 1995, 96)

The regularity of the process and the consistency of the result have remained a powerful point of departure among ecologists, while its actual mechanisms have been a subject of debate and research. The initial condition of the piece of land does not seem to matter much and the sequence of first species might differ, but the result is predictable if never exactly the same. The resulting forest is also remarkably resilient to certain amounts of logging, farming, and building: if you stop mowing your suburban lawn in my moist region, it will return to its forested condition in a matter of years. Thoreau had noted the sequence, as had earlier naturalists, although theories of the process were not developed until the 1890s when Henry Cowles at the University of Chicago described the sequence of vegetation that appeared on bare sand dunes near Lake Michigan (Cowles 1899). Frederic Clements subsequently formulated the notion of the *climax* forest as the goal of the process and its natural state if left undisturbed. Clements compared the stages of ecological succession with an individual organism that "arises, grows, matures, and dies" (Clements 1916).

Clements' ideas dominated the field for much of the first half of the twentieth century, and the appeal of the concept is evident. As research showed, the climax forest involves a complex web of interrelationships and exchanges: it provides food and habitat for an abundance of species, and it achieves nearly perfect recycling of materials. What a compelling model for a sustainable human civilization. Critics of the concept, beginning with H. A. Gleason, questioned the overwhelming determinism of the theory and the metaphoric nature of super organisms. For a start, the mechanisms of plant succession are more open than the genetic controls guiding the development of individual organisms. There are no seeds or genes for ecosystems, whose organization is guided by much looser forces.

It was not until the second half of the century, with the consolidation of cybernetics and systems theory, that it became possible to discuss the goals of complex, self-organizing systems in less deterministic ways. For generations of scientists trained in the identification of immediate, instrumental causes, the possibility of system goals was difficult to accept. Evolution based on natural selection provided a useful model and opened the door to explanations of properties or behaviors that emerge from interactions among large populations of actors and events. In the *Eighth Day*, R. N. Adams used the somewhat paradoxical term "final or selection cause" to describe a synergistic type of explanation that only exists as the goal of a process and only has a probability of ever occurring (Adams 1988, 38). The climax forest makes visible the selection goal of collective productivity and the many direct and indirect mechanisms of self-organization with which it is achieved.

Introduction

The energy systems language provides a powerful tool for understanding the interaction of human and natural systems, and is used to structure the sections of the book. The first section establishes the three thermodynamic principles that have emerged from systems ecology: the competitive and collaborative pursuit of maximum power, the development of energy transformation hierarchies, and the co-cycling of materials in pulses of energy transformation. In the second section, we apply these principles to three scales of building use or activity: shelter, setting, and site. Each of these scales presents different performance criteria for design, with each larger scale constraining the one below. The value of building energy efficiency, for example, is established by the households or institutions that use the building in their social and economic activities. Clarifying the three scales of performance helps distinguish among the very different kinds of work managed by buildings, for example, between the tempering of the climate, the preparation of food, or the processing of information.

The final section in the book considers the role of architecture within the different scales and anonymous processes of self-organization, including its symbolic aspects. Adams called the intertwining of technology and its social representations an "energy form"; however, the word "energy" is so bound up in utility bills and concentrated fuels that we have instead adopted the term "thermodynamic narratives" to broaden the description and to include the natural, industrial, and social channeling of power. Architectural narratives include the all-glass building, the survivalist retreat, and the suburban tract house, each of which describes a particular kind of living and working in the metropolitan system that constitutes the latest stage of cultural evolution. Narratives help situate the technical goals of enhanced performance within the pursuit of wealth and the fundamental indeterminacy of any design for the future. Thermodynamic narratives combine the maximization of power with the forms of its realization in a full-bodied account of environmental building design.

Bibliography

Adams, Richard N. 1988. *The Eighth Day: Social Evolution as the Self-Organization of Energy*. Austin, TX: University of Texas Press.

Banham, Reyner. 1965. "A Home is Not a House." *Art in America* 2: 70–79.

Banham, Reyner. 1969. *The Architecture of the Well-Tempered Environment*. Chicago, IL: University of Chicago Press.

Clements, Frederic E. 1916. *Plant Succession—An Analysis of the Development of Vegetation*. Washington, DC: Carnegie Institution of Washington.

Cowles, Henry Chandler. 1899. *The Ecological Relations of the Vegetation on the Sand Dunes of Lake Michigan*. Chicago, IL: University of Chicago Press.

Fuller, R. Buckminster. 1969. *Operating Manual for Spaceship Earth*. Carbondale, IL: Southern Illinois University Press.

Giedion, Siegfried. 1948. *Mechanization Takes Command: A Contribution to Anonymous History*. New York: W. W. Norton.

Hamowy, Ronald. 1987. *The Scottish Enlightenment and the Theory of Spontaneous Order*. Carbondale, IL: Southern Illinois University Press.

Jobard, Jean Baptiste Ambroise Marcellin. 1857. *Les nouvelles inventions aux expositions universelles*. 2 vols. Brussels: E. Flatau.

Kelly, Kevin. 1995. *Out of Control: The New Biology of Machines, Social Systems and the Economic World*. Reading, MA: Perseus Press.

Kiesler, Frederick. 1939. "On Correalism and Biotechnique: A Definition and Test of a New Approach to Building Design." *The Architectural Record* (September): 60–75.

Le Corbusier. 1991. *Precisions on the Present State of Architecture and City Planning: with an American prologue, a Brazilian corollary followed by The Temperature of Paris and the Atmosphere of Moscow*. Cambridge, MA: MIT Press.

Lescaze, William. 1939. "House at Tuxedo Park, NY, William Lescaze, Architect." *The Architectural Review* 86: 36.

Odum, Howard T. 1983. *Systems Ecology: An Introduction*. New York: John Wiley & Sons, Inc.

Oldfield, Philip, Dario Trabucco, & Antony Wood. 2009. "Five Energy Generations of Tall Buildings: An Historical Analysis of Energy Consumption in High-rise Buildings." *Journal of Architecture* 14(5): 591–613.

Rush, Richard D. 1986. *The Building Systems Integration Handbook*. New York: John Wiley & Sons, Inc./American Institute of Architects.

Saelens, Dirk. 2002. "Energy Performance Assessment of Single Storey Multiple-Skin Façades." PhD, Faculteit Toegepaste Wetenschappen, Katholieke Universiteit Leuven.

Sharp, Dennis, Ed. 1972. *Glass Architecture (1914) by Paul Scheerbart and Alpine Architecture (1919) by Bruno Taut*. New York: Praeger.

Figure 1.1: Two scales of environmental self-organization, weather, and urban settlements. A nighttime view of Tropical Storm Isaac and the cities near the Gulf Coast of the United States, August 28, 2012

NASA, Visible Infrared Imaging Radiometer Suite (VIIRS) image from Suomi-NPP satellite

Chapter One

Environments of maximum power

> We are taking "survival of the fittest" to mean persistence of those forms which can command the greatest useful energy per unit time (power output).
>
> (Odum and Pinkerton 1955, 332)

The reassuring images of a harmonious global environment, from the stable climate zones of the ancient world to NASA's "blue marble in space," have little to offer contemporary designers faced with a changing and self-organizing environment (see Figure 1.1). Even the productive agricultural civilizations of the last 10,000 years can be blamed for tipping many of the arid regions of the world into desert. Designers need help thinking about our situation in an endlessly changeable and changing climate, to grasp the interaction between our individual acts of building and the environment as a whole. The natural task of individual buildings, institutions, or economies is to determine the best use of the scarce resources that they compete to obtain, while the biosphere is working to dissipate the steady flow of energetic wealth from the sun and the planet's core. As Georges Bataille argued, the individual ethics of scarcity are simply different than the collective urgency of abundance, but the two can be linked by tracing the power that fuels them both (Bataille 1988).

We say that individuals "choose" while the environment "selects." But the environment can only select among things already birthed or built by the individuals that make up the whole. The environment that we encounter is the material result of the many arrangements constructed over time by different species, ecosystems, and human enterprises, each dissipating its share of energy to build for their particular purposes. The slow process of natural selection among species has been overtaken by the rapid adaptation tactics of humanity, which have liberated the power of information from the slow DNA mutations of speciation to the accelerated information cycles of technological innovation. The different rates of those techniques have been destabilizing. Aldo Leopold argued for an environmental approach that linked the two rates of adaptation, a "land ethic" based on a deeper understanding of the slower ecological food chain that the more rapid human enterprises have territorialized (Leopold 1949). A full account of the environment combines the ethics of the part and the whole, of the fast and the slow, in a thermodynamic analysis of the energy, materials, and information with which it is made.

Accounting for a living, self-organizing environment

The architectural profession has struggled to develop forms of environmental accounting that can guide the design process without overly burdening or complicating it. In addition to regulatory codes, a variety of approaches have emerged, which offer expanded forms of assessment: ecological footprints, carbon footprints, embodied energy, life cycle assessment (LCA), cradle-to-cradle, and ecosystem services review all offer enhanced methods for capturing some aspect of the environmental impact of materials, products, or buildings. The most widely recognized environmental standard for buildings is the US Green Building Council's (USGBC) Leadership in Energy and Environmental Design (LEED) program, which is an independent, "aspirational" standard meant to provide "building owners and operators with a framework for identifying and implementing practical and measurable green building design, construction, operations and maintenance solutions." (USGBC) LEED largely draws on existing standards—such as the model energy codes developed by the American Society of Heating Refrigerating and Air-conditioning Engineers (ASHRAE) and the EPA's EnergyStar rating system—and assigns subjective points to reconcile the differences between measurements of energy use, water consumption, or indoor air pollution.

The very variety of codes and standards—and especially the competition among voluntary evaluation systems like LEED, BREEM®, Green Globes, and others—is symptomatic of the lack of a comprehensive science of environmental sustainability. LEED has achieved pragmatic clarity at the expense of a more comprehensive assessment or more ambitious goals. By providing checklists of contemporary best practices, LEED has increased market penetration but does little to foster innovation or the radical change that is needed.

To the USGBC's credit, one of the most ambitious, aspirational standards has emerged from its own "left wing"—the International Living Future Institute, which administers a performance standard called the Living Building Challenge (LBC). The goal of the LBC is to promote buildings that contribute as productively to their ecosystems as trees and plants. To realize this challenge, the LBC developed a suite of 20 or more performance-based "imperatives" that are instructive both for their environmental ambitions and the limitations they reveal (LBC 2012). The first five categories of the challenge are similar to those used in the LEED program—site, water, energy, health, and materials; two additional categories, equity and beauty, seek to extend the challenge into social and cultural conditions. Taken together, the seven categories capture most of what we would expect in an environmental metric and, within each imperative, the LBC has adopted the most ambitious current approach: net zero energy, net zero water, and a "red list" of prohibited materials. Despite the ambition of the 20 imperatives, however, the LBC provides no objective method for comparing the value of one imperative with another, for assessing the total environmental impact of a building project, or ultimately for optimizing a particular design.

The Living Future Institute is admirably clear that it is setting goals, rather than offering a complete method through the LBC. But the lack of a fundamental environmental value is a problem common to most of the building standards, metrics, and tools currently in use. Broadly speaking, those measures can be divided into two classes: objective and reductionist, and those with some degree of subjective weighting. LEED and the LBC both apply subjective evaluations to the results of reductionist calculations of energy consumption, water use, or embodied carbon, and use professional judgment or current practices to establish the relative importance of the different criteria.

When the Living Building Challenge offers life as a goal for design, it invokes the longstanding use of biological analogies in design—from biotechnics and biotechniques to bionics and biomimicry—and points the way to an ecological form of design based on a deeper understanding of the place of buildings in the environment (Steadman 1979; Mertins 2004). It is telling that the LBC refers to trees and other plants, and not animals, especially not predators, as the model for "living" buildings. The immobility of plants strengthens the analogy, but most buildings are more like herbivores that consume plant products, while some high-powered buildings are more like carnivores or carrion eaters that feed at higher levels or on the detritus of the food chain.

While useful as a starting point, analogies are not entirely sufficient to imagine an ecological form of building for the anthropocene. We need to understand the mechanisms that drive the operation of ecosystems, as well as the ways in which human designs differ from (and resemble) the evolution of species or the self-organization of ecosystems. Over the last century, biology, ecology, and economics have developed new techniques to describe the behavior of self-organizing systems, based on the thermodynamic exchanges of food, energy, money, and information, which can reveal the organization and trajectories of those systems.

Thermodynamics of living systems

Precisely because of its universality, energy can be confusing. It combines common-sense understandings of work with a number of more precise concepts such as heat, exergy, entropy, power, and embodied energy. In the formal definition, energy uses heat to establish equivalencies between vastly different scales of activity, from the formation of stars and the rusting of metals to the "vital force" of living creatures. The power of those comparisons can obscure other principles, such as the quality of different energy sources, their relative utility, and the conversion of energy into products, services, and forms of order with little measureable energy content. Each of these concepts helps illuminate critical aspects of environmental building design for which energy use or conversion efficiency are insufficient. To sort them out, we need to start at the beginning.

Thermodynamics really began in the shop, or rather at the mine head, when Thomas Savery, Thomas Newcomen, and James Watt developed steam engines to pump water from coal mines in the seventeenth and eighteenth centuries. Miners needed the engines because they had exhausted the easier-to-reach surface coal, driving miners below groundwater levels in search of coal (Galloway 1882). Of course, digging more aggressively for coal had only become necessary after loggers had depleted the forests of wood, which had helped fuel the growth in populations and industries that were hungry for other sources of power. In other words, steam made by burning coal was the latest step in which technical capacities and sources of available energy were developing together.

The foundation of thermodynamics was not the so-called "first" or universal law of energy conservation. Rather, it was the "second" law that developed first and explained the maximum efficiency with which those engines could convert the heat from burning coal into the work of pumping water. Sadi Carnot, in *Reflections on the Motive Power of Fire* (1824), first worked out the mathematical formulation of that efficiency, and Rudolf Clausius and Hermann von Helmholtz later formalized the definition of entropy that explained the second law of thermodynamics.

Twenty years later, in the 1840s, James P. Joule, Julius von Mayer, and Helmholtz consolidated a great deal within the sciences when they formalized the equivalency between heat and work in the "first" law of energy conservation. Ultimately, however, it is the second law that is actually useful. As the ecologist Robert E. Ulanowicz argues, "In ecology, as in all other disciplines that treat dissipative systems, the first law is not violated, but it simply does not tell us very much that is interesting about how a system is behaving" (Ulanowicz 1997, 24). The important question for the shop, the tidal estuary, or the human economy is how much energy is available to do useful work and how does it create systems of such intricacy? The interesting thing about the second law is that it depends on the conditions surrounding the work we hope to accomplish. In terms worked out by Carnot, the efficiency of a heat engine is limited by the temperatures in its immediate surroundings (the greater the temperature difference, the higher the efficiency). The second law also implies a broader account of the capacities for work that are available in the coal that is burned, the iron of the engine, or even in the social arrangements that made it possible to put the two together. Each of those examples, a concentrated fuel, a purified metal, and a working economic system, requires a considerable prior investment of work to make it available and represent a substantial amount of energetic potential.

Clausius' simplest statement of the second law, that "heat cannot of itself flow from a colder body to a warmer one," may not seem to capture all those different potentials (Clausius and Hirst 1867). Its fuller implications emerge from the concept of entropy, which is a quantification of the capacity that is lost when heat flows from a hotter to a colder body. Any transformation of energetic potential, whether into useful work or simply into lower temperature heat, irreversibly increases entropy. You cannot turn ashes back into coal or rust into iron without doing even more work to reassemble all the capacity that was released in the burning or rusting. The term "entropy" is somewhat counterintuitive: it describes the amount of energy that is *unavailable* to do work; it is often used synonymously with disorder or uncertainty; and it leads to the use of opposite terms such as negentropy, order, and information to describe the capacity for work that is built up throughout the environment. What we are interested in, however, is the capacity *available* to do work, whether of wood to heat a house or money to buy food.

Limitations of efficiency: the roles of entropy and exergy

Thermodynamics has largely been implemented with the measure of efficiency, and it has been one of the fundamental tools of technological innovation. Reviewing the different uses of efficiency helps reveal the difference between the different principles of thermodynamics. Count Rumford observed the heat equivalence of work in 1798, based on his measurements of the frictional heat released while boring cannons. The theory that forms the basis of the first law was not accepted until the 1840s, when Joule and Mayer independently showed the same correspondence (with more precision) in the interactions between mechanical work, electricity, magnetism, chemical reactions (combustion and digestion), and heat. The energy defined in the first law is ultimately the abstract quantity that is conserved in all those interactions, which is measured as heat. Efficiency measurements of the first law are therefore expressed in heat equivalents, comparing, for example, the heat content of the fuel burned in a machine to the heat value of the work delivered at the end.

What first-law equivalencies miss is the amount of work originally available in that fuel, which is the role of entropy. Entropy forms the basis of the second law of thermodynamics, whose definition was completed in the 1870s by J. Willard Gibbs when he added chemical potential to the description of a thermodynamic state. This enabled Gibbs to quantify the total free or available energy, which is now more commonly called *exergy*, and it better describes what energy means in common language (Rant 1956). According to the second law, exergy is destroyed in any process of energy conversion (while entropy increases). The second-law (or exergy) efficiency is the ratio of the work output to the exergy input. It has proved to be a more useful tool for the engineering of chemical processes and mechanical energy conversions, since it describes how much of the available energy has actually been exploited.

For building performance, exergy analysis is typically applied to explicit energy conversions, such as the burning of fuels or the use of electricity in mechanical and electrical equipment. The first-law efficiency of a natural gas furnace, for example, has increased dramatically in recent decades, from delivering 65% to 80% of the fuel's heat content to ratings of around 97% today. But this only highlights the inadequacy of first-law measurements. A second-law efficiency would compare that delivery to the performance of an ideal heat pump working at its Carnot-defined coefficient of performance (COP) of about seven, meaning that it provides seven units of heat for each unit of electric power it consumes. This means that the most efficient natural gas furnace is only providing about 14% of the heat that could be delivered by an ideal heat pump.

Energy quality and the scope of analysis

Calculating second-law efficiencies highlights the importance of the boundaries of analysis that are used. For instance, the evaluation of the natural gas furnace could be put in larger context by including the fuels that were burned to produce the electricity to drive the heat pump, or even the work and resources required to build and operate the furnace. To understand the full environmental cost of a product or service, the boundaries of analysis have to be expanded to include the full array of inputs and effects required to provide the heat. The biosphere establishes the ultimate boundary of environmental analysis, while each expansion of the scope adds complexities and uncertainties to the accounting. However, these accounting questions point to a deeper topic: the quality of different sources of energy. Engineering practice already makes qualitative distinctions about energy based on economic value, matching the costs of energy sources to the thermodynamic quality of the work being accomplished. For example, in one of the first Solar Decathlon buildings, direct sunlight was used for daylighting, it was also converted to heat in evacuated-tube solar collectors for heating and cooling, and more expensive photovoltaic panels were used to concentrate sunlight into electricity to power motors, lights, and electronics (DOE 2007) (see Figure 1.2).

The "quality" of an energy source is an extremely important and complex idea, used to bridge the gap between the goals of individual buildings and of the biosphere and between selfish efficiency and overall prosperity (Odum 1983a). A common measure of the energy quality of a fuel or power source is the ratio of exergy to energy content; this indicates the "richness" of a potential energy source but offers little measure of its environmental effects or insight into the

Environments of maximum power

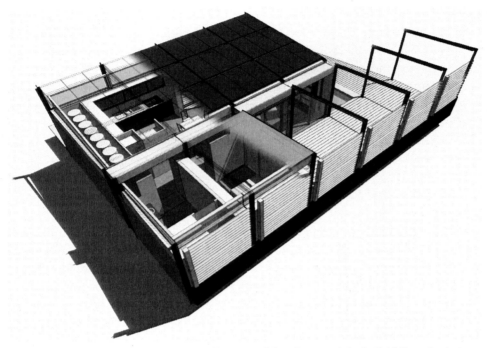

Figure 1.2: Sunlight converted into three different qualities of energy: into daylight through windows, hot water through vertical solar-thermal collectors, and electricity through photovoltaic panels

Solar Decathlon, University of Cincinnati, 2007

value of materials or services that are not used as energy sources, like fresh water or steel. Over the last 60 years, a variety of additional approaches have been developed to quantify the costs and impacts of different materials and services. These range from embodied energy calculations and life cycle analysis to e[m]ergy analysis, each of which involves an expanded scope of analysis. Every boundary change adds complications and alters the determinations of value. Broadly stated, there are four nested scales by which the quality of a product or service can be determined, and each method has a particular history of development and corresponds to a specific field of approach and source of information (see Figure 1.3).

The narrowest scope of analysis is the tracking of energy/exergy flows for individual buildings or processes, typically using efficiency measurements and consumption norms as a guide. Concern with explicit energy consumption for

Environments of maximum power

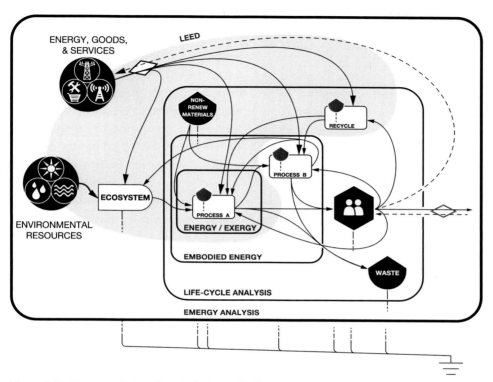

Figure 1.3: Four boundaries of analysis for evaluating the upstream costs of materials, products, and services, with general scope of LEED and LBC indicated as overlay, after Buranakarn

heating, cooling, lighting, and plug loads has dominated the field since the energy supply crises of the 1970s, due not only to its immediacy and cost, but also because it is easy to track through utility bills. From the beginning, designers, researchers, and regulators recognized that energy is also used indirectly in the many "up stream" processes involved in building. In *Architecture and Energy* (1977), Richard Stein demonstrated that the work and energy expended in the construction of buildings could be as important as that used for their conditioning; Stein introduced the concept of "embodied energy" to the field, defined as the energy used up indirectly in the process of preparing, delivering, and assembling buildings. Luis Fernández-Galiano called it the "fire that builds the building" (2000).

Embodied energy calculations grew out of two methods: the economic input–output (I–O) analysis methods developed by Wassily Leontief in the 1930s and the physically based process analysis methods elaborated by engineers through the same period (Leontief 1966). In the 1970s, the Center for Advanced Computation (CAC) at the University of Illinois adapted the calculations for explicit energy studies, and called the result "energy intensity." As the documents describing the center's methodology explained, "it takes energy to manufacture, deliver, and sell all types of goods and services. It is possible to add up the energy required at each step of the production process to determine the total 'energy cost' of particular goods and services" (Bullard et al. 1976, 1). In practice, the CAC analysis used an input–output matrix of dollar flows through the US economy to calculate energy intensities by sector. For finer grained analysis of individual products or services, they incorporated process analysis methods with physical units of energy and material flows. Theoretically, the two methods would yield the same results, but the different sources of data rarely agree, so the risks for error and uncertainty abound. The energy intensity or embodied energy of products and services establishes the energy cost of the materials that are not used as fuels. But as Buranakarn observed, it still excludes that "indirect energy required in the past to produce energy or machinery," as well as environmental costs. For these costs, the methods of life cycle assessment (LCA) were developed (Buranakarn 1998, 9).

There are numerous forms of life cycle assessment, with different boundaries of analysis—cradle-to-gate, cradle-to-grave, and now even cradle-to-cradle. The tracking of the work and resources expended in building materials has its roots in the analysis of commercial products in the 1960s, and has been readily extended to the many products used in construction. As the National Renewable Energy Laboratory (NREL) explained it, "Life-cycle assessment is a holistic and systematic method for analyzing the environmental and human health impacts of a product or process across its life cycle." Like I–O and Process analysis, the challenge has been to acquire comprehensive enough data to provide guidance for design.

In 2001, NREL and the Athena Institute developed a roadmap for a US "life-cycle inventory (LCI) to track the input and output material and energy flows associated with each step in a process or in the production of a product" (Deru 2009, 2). A life cycle analysis of a cardboard box, for example, may link "dozens of LCI data sets to study the raw materials extraction, production, transportation, use, and recycling or disposal life cycle stages." Once the data are gathered, however, the critical aspect of life cycle analysis is the assessment of human and ecological impacts. The Eco-Indicator 99 methodology, a widely used, "damage-oriented" protocol developed in the Netherlands, catalogs impacts in three broad categories: "human health, ecosystem quality, and resources" (Ministry of Housing 2000).

The effects are assigned "eco-indicator values," points based on subjective estimates of the relative damage they will cause. This allows comparison between the total life cycle impact of different materials, products, or aspects of production. The approach has been increasingly refined and incorporated into software tools that produce easily interpreted scores for designers to use, with the goal of minimizing the total resource use and eco impact of the product or process. Life cycle assessment methods further expand the scope and time frame of analysis, producing weighted comparisons of the environmental cost of specific materials or products. But even cradle-to-cradle analyses have no method for including "the work of the environment in producing 'natural capital' as inputs or for environmental services in processing waste byproducts." The most recent development has been the move to establish economic values for these different "ecosystem services" (Buranakarn 1998, 8).

The implicit argument of first- or second-law efficiency measurements of energy use, embodied energy accounting, life cycle analysis, ecosystem services, and sustainable design generally is that growth will continue to occur, so its costs and effects should be minimized. This is a natural design imperative for individual machines, buildings, or human institutions for whom greater efficiency means more available resources. But it offers little insight into the relentless nature of growth itself. Consumption to the limits of resources characterizes both human and natural systems and, in most cases, greater efficiency only serves to enhance growth, not reduce it. As outlined in the Introduction, environmental building design can only be understood within our tremendous contemporary accumulation of wealth, which, as Bataille pointed out, eventually has to be spent on something.

Bioenergetics

Understanding the nature of living systems has been called a choice between Carnot and Darwin, between the apparent inevitability of entropic decline and the emergence of ever more complex, living creatures and ecosystems (Fernández-Galiano 2000). The philosophical debate about entropy seems to divide the hard sciences from those concerned with life. Carnot and Darwin were really working on different problems: Carnot with the efficiency of devices operating near equilibrium, and Darwin with the evolution of species in large, dissipative systems. The first-law equivalence between heat and work, which made energy a unifying principle in physics, was just one tool among many for decoding the work of living. Antoine Lavoisier's link between the heat output of animals and their feed (1778), which was subsequently quantified by Mayer, helped fit animals into the physics of steam engines (although the determination of their first-law efficiency, about 20%, seems to beg for improvement).

Contemporary calorie counting and advances in sports medicine are extensions of the insight that animals are a kind of heat engine, but measurements of first- or second-law efficiency do not begin to explain the appearance of more complex and costly creatures. An explanation began to emerge in the 1870s when Ludwig Boltzmann developed statistical thermodynamics. Boltzmann used probability theory to provide a mathematical description of molecular "orderliness" or, really, to measure how different it was from total disorder. In 1944 Erwin Schrodinger extended that statistical approach in his speculations on the question, "What is life?" He considered the controlling power of genetic material and concluded that "the device by which an organism maintains itself stationary at a fairly high level of orderliness (= fairly low level of entropy) really consists of continually sucking orderliness from its environment."

The chemist Ilya Prigogine subsequently coined the term "dissipative system" to describe the dynamic structures or systems that decrease their internal entropy by producing and exporting entropy to elsewhere in the environment (Prigogine and Stengers 1984). This is an easily recognized characteristic of living creatures and ecosystems, which depend on the steady flow of low-entropy resources in the form of food.

Orderliness also characterizes many inanimate processes, from chemical clocks to tornadoes. In 1948 Norbert Wiener firmly consolidated the use of probabilistic descriptions of order for living and non-living systems in *Cybernetics or Control and Communication in the Animal and the Machine* (1948). That same year, C. E. Shannon generalized the mathematical descriptions of order in his work on information theory at Bell Labs, although its connection to communications initially limited its adoption in fields such as ecology (1948). The transition from a thermodynamics of work and efficiency to a thermodynamics of life and order marks a critical step to an ecological form of design.

The value of energy analysis for understanding living systems became increasingly clear through the twentieth century, beginning with Alfred Lotka's work in the 1920s, putting Darwinian evolution in thermodynamic terms. Lotka was a statistician, demographer, and biologist, best known for developing mathematical models describing predator–prey dynamics. The relatively simple interaction over time between the numbers of a prey species, such as hares, and the numbers of a predator species, such as lynx, helps illustrate how the behavior of ecosystems can differ from the goals of individual species. As the population of hares rises, so does the population of the lynx that feed on them, up to some critical threshold; when the larger number of lynx begin to kill hares more quickly than they can breed, the population of hares declines rapidly from being eaten, followed by a crash in the lynx population from the collapse of their food supply. Once the number of lynx drops far enough, however, the number of hares begins to increase again, and the cycle starts over. The behavior of real ecosystems includes additional limitations imposed by the rate of growth in the grasses eaten by the hares, and competition among other prey or predators. But the linked, oscillating populations of the two species is a feature of their interaction that could not be predicted from a study of either hares or lynx alone. Individually, the hares would just as soon not get eaten, while the lynx would rather not starve, but they are bound together in a "sustainable," oscillating relationship. The balance is achieved through cycles of growth, overshoot, and contraction fed by the available energy of the grasses eaten by the hares.

Among the most challenging questions posed in debates about environmental design is whether humanity is like other top predators, always overshooting the limits of available resources, or whether we can adapt and plan for resource and pollution limits. This question is most closely associated with Thomas Malthus, whose *Essay on the Principle of Population* (1798) predicted a predator–prey-type contraction in human population when it grew beyond the agricultural capacity of the late eighteenth century, summarized in his elegant syllogism:

> That the increase of population is necessarily limited by the means of subsistence,
>
> That population does invariably increase when the means of subsistence increase, and,
>
> That the superior power of population is repressed, and the actual population kept equal to the means of subsistence, by misery and vice.
>
> (Malthus 1798)

Quantifying the energy value of foods added a new level of precision to Malthus' observations, in a form that calorie counters will recognize. But he has been much criticized for the apparent failure of his predictions, since populations have obviously continued to grow exponentially since the eighteenth century. His inaccuracy is frequently attributed to his neglect of technical innovation, which distinguishes men from other kinds of biological population. The "cornucopian" argument points to the dramatic increases in agricultural output and human population through the nineteenth and twentieth centuries as evidence that for humanity increased scarcity inspires the increased technological innovation needed to overcome resource limitations. The cornucopian criticism overlooks the equivalence between food and energy, and the degree to which increases in agricultural productivity over the last 200 years have come as much from the use of more fuels as from technical or genetic advances—fuels to produce fertilizers and to drive more powerful techniques of tilling, weeding, harvesting, and transporting food products. As Odum once observed, over 60% of the modern potato is oil (Odum 1970). So while Malthus was correct in principle, he had no idea that food could effectively be extracted from coal mines or oilfields, deferring the encounter between human populations and limits to the means of subsistence. Malthus' failed eighteenth-century prediction should reinforce one of the lessons of systems theory: there are no simple limits, only complex thresholds of transition.

Natural selection as a thermodynamic principle

Lotka's great achievement was to establish natural selection as a general principle of thermodynamics, which provided a goal for self-organization and clarified the role of energy efficiency. His point of inspiration was Boltzmann's observation in the 1880s that "available energy" was the "fundamental object of contention in the life-struggle" (Lotka 1922a, 147). Lotka pointed out that the Mayer–Joule (first) and Carnot–Clausius (second) laws of thermodynamics only explained what was not possible, but they were inadequate for understanding the tendency of systems to grow in size and complexity. In his view, the populations that would succeed and grow were not only those effective at capturing available energy, but those "suitably constituted" to increase the total energy flux through the systems in which they live. The second point is critical. It can occur through indirect means, such as species that unintentionally support other energy-capturing populations with their waste products or behavior; or it can occur by direct means, such as the increased cycles of planting and harvesting implemented in human agriculture. The mechanisms of natural selection explain how overall system behavior or "goals" can emerge from the interactions of species that are otherwise acting in their own self-interest.

Natural selection is only half of the evolutionary mechanism described by Darwin; the other half is the generation of variations. In the classic view, the variations in biological life are generated by random mutations in the genetic code and the "fittest" are selected by their environment, allowing them to continue to reproduce. The criteria of fitness have been much debated, as has the scale of entity to which selection applies: individuals, species, or ecosystems? Lotka argued that the principle of environmental selection applied to any coherent system that converted available power and generated variations, from inanimate chemical reactions to organic life and human technology. This argument enabled him to reframe the goal of natural selection and the environmental dilemma of humanity as a general question of thermodynamics. As Lotka wrote:

> The influence of man, as the most successful species in the competitive struggle, seems to have been to accelerate the circulation of matter through the life cycle, both by "enlarging the wheel," and by causing it to "spin faster." The question was raised whether, in this, man has been unconsciously fulfilling a law of nature, according to which some physical quantity in the system tends toward a maximum. This is now made to appear probable; and it is found that the physical quantity in question is of the dimensions of power, or energy per unit time.
>
> (Lotka 1922a, 149)

Like tornadoes, animal populations, and ecosystems, human civilization is a form of self-organization where variations are selected over time for their ability to maximize the flow of useful power. This simple proposition requires quite a bit of elaboration (from the proper measures of useful power to the specific mechanisms of selection), but it puts environmental building design in its correct scale and context: more efficient buildings and components contribute to the power of the institution or society for which they are built. It also highlights the deeper challenge, which Lotka called "unconsciously fulfilling a law of nature."

Can a clearer understanding of emergent system goals such as maximum power help us maintain the healthy productivity of humans in the biosphere?

Lotka ultimately proposed that selection for maximum power could be a fourth law of thermodynamics (the third is the definition of absolute zero), a general principle in the "persistence of stable forms" (Lotka 1922b). He added a number of distinctions to the principle, the most important being that growth in size and increases in total power flow succeed only when there are sufficient available resources (matter and energy). Wrote Lotka: "Where the supply of available resources is limited, the advantage will go to that organism which is most efficient, most economical, in applying to preservative uses such energy as it captures" (150). Increased energy efficiency can be effective for either maximizing power or competing for scarce resources, a critical distinction visible in the different ways in which efficiency has been explained. Take the design of cars and buildings, for example. In the periods of higher energy prices over the last century (1948–50, 1973–79, 2006–08), the availability and numbers of smaller, more efficient cars and buildings increased quickly, while in periods of lower price, greater efficiency has been used to increase the power of engines and the size or capacity of buildings.

Lotka's law, however, is enforced inconsistently. In fact, it seems confusing to call maximum power a "law" in the same sense as the Carnot–Clausius law. The second law explains that entropy always increases, that all energy conversions involve waste, and it admits no exceptions, no temporary instances of perpetual motion. The principle of maximum power is a different kind of explanation, which describes the final or selection goal toward which the process, species, or system evolves over time. In a selection process, many variations will exist that do not deliver maximum power, but if the conditions of the environment remain relatively stable over many generations of variations, the more successful configurations will succeed and persist. If conditions change more quickly, then the selection goal will shift and other strategies will eventually persevere. The contingency of even the simplest selection process, such as the interaction between predators and prey, helps illustrate why natural ecosystems are constantly changing and why the restless generation and testing of alternate arrangements are parts of the principle.

When faced with conditions of scarcity, individuals have such a fundamental instinct for frugality and efficiency that the conservation of available energy (or the minimization of entropy) is often assumed to be the real goal of a successful species (or of environmental building design). Lotka and others pointed out that when it comes to minimizing entropy, simple plants are far more effective than most mammals or even more complex plants, so selection for greater efficiency would suggest that the earth should be covered with plant forms such as algae (Lotka 1922a). We have only to look around us to realize that the complex, hierarchical arrangements of less efficient but more powerful plants and animals have succeeded over time. Far from minimizing the use of available energy, they have dramatically increased the populations that can be supported as well as the flow of resources through ecosystems. Building on the analysis of energy exchanges in this way led to the recognition that the food chains themselves might be a thermodynamic principle of ecosystem organization.

In 1942, Raymond Lindeman published a short article, "The Trophic–Dynamic Aspect of Ecology," based on his doctoral study of the succession of plant species in Minnesota's Cedar Creek Bog. Lindeman died not long after publishing the article, which was recognized as a classic paper establishing the value of energy flow in ecosystems (see Figure 1.4). Some 35 years later, R. E. Cook observed that "the work's most enduring contribution is that it provided a common currency (organic matter or energy flow) for studying interactions among trophic levels ... thus establishing a theoretical orientation in ecology" (Cook 1977, 25). At the time of the publication, Lindeman was working as a postdoctoral student at Yale University under limnologist G. Evelyn Hutchinson, who immediately recognized its importance for comparing the organization of different aquatic systems. But it was Hutchinson's doctoral student, H.T. Odum, who later embraced and generalized Lindeman's approach.

The basic principle of the trophic–dynamic approach was the tracking of energy exchanges between the elements of an ecosystem, taking into account every exchange, storage, and conversion of available energy. This principle revealed the now familiar hierarchical arrangements between primary producers that fix sunlight and nutrients into organic molecules, herbivores that feed on plant matter, and higher levels of carnivores that feed on herbivores and on each other. Energy flows also helped reveal indirect connections through the recycling of waste and the interaction between ecological processes operating at different spatial and temporal scales. Over the next 30 years, Odum generalized the use of energy exchanges for understanding the organization of complex systems, testing and restating Lotka's maximum power principle. Odum finally identified the trophic web or energy transformation hierarchy itself as a selection principle for open, thermodynamic systems (see Figure 1.5).

Environments of maximum power

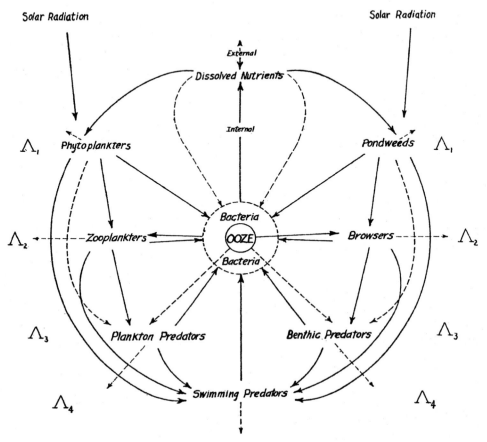

Figure 1.4: "The trophic–dynamic viewpoint [. . .] emphasizes the relationship of trophic or 'energy-availing' relationships within the community unit to the process of succession" (399)

R. Lindeman, *Ecology*, © 1942 Ecological Society of America

Maximum power

Odum's first advance on Lotka's maximum power principle was a startling 1955 paper, prepared with the physicist R. C. Pinkerton. In this paper, Odum and Pinkerton considered the way the rate of energy dissipation (or entropy increase) was actually regulated, since the second law provided little guidance. As they observed:

> One of the vivid realities of the natural world is that living and also man-made processes do not operate at the highest efficiencies that might be expected of them. Living organisms, gasoline engines, ecological communities, civilizations, and storage battery chargers are examples. In natural systems, there is a general tendency to sacrifice efficiency for more power output. Man's own struggle for power is reflected in the machines he builds. In our energy-rich culture, most of our engines are designed to give maximum power output for their size.
>
> (Odum and Pinkerton 1955, 331)

Using a variety of natural and technological examples with rates of energy use proportional to the forces or populations driving them, Odum and Pinkerton demonstrated that maximum power occurs at intermediate levels of efficiency. In conditions with abundant available energy, efficiency is sacrificed for power, while under conditions of scarcity, efficiency becomes the more effective strategy. In their words, "We are taking 'survival of the fittest' to mean persistence of those forms which can command the greatest useful energy per unit time (power output)."

It would be hard to find a drier statement to describe the remarkably frustrating dilemma that faces environmental activists and designers who advocate efficiency as a solution to excess consumption. Efficiency is a strategy that makes sense to everyone when energy prices are high, but the appeals of power apparently take over during periods of abundance. In 1856, the economist William Stanley Jevon first observed that the steadily increasing efficiency of coal-powered steam engines had already led to decades of increasing coal usage, rather than a reduction. In "Jevon's paradox," also called the rebound effect, the savings produced by greater efficiency are reinvested to increase production. The rebound effect has been much debated since being introduced, and economist Harry Saunders gave Jevon's work a sharper definition in the 1990s when he distinguished between direct and indirect effects, between a direct encouragement of increased energy consumption by the reduction of energy prices and indirectly through increased economic growth. Saunders dubbed it the "Khazzoom–Brookes Postulate" after two earlier economists who were interested in the paradox (Saunders 1992).

Saunders' argument about indirect effects has been strengthened by the work of economists Robert Ayres and Benjamin Warr. Their work shows that the

Environments of maximum power

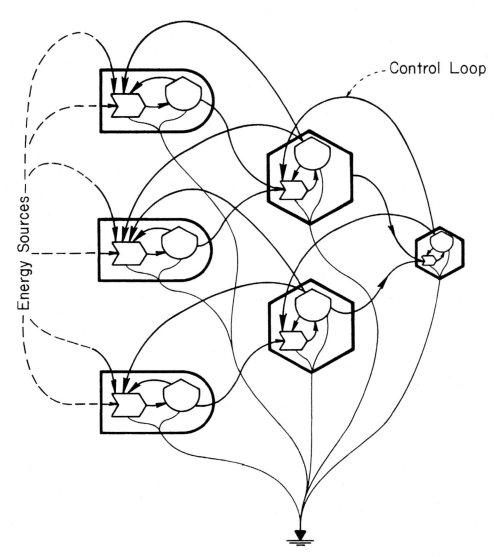

Figure 1.5: "A characteristic web of converging energy transformations and feedback of interaction control loops found in self-organizing systems" (17)

H. T. Odum, *Systems Ecology*, © 1983 John Wiley & Sons

spectacular growth of wealth in the United States through the twentieth century did not correlate to primary energy consumption, but rather to the "useful" work actually delivered, which results from the increasingly efficient conversion of increasing amounts of fuels (Ayres and Warr 2009). The debate about rebound mechanisms remains active among economists and environmentalists (Ayres and Warr 2008). A recent book by David Owen, *The Conundrum: How Scientific Innovation, Increased Efficiency, and Good Intentions Can Make Our Energy and Climate Problems Worse* (2012), sparked a heated debate with Amory Lovins, the authoritative advocate of building energy efficiency since the 1970s. Lovins argued that for most of the efficiency improvements in buildings, there are natural limits to consumption; we cannot wash more loads of dishes or laundry, neither do we exceed a comfortable temperature once it is achieved (Vaughn 2012).

Much of the argument involves the scale at which the analysis is conducted, and whether it focuses on the use and efficiency of individual products or on the behavior of larger systems. The growth in size of cars and houses in the US over the last few decades has absorbed much of the efficiency gains achieved through more efficient design, while the development of new categories of labor-saving and power-consuming devices (the "other" category in energy usage surveys) has taken up much of the rest. But the focus on the success or failure of efficiency misses the important lesson offered by Lotka, Odum, and other ecologists: the overall goal of communities and societies can be dramatically different from the goals or beliefs of its members.

Hierarchies of production, and e[m]ergy

Food chains and other energy-transformation hierarchies increase the total flow of power, just as Lotka described. But the very fact that these hierarchies existed is what Odum explored for the rest of his career and used as a tool for evaluating complex, self-organizing ecosystems. Odum actually began his career studying energy exchanges in weather formation and ecosystems, and then started in the 1960s to apply those techniques to human activities. Despite the power of energy accounting to reveal the structure of systems, he quickly recognized that tracking energy according to its first-law heat equivalence overlooked the very different cost and quality of different energy sources. The simplest example in building operation is the difference between the energy content of fuels burned for heating or cooking and the energy content of electricity used to power motors or electronics. Electric energy is different in two senses: first, more energetic potential is used up in its production and delivery, and second, it is a cleaner, more concentrated, and more flexible form of power. Electricity is typically generated by burning fuels at a conversion efficiency of about 35%; for each unit of electric power used in a building, three units of fuel are burned back at the power plant. Odum's general proposition was that in a mature system (such as a climax forest, which had developed over a long period of time), the higher cost of a particular food or energy resource would be an indicator of higher quality and of a more valuable role in the production hierarchy.

Differences in energy quality are not limited to explicit power sources such as gas or electricity, but apply to every useful resource or service in an ecosystem. Meat is a higher quality of food than plants because herbivores have to consume many calories of plant matter for each calorie of their flesh. Carnivorous fish represent an even higher cost, because they eat even higher in the food chain. The large numbers of lower level producers in trophic webs are needed to support the smaller numbers of higher quality entities at the top. While this makes the predators more expensive, quality is not merely a measure of energy cost. As Lotka's predator–prey dynamic illustrated, predators and other specialized creatures also serve a balancing, regulatory role in ecosystems. Top predators are the products of an ecosystem—not their rulers—and they are the first to suffer when their ecosystem is stressed. In fully developed ecosystems, small amounts of higher quality energy are expended to regulate other levels and to amplify the flow and storage of available resources through the whole system. A significant difference between natural and human ecosystems is that social roles are not filled by the evolution of new species but by the adaptation and retraining of individuals. Since the first nomadic tribes, human societies have been increasingly hierarchical, developing increasingly specialized roles and social arrangements.

Odum's proposition was an extension of Lotka's selection principle: energy transformation hierarchies develop and succeed over time because they maximize the flows of useful power. If we call the maximum power principle a "final cause" or the selection goal of a self-organizing system, then energy transformation hierarchies are a kind of "formal cause," a form of organization that systems evolve toward over time in conditions with available energy. As Lindeman demonstrated, those hierarchies could be understood and diagrammed by following the chains of energy exchanges, but Odum recognized that tracking the cumulative energy dissipated in the support of each subsequent level could be used to indicate its value or quality within a production hierarchy. Odum subsequently coined the term "emergy" to distinguish the accounting of cumulative dissipated energy from first-law measurements of energy based on heat content, or second-law measurements of available energy (or exergy).

E[m]ergy is a system concept, developed to understand and reveal the production hierarchies that emerge over time in natural and human ecosystems. The concept of e[m]ergy is inseparable from the "energy systems language" that Odum used to understand and explain the direct and indirect interactions that constitute systems and the "algebra" of its accounting. He began developing the diagramming language in the 1950s—drawing on the conventions of electrical circuit diagrams, general systems theory, and Jay W. Forrester's *Industrial Dynamics* and *World Dynamics* (1961, 1971, used for the world model in *Limits to Growth* 1972)—and settled on its basic form in the 1970s in conjunction with the principle of tracking embodied or cumulative dissipated energy (Brown 2004). The development of the energy systems language was fully complete with the publication of his book *Systems Ecology* (1983b). Odum continued throughout the following decade to steadily refine the rules of its accounting, culminating in the publication of *Environmental Accounting* (1996), which elaborated the basic principles of e[m]ergy "algebra." The diagrams became fully expressive of energy quality hierarchies when they adopted the convention of organizing the energy sources, flows, and storages left-to-right according to their e[m]ergy intensity, with original sources and primary producers at the left and higher level consumer and products to the right. The symbols and conventions of the energy systems language will be used throughout the rest of this book (see Appendix A for a more complete description).

In Odum's original definition from 1986, "EMERGY is the available energy of one kind previously used up directly and indirectly to make a service or product." There are many accounting challenges in accurately determining such a complex property, but it provides a powerful tool for comparing very different energy sources and materials when the accounting is normalized to the original solar energy fueling the system, making the basic unit of e[m]ergy the "solar emjoule" (sej). As noted previously, the measurement of dissipated energy is typically called "embodied energy" (evoked by the "m" in e[m]ergy); however, that term is largely associated with the input–output analysis of energy flows within the economy, which counts environmental energies as "free," so Odum adopted his neologism to describe the cumulative dissipation of all available energies within the biosphere. E[m]ergy is a powerful, analytical tool, but one easily confused with the terms energy and exergy (especially in a world of auto-correction). To keep the focus on principles, this book mostly uses more cumbersome descriptions, such as cumulative dissipated energy, total expended work and resources, or total costs. In cases where the term has to be used for precision, the brackets around the [m] will be included.

The cumulative amount of dissipated energy becomes an indicator of quality when the intensity per unit of energy or material is determined (sej/J, sej/g, sej/$). Unit e[m]ergy intensities provided a systemic metric of environmental quality or efficiency, which can be used to guide the selection of materials and fuels. Coupled with the diagramming language, they can reveal production hierarchies, dependencies, interconnections, and relative values. Higher intensity fuels, materials, and services can serve critical, regulatory roles in self-organizing systems or their higher unit intensity can simply indicate the unproductive dissipation of excess capacity. The distinction turns on the different kinds of work involved.

Useful work

Energy is the capacity to do work, but it is worth recalling the pragmatic origins of thermodynamics that established the focus on physical forms of work. Watt's engines lifted coal and pumped water. Joule wondered about the economics of switching his brewery from steam to electric motors. Mayer was intrigued by the human body's greater food efficiency in warmer climates. The focus on the heat equivalence of work often discounts the many other activities we typically call work, such as the reading, writing, counting, processing, and ordering that require little physical work. There are many even less physically measureable aspects of work that nonetheless rightly belong to a more complete description, such as the value of timing, organization, or the availability of necessary materials to accomplish work. The second law explains the limiting role of environmental temperatures in determining the maximum efficiency of conversion, but a full account of the capacity for work requires an assessment of all the other limiting factors of production—matter and information—and the history of their availability.

The work of constructing even the most efficient or renewably sourced building can be wasted if it is located in the wrong place, meets the wrong needs, or is operated incorrectly. Its effectiveness is as much a property of its context

Environments of maximum power

and timing as of its raw resource efficiency. It takes a relatively small amount of physical work to decide where and when to build, but the right decision at the right time can make the difference between waste and productivity. These forms of work involve a similar, hierarchical chain of production as found in the upper levels of a food chain, with large amounts of low-quality energy dissipated in activities like heating and cooling to support the development of work and information that is useful to the economy. The detection of production hierarchies in successful ecosystems can be extended to the evaluation of hierarchies in human work, but because the modern, metropolitan environment has developed over such a short period, we have to proceed with care. There is no reason to assume that the current configurations and use of resources are optimal for anything but rapid growth.

Odum's argument about hierarchical forms of production has two aspects: as a selection goal of self-organization, and as a definition of the property to help detect and evaluate those hierarchies. As M.T. Brown explained, "Odum redefined work as an energy transformation where an input energy is transformed to a new form (or concentration) of 'higher quality'" (2004, 85). In other words, e[m]ergy is a system concept, which describes the work of a production hierarchy, with greater e[m]ergy intensity measuring levels of quality within the system. That led to the reformulation of the fourth principle as the principle of maximum em-power, which helps explain the competitive success of more mature ecosystems that may have a lower throughput of raw power, but whose greater complexity of interconnection involves much greater amounts of e[m]ergy. However, the cumulative nature of e[m]ergy calculations makes it more difficult to evaluate the intensity of higher quality resources that develop over larger areas and time spans, especially information.

Information in systems

One of the basic distinctions between a tool and a machine is the capacity of the machine to regulate itself, which requires a theory of information to explain the power of feedback. The importance of information in the regulation of useful energy processes was written into thermodynamics from the beginning. A key part of Watt's steam engine was the mechanical governor he developed to automatically "throttle" the steam feeding the engine so that its velocity stayed constant. Many refinements and variations were developed over the following century to reduce the oscillations that such governors produce as they over- and undershoot the target velocity, behaving like a predator–prey system. Both the control of velocity and its oscillations around the target are effects that emerge from the operation and configuration of the engine, but neither is described by the first or second law of thermodynamics.

Although the importance of information in thermodynamics was recognized from the start, the mathematical tools to describe information's thermodynamic role were only developed in the twentieth century. J. C. Maxwell first explored the mathematics of the dynamics in 1868, which set the basis for cybernetics and systems theory in the mid-twentieth century. For his first project at Yale in 1869, Willard Gibbs designed an improved mechanical governor; however, without any principles on which to build a system theory, he soon shifted to the description of available energy for which he is known (Gibbs' free energy). Any ongoing energy transformation requires regulation, which could be accomplished by the operation of a simple tool by its user or an autonomous feedback device like a thermostat or governor.

As the ecologist Robert Ulanowicz observed, "Information refers to the effects of that which imparts order and pattern to a system" (1997, 65). The information coded in biological genes, for example, involves very small amounts of material and chemical potential, but exerts tremendous influence over the development and behavior of living systems. Schrodinger's great insight recognized the power of genetic information to regulate the statistically improbable decrease of a cell's entropy, keeping itself alive by importing low-entropy resources such as food from its environment. Like work, the word information means many things in everyday language, but in this context it represents a high-quality form of stored energetic potential that can accomplish useful work by channeling and regulating lower quality flows. Schrodinger himself noted that his argument was more correctly framed in terms of "free energy" (or exergy), but the link between low entropy, order, and information has a metaphoric appeal that has obscured the subject ever since.

Odum pointed out that Boltzmann's statistical definitions of entropy only serve as a useful indicator of order at a microscopic scale, where the entropy of molecules increases as temperatures rises; but it fails to describe the utility of many arrangements at macroscopic scales (Odum 2007). For example, the higher internal temperature of a house or mammal in winter has greater entropy than a cold one, even though it takes considerable work and information to maintain that temperature. The organization of the gene, the building, and the mammal all operate far from thermodynamic equilibrium, and their value can only be explained with a more complete description of the information with which they are maintained. Part of the confusion arises from the expression for probabilities used in statistical thermodynamics and in information theory ($s = -k \log p$). The thermodynamic expression for entropy uses the Boltzmann constant to relate the average energy of the molecules in the material to the macroscopic temperature measurement, giving it a precise physical meaning ($k = 1.38065 \times 10^{-23}$ J/°K). In contrast, information theory adopted a proportional constant that disconnects it from any physical correspondence, resulting in the wholly abstract measurement of "bits."

As an ecological tool, Ulanowicz instead adapted a statistical measure of system complexity, "average mutual information," and then used the total matter–energy throughput as a scaling constant for applying it to ecosystems (1997). Multiplying them together, he produced an index called "ascendency," which combines the system's total complexity and power flow. In a proposition similar to the maximum power principle, he argued that "in the absence of overwhelming external disturbances, living systems exhibit a natural propensity to increase in ascendency" (65). Among the many different strategies explored by ecosystems in their development, he argued, arrangements are selected to increase the total throughput of power (growth), their complexity (development), or both. This is conceptually consistent with Odum's maximum empower principle where information ordering and regulating a system has a higher e[m]ergy intensity, even though it has proved difficult to quantify.

The theory of ascendency was based on empirical observations about ecological succession. Like the maximum empower principle, it has also been used to describe the growth and development of social systems. In *The Collapse of Complex Societies*, the anthropologist Joseph Tainter used the related economic concepts of excess overhead and declining marginal returns to explain the sudden loss of order in state societies (Tainter 1988). However, analogies such as these between biological, technological, and social systems have to be drawn with care, recognizing their differences and evaluating the actual mechanisms for creating order and using information. The methods of copying and maintaining information mark a critical distinction between the information that organizes biological reproduction, the emergence of ecosystems, and human enterprises such as building design or social organization. The information coded in genetic material is reproduced with very high fidelity and (mostly) follows precise rules of recombination. The information organizing ecosystems only exists in the relationships among its geological and biological elements, so the process directing ecosystem succession is less precise and unfolds differently each time, arriving (eventually) at a functionally similar arrangement. The reproduction of cultural products such as buildings is an even more open and promiscuous process, involving many different kinds of copying and variation among many different scales of interaction. There have been numerous attempts to explain technological development by analogy to genetic evolution, using concepts such as "memes," but design is far more indeterminate, and not only involves the reconstruction and reinterpretation of symbolic information but is also partly directed towards specific goals. Explicitly stated environmental goals are themselves a form of information regulating the reproduction of human artifacts.

Buildings are embodied forms of information as well as settings in which concentrated forms of information are processed, stored, and applied. In contrast to genetic coding, human society has externalized the storage and transmission of information, enhancing its capacity to adapt and grow. In this sense, all forms of technology, from buildings to social arrangements, can be described as forms of information, but the term can be confusing, suggesting the complete abstraction from material and energy flows. R. N. Adams preferred the more general term *energy form*, which combines "matter and information" and includes anything "that has the potential of releasing energy and is, therefore, theoretically capable of doing work" (1988, 15). This distinction helps clarify the nature of information, which is coded in material forms even when that material is the subtlest variation of an electromagnetic field. The flexibility that results from its concentration helps explain its powerful role, while the abstraction can conceal its energetic basis. As Adams argued, "*Energy forms* are of interest to people principally because of their meanings and functions, and only occasionally does this include their energy dimensions."

We cannot measure information directly. The heat released when a book is burned, for example, only describes the heat equivalence of the paper and not the information it conveys, which dissipates without a trace (unless there are copies). Information theory can be used to establish the capacity of a particular channel of communication, the number of bits stored in a book or the gigabyte flow through an internet connection, but not its effects or utility. The key to understanding information in buildings is the power of its reproduction and transmission. The architect in that mythical tribe who first figured out how to build a shelter could continue building shelters for as long as he lived and had sufficient resources, but he increased the effect of his discovery by helping others learn how to build as well. That process is enhanced by coding the instructions in drawings, and further amplified by making and distributing copies of the information in manuscripts, books, and now building information models (BIM).

The value of information can be partly explained by considering the costs of its replacement (Odum 2007). There is considerably more time and work involved in redrawing the plans of the Villa Rotunda than in acquiring a copy of Palladio's *Four Books*. But even a well-made book is still subject to decay, and so its materials have to be maintained. The astonishing power of information is the ability to make many copies at relatively low cost, recognizing that each copy has the same capacity as the original, can extend its reach, and reduce the rate of depreciation. Without the *Four Books*, Palladio would only have been a successful architect of the Veneto; the first copy of his book required the most work to develop, roughly half of his career, and also makes evident the role of previously developed information. Palladio's work was not possible without his teachers and the tradition of building in the region.

Like other thermodynamic transformations, the potential value of information depends on its history and context. Publishing Palladio's work in BIM form in the seventeenth century would have had no effect without the tools of the information society. Buildings cannot be wholly reduced to the information describing them. Their value is determined by the particular production hierarchy, in which the information is applied, including building codes, trade practices, conventions of work, cultural norms, and a host of other kinds of information. The success of human civilization has involved progressive refinements in assembling and transmitting non-genetic information to successive generations, from the invention of language to writing, social organizations, and technological inventions. Each stage in the intensification of information transmission has amplified the reach of humanity, but its power still rests on the material capacities and cycles of the planet we occupy.

Material cycles and pulsing of systems

In Odum's exploration of Lotka's maximum power principle, the final systems concept he considers is the tendency of complex systems to cycle or pulse over time as their many feedback and reinforcement mechanisms interact. Like populations of predators and prey, the velocity of a steam engine, or the temperature regulated by a household thermostat, systems typically oscillate, over- and undershooting their target state. Systems can also cycle through recognizable stages of development, such as the life cycle of individual creatures or the succession of species on virgin land. These kinds of cycling are a much described aspect of ecosystems. C. S. Holling's "adaptive cycle," first published in the 1980s, has come to exemplify the principle, showing the movement of ecosystems through four characteristic stages of "exploitation, conservation, release, and renewal" (1992) (see Figure 1.6). That memorable formulation emerged from his 1973 paper on *Resilience and Stability*, which applied the mathematics of non-linear dynamics to understand the resilience of successful ecosystems as they cycled through the stages of adaptation. The concept of resilience not only explained the ability of ecosystems to survive events such as wildfires and insect plagues, but identified such events as integral aspects of self-organization.

The principle of resilience is increasingly offered as substitute for the goal of sustainable development, exchanging the steady state of the climax forest for a

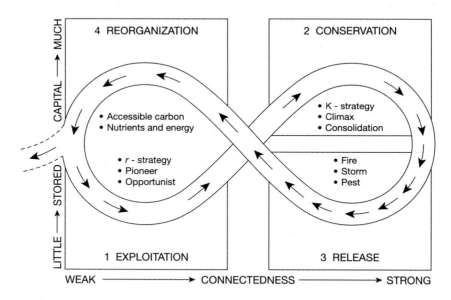

Figure 1.6: "The four ecosystem functions and the flow of events between them" (481)
C. S. Holling, *Ecological Monographs*, © 1992 Ecological Society of America

Environments of maximum power

dynamic process of growth, collapse, and renewal. Holling's adaptive cycle exemplifies the shift in thinking from an ecology of species or specific populations to the behavior of whole communities and ecosystems. The "figure eight" of his diagram, showing balanced exchanges between the stored capital of ecosystems and their connectedness, distinguishes the work invested in the growth of biomass from the work invested in organizing the ecosystem as stages of the cycle. Ulanowicz added a finer level of precision to the adaptive cycle in the 1990s, using the statistical measure of "average mutual information" to evaluate the level of structural organization. That version of the adaptive cycle makes visible the asymmetry between "release" and the three stages of growth and development and the energy required to drive them (see Figure 1.7).

Many have been inspired to use the four stages of the cycle to describe the adaptive behavior of social and business cycles of all kinds, from personal growth to stock market analysis, and the common-sense appeal is apparent. In principle, cycles of release and renewal continue for as long as there is a supply of available energy and the system is not otherwise stressed beyond its capacity to adapt.

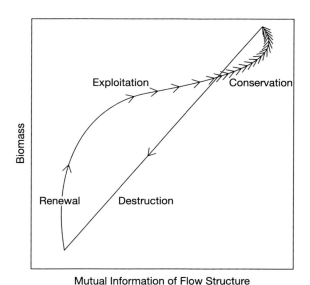

Figure 1.7: "Hypothetical counterpart for Holling's diagram, created by plotting the biomass of the system against the mutual information inherent in the flow structure" (90)

From R. E. Ulanowicz, *Ecology: The Ascendent Perspective*. Copyright © 1997 Columbia University Press. Reprinted with permission of the publisher

Environments of maximum power

The appeal of endless cycles reveals again the tension between system strategies and the interests of the individuals who are released or destroyed in the process of renewal. Bataille observed that "the very word interest is contradictory with the *desire* at stake under these conditions," by which he meant the "pressure" of accumulated resources to dissipate (1988, 30). The pressure of second-law depreciation is countered by increasingly complex arrangements that also serve to increase the flow of power and the dissipation of available energy.

Odum argued that the cycles of release and renewal were another strategy for maximizing power flow, which could be understood by studying the movement and concentration of materials within the pulsed cycles of adaptation. In the classic example of the forest fire, the available energy in the biomass is rapidly oxidized, converted to heat, and dissipated in the atmosphere. The energy that had earlier been expended to build and organize the trees, forest, and habitats—their order or information content—is even more decisively dissipated. The energy and information of the forest is coded in its material arrangements, in the available energies of organic molecules, and in the organization of the forest and animal populations. Depending on the severity of the fire, the reordering of the forest is passed on through the information coded in seeds, in the trees left standing, in the animals that could flee, and in the communities of soil microorganisms that survived. Over time, the flows of available environmental resources—sun, rain, and nutrients—are used to recycle the degraded materials and reassemble the forest.

Research has shown that fire prevention in alpine forests simply defers the inevitable fire, increases its intensity, and makes renewal slower, though many subalpine forests have longer, natural periods between large fires (Schoennagel et al. 2004). The frequency and severity of fires corresponds to the amount of biomass (fuel) built up in the forest, the structural mix of species, and local climate patterns. In Bataille's terms, when available resources are in excess and growth has slowed, "the excess energy (wealth) ... must necessarily be lost without profit; it must be spent, willingly or not, gloriously or catastrophically" (Bataille 1988, 21). The principle that Odum discerned in these cycles begins with the established link between the amounts of accumulated fuel, the period of the cycles, and the intensity of the release, and is expanded by including the total amount of work and resources expended to assemble the forest ecosystem in the first place.

In other words, energy and material cycles are inextricably linked; in self-organizing systems, materials will be organized in hierarchies of concentration and intensity that follow the hierarchies of energy transformation. This can be illustrated even more clearly by tracking the concentrations of an individual material such as iron. The majority of iron in the geobiosphere exists in a diffuse background concentration, but the energy expended through geological and biological cycles has gathered small amounts of iron in the more concentrated mixes that we call ores, which can be mined and further concentrated with the expenditure of more work and energy. With each increase in concentration, more energy is required and some material is lost to lower levels of concentration, producing a hierarchy of materials of higher concentrations and e[m]ergy intensity.

Odum's general statement of the principle linked the spectrum of the e[m]ergy intensity of materials to "mass flows, concentrations, production processes, and frequency of pulsed recycle" (Odum 2002). He debated whether this constituted a sixth principle of self-organizing systems or a corollary to the fifth principle of energy hierarchies, but it will be listed separately in this book because the distinction between energy and material intensity hierarchies is so useful for describing buildings. The interaction between materials and fuels in buildings, or between urban centers and less intensive land uses, can be detected through material concentrations. The sixth principle explicitly connects material and spatial practices with energy transformation hierarchies and selection for maximum power, revealing the dynamic cycles that use pulses of available energy to shape and concentrate material structures that in turn contribute to the further enhancement of power flow.

The climax forest as a resilient system continues to offer a powerful model for environmental design, especially the nearly perfect recycling of materials accomplished with hierarchical cascades of energy transformation (food chains). Systems tend toward such productive hierarchies over time in order to maximize their power, whether they ever arrive at the perfected state. The development or emergence of such systems has to be traced backwards as well. Ecosystems and civilizations are built within the remnants of the previous situation. Design is thermodynamic in this fundamental sense, linking "fire and memory" in Fernández-Galiano's apt phrase (2000). Every project and building is a renovation of already existing, historical conditions. They use some amount of current energies to reorder the local situation, export their wastes (entropy), and accumulate wealth. Environmental building design begins with the historical, accidental conditions of the current environment and projects a potential future.

System principles in the built environment

The theory of material concentration cycles completes the trilogy of thermodynamic system concepts that Odum developed from Lotka's original proposition. To summarize, there are three classic laws of thermodynamics:

1. The Mayer–Joule principle of the conservation of energy measured as heat equivalents.
2. The Carnot–Clausius principle of the increase of entropy, or loss of available energy, in any energy conversion or work process.
3. The principle of an absolute zero temperature at which the entropy of a perfect crystal is zero.

To add to these three classic laws, Odum proposed three additional system principles:

4. The Lotka–Odum principle of maximum empower as the selection goal toward which self-organizing systems evolve over time.
5. The Lindeman–Odum principle of energy transformation hierarchies, which emerge over time to achieve maximum power.
6. The principle of material concentration hierarchies, closely coupled to energy transformation hierarchies, which cycle or pulse at different spatial and temporal scales to achieve maximum power.

Self-organization

The principles of maximum power, production hierarchies, and material cycles of renewal situate the design of more efficient buildings in their social and environmental context. Asking environmental questions shifts from the efficiency goals of individuals concerned about scarcity to the productivity sought by the overall ecosystem. That shift alters the nature of building design. The energy systems language and e[m]ergy accounting methods are techniques that Odum developed to detect the structure of self-organizing systems. The next chapter applies these techniques to understand the ways in which buildings result from and contribute to thermodynamic self-organization. The real fruit of systems ecology is to discern the behavior of the built environment as it develops from the activities of different actors. This includes the historical evolution of building types and styles, market preferences for specific materials and methods of construction, and real estate dynamics. Each of these directs, limits, and shapes the buildings that we actually build.

Bibliography

Adams, Richard N. 1988. *The Eighth Day: Social Evolution as the Self-Organization of Energy*. Austin, TX: University of Texas Press.

Ayres, Robert U., & Benjamin Warr. 2008. "Energy Efficiency and Economic Growth: The 'Rebound Effect' as a Driver." In *Energy Efficiency and Sustainable Consumption: The Rebound Effect*, edited by Horace Herring and Steve Sorrell. Basingstoke: Palgrave.

Ayres, Robert U., & Benjamin Warr. 2009. *The Economic Growth Engine: How Energy and Work Drive Material Prosperity*. Cheltenham: Edward Elgar.

Bataille, Georges. 1988. *The Accursed Share: An Essay on General Economy*. New York: Zone Books.

Brown, Mark T. 2004. "A Picture is Worth a Thousand Words: Energy Systems Language and Simulation." *Ecological Modelling* 178: 83–100.

Bullard, Clark W., Peter S. Penner, and David A. Pilati. 1976. *Net Energy Analysis: Handbook for Combining Process and Input–Output Analysis*. Urbana, IL: Energy Research Group, Center for Advanced Computation, University of Illinois at Urbana-Champaign.

Buranakarn, Vorasun. 1998. "Evaluation of Recycling and Reuse of Building Materials Using the Emergy Analysis Method." PhD, University of Florida.

Carnot, Sadi. 1824. *Réflexions sur la puissance motrice du feu et sur les machines propres à développer cette puissance*. Paris: Bachelier. Microform.

Clausius, R., & Thomas Archer Hirst. 1867. *The Mechanical Theory of Heat with its Applications to the Steam-engine and to the Physical Properties of Bodies*. London: J. van Voorst. Microform.

Cook, Robert E. 1977. "Raymond Lindeman and the Trophic–Dynamic Concept in Ecology." *Science* 198(4312): 22–26.

Deru, Michael. 2009. "U.S. Life Cycle Inventory Database Roadmap." US Department of Energy/National Renewable Energy Laboratory, Washington, DC.

DOE. 2007. *Solar Decathlon 2007*. http://www.solardecathlon.gov/past/2007/team_cincinnati.html.

Fernández-Galiano, Luis. 2000. *Fire and Memory: On Architecture and Energy.* Cambridge, MA: MIT Press.

Forrester, Jay Wright. 1961. *Industrial Dynamics.* Cambridge, MA: MIT Press.

Forrester, Jay Wright. 1971. *World Dynamics.* Cambridge, MA: Wright-Allen Press.

Galloway, Robert Lindsay. 1882. *A History of Coal Mining in Great Britain.* London: Macmillan.

Holling, C. S. 1973. "Resilience and Stability of Ecological Systems." *Annual Review of Ecology and Systematics* 4: 1–23.

Holling, C. S. 1992. "Cross-Scale Morphology, Geometry, and Dynamics of Ecosystems." *Ecological Monographs* 62(4): 447–502.

Jevons, William Stanley. 1866. *The Coal Question*, 2nd ed. London: Macmillan.

LBC. 2012. "Living Building Challenge 2.1: A Visionary Path to a Restorative Future." Seattle, WA: International Living Future Institute.

Leontief, Wassily. 1966. *Input–Output Economics.* New York: Oxford University Press.

Leopold, Aldo. 1949. *A Sand County Almanac, and Sketches Here and There.* New York: Oxford University Press.

Lindeman, Raymond L. 1942. "The Trophic–Dynamic Aspect of Ecology." *Ecology* 23(4): 399–417.

Lotka, Alfred J. 1922a. "Contribution to the Energetics of Evolution." *Proceedings of the National Academy of Sciences of the United States* 8: 147–151.

Lotka, Alfred J. 1922b. "Natural Selection as a Physical Principle." *Proceedings of the National Academy of Sciences of the United States* 8: 151–154.

Malthus, T. R. 1798. *An Essay on the Principle of Population as it Affects the Future Improvement of Society, with Remarks on the Speculations of Mr. Godwin, M. Condorcet and Other Writers.* London: J. Johnson.

Meadows, Donella H., H. Randers, Jorgen, Dennis L. Meadows, & William W. Behrens III. 1972. *The Limits to Growth: A Report for the Club of Rome's Project on the Predicament of Mankind.* New York: Universe Books.

Mertins, Detlef. 2004. "Bioconstructivisms." *NOX: Machining Architecture*, edited by Lars Spuybroek. London: Thames & Hudson.

Ministry of Housing, Spatial Planning and the Environment. 2000. *Eco Indicator 99 Manual for Designers: A Damage-oriented Method for Life Cycle Assessment.* The Hague, Netherlands.

Odum, Howard T. 1970. *Environment, Power, and Society.* New York: John Wiley & Sons-Interscience.

Odum, Howard T. 1983a. "Maximum Power and Efficiency: A Rebuttal." *Ecological Modelling* 20: 71–82.

Odum, Howard T. 1983b. *Systems Ecology: An Introduction.* New York: John Wiley & Sons, Inc.

Odum, Howard T. 1986. "Emergy in Ecosystems." In *Ecosystem Theory and Application*, edited by N. Polunin. New York: John Wiley & Sons.

Odum, Howard T. 1996. *Environmental Accounting: EMERGY and Environmental Decision Making.* New York: John Wiley & Sons, Inc.

Odum, Howard T. 2002. "Construction Ecology: Nature as a Basis for Green Buildings." In *Construction Ecology*, edited by C. J. Kibert. London and New York: Spon Press.

Odum, Howard T. 2007. *Environment, Power, and Society for the Twenty-First Century: The Hierarchy of Energy.* New York: Columbia University Press.

Odum, Howard T., & R. C. Pinkerton. 1955. "Time's Speed Regulator: The Optimum Efficiency for Maximum Output in Physical and Biological Systems." *American Scientist* 43: 331–343.

Owen, David. 2012. *The Conundrum: How Scientific Innovation, Increased Efficiency, and Good Intentions Can Make Our Energy and Climate Problems Worse.* New York: Riverhead Books.

Prigogine, Ilya, & Isabelle Stengers. 1984. *Order out of Chaos: Man's New Dialogue with Nature.* New York: Bantam New Age Books.

Rant, Zoran. 1956. "Exergie, Ein neues Wort für 'technische Arbeitsfähigkeit.'" *Forschung auf dem Gebiete des Ingenieurswesens* 22: 36–37.

Saunders, Harry D. 1992. "The Khazzoom-Brookes Postulate and Neoclassical Growth." *Energy Journal* 13(4): 131–148.

Schoennagel, Tania, Thomas T. Veblen, & William H. Romme. 2004. "The Interaction of Fire, Fuels, and Climate across Rocky Mountain Forests." *BioScience* 54(7): 661–676.

Shannon, Claude E. 1948. "A Mathematical Theory of Communication." *Bell System Technical Journal* 27 (July, October): 379–423, 623–656.

Steadman, Philip. 1979. *The Evolution of Designs: Biological Analogy in Architecture and the Applied Arts.* Cambridge Urban and Architectural Sudies. New York: Cambridge University Press.

Stein, Richard G. 1977. *Architecture and Energy.* New York: Anchor Press/Doubleday.

Tainter, Joseph A. 1988. *The Collapse of Complex Societies*, New Studies in Archaeology. Cambridge and New York: Cambridge University Press.

Ulanowicz, Robert E. 1997. *Ecology: The Ascendent Perspective*. New York: Columbia University Press.

USGBC. http://new.usgbc.org/leed.

Vaughn, Kelly. 2012. "Jevon's Paradox: The Debate That Just Won't Die." *RMI Outlet, Plug into New Ideas*, March 20. http://blog.rmi.org/blog_Jevons_Paradox.

Wiener, Norbert. 1948. *Cybernetics or Control and Communication in the Animal and the Machine*. Cambridge, MA: MIT Press; 2nd ed., 1961.

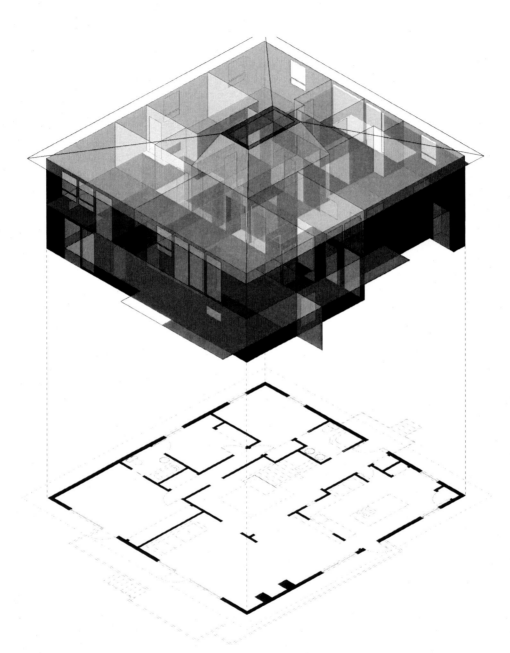

Figure 2.1: Axonometric of the "Ellis House," a mid-century house designed on a nine-square grid around a central, skylit atrium with front and back porches cantilevered on steel beams. Every room in the house has at least two doors (including bathrooms), and there are seven doors to the outside

Mather Lippincott, Architect

Chapter Two

Buildings in three parts

> In human design, we could conceivably see organic evolution continued, and extending into a man-shaped future ... All our expensive, long-term investments in constructed environment will be considered legitimate only if the designs have a high, provable index of livability. Such designs must be conceived by a profession brought up in social responsibility, skilled, and intent on aiding the survival of a race that is in grave danger of becoming self-destructive.
>
> (Neutra 1954, 3)

Buildings have evolved in fits and starts since humans built the first shelters, improving and elaborating huts and caves, steadily inventing new types of shelter, and enhancing their capacities until we all arrive at the modern metropolis. The comparison between design and evolution is not meant metaphorically, but we have to distinguish carefully between those aspects of building design that are consciously determined by architects (and others) and those that are determined by collective processes (such as real estate markets, fashion trends, and urban expansion) in which one class of variations succeeds for reasons well beyond individual design decisions. Through the many dimensions of cultural evolution, we can discern the thermodynamic principles of self-organization outlined in the first chapter. Hierarchical arrangements of energy transformation and material concentration are evident throughout the built environment, where the conflict between the collective and individual pursuit of maximum power remains an enduring ethical dilemma. Systems ecology helps to reveal these kinds of patterns, and as Odum once observed, aspires to become "the means by which the system visualizes an image of itself" (Odum 1977, 118).

Analogies to biology and evolution have been part of architectural theory from the beginning of the modern period. Even contemporary biologists, such as Jablonka, now distinguish among "four dimensions" of evolution—genetic, epigenetic, behavioral, and symbolic—where natural selection itself can be said to have evolved, adopting mechanisms that operate more quickly and with greater freedom (Jablonka 2005). Recognizing that buildings are products of cultural evolution does not exempt them from the dictates of thermodynamics—quite the opposite. By identifying the actions of self-organization at multiple scales throughout the built environment, we are able to connect the technical tracking of resource flows with the social and cultural pursuit of wealth, which buildings both facilitate and come to represent. Systems ecology links the longstanding environmental concerns with resource scarcity and pollution effects to the social and cultural dimensions in which buildings operate, and reveals the often conflicting criteria with which they are conceived.

Kiesler called the evolving ecosystem of the built environment a *correalism*, and his diagram showed mankind, not buildings, at the center of the three coevolving environments. That simple displacement marks a critical step in the formulation of an explicitly environmental form of building design, establishing buildings as one of many tools of human evolution. Kiesler was not yet aware of limitations to the biosphere, so his diagram can be updated by incorporating the thermodynamic sources and hierarchical nature of those environments. The natural environment, meaning the whole biogeosphere, forms the context, resource base, and destination for the wastes of humanity's social and cultural arrangements, which, in turn, provide the setting for the restless evolution of our technologies, from shirts and shelters to information systems (see Figure 2.2).

Three aspects of buildings: site, shelter, setting

We begin to unravel the ecosystem of the built environment by asking one simple question: What do buildings do? Examining the work and resource transformation hierarchies involved, we can distinguish among three nested scales of purpose for the construction and use of buildings: first, to occupy and intensify the characteristics of a particular *site*; second, to provide *shelter* from the climate; and third, as a *setting* for work and living (see Figure 2.3). These activities

Buildings in three parts

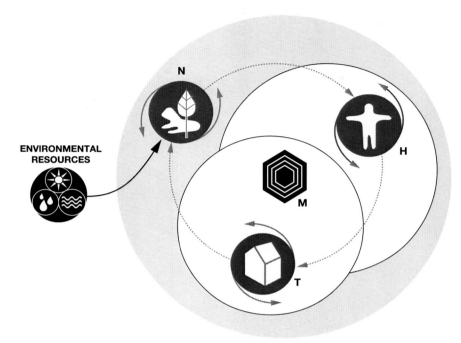

Figure 2.2: An updated version of Kiesler's correalism diagram, showing the biophysical interactions among the three coevolving environments: natural, human, and technological

are hierarchical and interconnected, meaning that the work of securing a building site is necessary for the construction of shelter, and both are needed to accommodate the activities of work and living. Conversely, the social and economic value of the activities that are housed in a building actually constrain the choice of the site, as does the climate in which it is located. The dynamics of real estate—with its steadily shifting values, locations, and patterns—provide one of the most easily recognized examples of self-organization in the built environment, which designers, planners, economists, and politicians struggle to understand and anticipate.

The central portion of this book is divided into chapters that elaborate on each of these three categories. Although the selection and preparation of the site logically precedes the construction and operation of buildings, we begin in the middle, with the building as a shelter. Why? Because building-as-shelter is the tangible focus of architecture. It is also easier to discuss the thermodynamics of sites after developing an understanding of the thermodynamics of shelter, which

Buildings in three parts

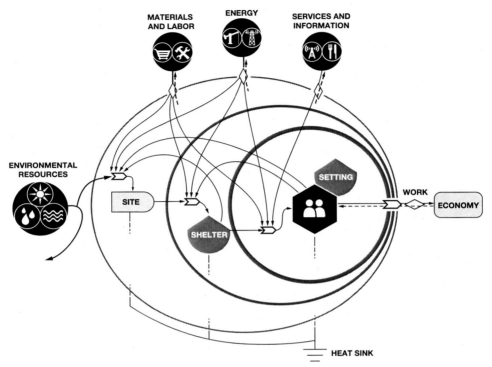

Figure 2.3: Diagram of the three, nested scales of purpose for the construction and use of buildings: intensification of a site, shelter from the climate, and setting for work and living

are a particular intensification of their location within an urban system, and that location, in turn, dictates decisions about building type, size, and quality. The link between the dynamics of urban agglomeration and environmental design is established by the capacity of sites to gather environmental energies. Unlike fuels that can be mined or logged (and depleted) from sites, the energies that arrive (more or less) continuously through sun, wind, and rain require land area to gather and concentrate them. The contrast between the energy intensity of contemporary buildings, based on concentrated fuels, and the diffuse nature of the environmental energies available on building sites, explains the radical urban reorganization required to effect any real transition to renewable energies.

Tracking the cascades of energy exchanges and treating the built environment like an ecological food web are the underlying techniques for organizing this book. Broadly speaking, the book explores six different kinds of environmental flow and service, from those involved in construction and operation to those required for the activities housed by buildings to those dictated by their urban and economic situation. Analyzing the building-as-shelter involves a categorical distinction between the work and resources invested in the construction of the building and the energy flows used to modify the climate. We divide the energies used for the building as a setting for work and living into two categories—material services and concentrated power—based on the material intensity of the resource flows. The analysis of the building-as-site distinguishes between the work and resources involved in the spatial hierarchies of urban organization and those reflecting the social and economic hierarchies of wealth, which also reflect degrees of materialization.

As it does for ecological systems, the matter of material and energy intensity appears again and again through analysis of the built environment, and helps to reveal the hierarchies among the activities for which buildings are built. In each of the three categories presented here, the flows of work and resources are differentiated by their degrees of dematerialization, with the heavier flows typically moving on slower cycles than the lighter and more concentrated ones. In summary, here are the sections of the analysis:

- Building-as-shelter from the climate
  Construction and maintenance
  Climate modification: heating, cooling, air-conditioning, ventilation, illumination
- Building-as-setting for work and living
  Material services: water, wastewater, food, supplies, trash
  Concentrated flows: fuels, power, information, money
- Building-as-site, the intensification of location
  Spatial hierarchies: urban self-organization
  Social and economic production hierarchies

Systems ecology establishes a context in which the many kinds of building performance assessment, developed over the last few decades, can be compared in order to better guide design. By assessing the cumulative work expended for each kind of resource flow, it becomes possible to estimate the environmental cost of a project and determine its relation to larger processes of self-organization. Each of the categories draws on bodies of existing research, databases of information, and the work of professional organizations and institutions. The flows of work and resources will be examined individually to identify their thermodynamic aspects and the different criteria for building performance they present.

The Ellis House

As the primary case study throughout the book, this project uses the Ellis House, a free-standing, two-story residence located in the Philadelphia suburbs that my family acquired and substantially renovated in 2005. Architect Mather Lippincott designed the original building in 1964 for a Dr. Ellis (hence the name), and I eventually used it as an example in so many classes that it accidentally became the basis for exploring the potential of systems ecology. Since houses embrace nearly every human activity from leisurely entertainment to paid work, they offer something of a microcosm of contemporary life. And since the Ellis House was not a particularly high-performance building, using it as an example helped illustrate normative behavior and the effects of different kinds of improvement. No single project can represent the wide array of building types, generations of construction, and climates, but the Ellis House serves as an introductory example for the application of ecological accounting to buildings (see Figure 2.1).

Three versions of the Ellis House have been developed to demonstrate the method of e[m]ergy accounting for buildings (see Appendix B). The first is a normative version, based on the actual construction of the original, barely insulated building with typical consumption and occupancy values for a contemporary house in the mid-Atlantic region. The second version represents the building that was renovated in 2005, largely according to conventional economic incentives; this achieved a substantial reduction in utility use and improvements in transportation, water, and food consumption. The third Ellis House version is a hypothetical example, using the same building now renovated to *Passivhaus* standards and equipped with sufficient photovoltaic panels to achieve a net zero energy (NZE) rating and comparable reductions in nearly every other category of consumption. *Passivhaus* is a well-codified approach to super-insulated building construction, first developed in the US in the 1970s and refined in Germany in the following decades (Shurcliff 1979; Passive House Institute 2014). A newly renovated neighboring building has recently received a *Passivhaus* rating, so the third version represents a current, environmentally ambitious approach (see Appendix B). Taken together, the three versions of the

Ellis House—normative, improved, and *Passivhaus* NZE—provide an illustrative range to explore the principles of environmental building design.

Of course, there are many, highly specialized forms of contemporary building that are not represented by the Ellis House. Because the scope of ecological analysis is so broad and the topics it reveals are so fundamental, we were determined to limit the number of examples. The ambition of the Ellis House case study is to identify principles of environmental building design and topics for future research. Nearly every aspect of the systems ecology applied to buildings demands more work and information, from the materials of modern construction and the characteristics of the contemporary workplace to a full accounting of the metropolis.

Bibliography

Jablonka, Eva, 2005. *Evolution in Four Dimensions: Genetic, Epigenetic, Behavioral, and Symbolic Variation in the History of Life*. Cambridge, MA: MIT Press.

Neutra, Richard. 1954. *Survival Through Design*. New York: Oxford University Press.

Odum, Howard T. 1977. "The Ecosystem, Energy, and Human Values." *Zygon* 12: 109–133.

Passive House Institute. 2014. *Active for More Comfort: Passive House. Information for Property Developers, Contractors, and Clients*. Darmstadt, Germany: International Passive House Institute.

Shurcliff, William. 1979. *Superinsulated Houses and Double-Envelope Houses: A Preliminary Survey of Principles and Practice*, 2nd ed. Cambridge, MA: Shurcliff.

Figure 3.1: "Two basic methods of exploiting the environmental potential of that timber exist: either it may be used to construct a wind-break or rain-shed—the structural solution—or it may be used to build a fire—the power-operated solution" (Banham 1969)

Photo: Robert Kerton, CSIRO

Chapter Three

Building-as-shelter

In his well-known parable of building environmental management, Reyner Banham imagined a "savage tribe, of the kind that only exist in parables" in a clearing, faced with a pile of timber (see Figure 3.1). "Two basic methods of exploiting the environmental potential of that timber exist," he wrote. "Either it may be used to construct a wind-break or rain-shed—the structural solution—or it may be used to build a fire—the power-operated solution" (1969, 19).

With this parable, Banham set up his discussion of the high-powered buildings of the mid-twentieth century, the ones based on a steady supply of fuels and electricity, and remarked that pre-industrial civilizations never really had enough ready fuel to opt for the power-operated solution. Pre-industrial designers invested most of their effort and resources in the durable and massive buildings of the structural solution; that work is said to be "embodied" in the substance and configuration of the building, which then modifies the local climate, keeping out the rain and enhancing the effects of the more modest fires that are built inside. Only with the modern luxury of excess capacity—of sufficient food, fuels, time, and knowledge—did the power-operated solution even become an option. With each decade since Banham first recounted his parable, contemporary buildings have become increasingly powerful and increasingly efficient at delivering that power.

The current promise of the power-operated solution is the growing intelligence with which enhanced power is delivered, exemplified by the development of the thermostat and the increasingly powerful information and control systems it has spawned. Buildings embody information in an even more fundamental way—in their shape, materials, and the arrangement of their parts—which the energy systems language makes visible and measurable. This chapter examines the thermodynamics of shelter in the interaction between building construction and climate modification, using the three versions of the Ellis House—normative, improved, and *Passivhaus* NZE—to put design strategies in a larger context.

Building construction

Accounting for the embodied work and resources of construction involves a critical distinction. As Banham's example illustrated, there is a difference between investing timber in the construction of a building that provides environmental services over time (the structural solution) and burning it quickly to provide heat or perform work (the power-operated solution). In the structural solution, the energetic potential in the wood is not consumed immediately by its use in the building. Some of the potential is discarded as waste during construction, but the capacity of the timber has been invested in a configuration that moderates the local climate for as long as its integrity can be maintained. In the power-operated solution, when the wood (or coal, oil, gas, etc.) is burned to produce heat, the energetic potential is simply exhausted, leaving only residual heat. In an economist's terms, the building is a "fund-of-services," while the fire is a "flow or expenditure from a stock" (Georgescu-Roegen 1971, 226). Both are subject to the irreversible dissipations of the second law, but the difference between them is in the rates at which they can be used. For example, the building as a fund-of-services might shelter one tribe for 10 years, but it cannot be used more quickly to shelter ten tribes for one year (without more wood). Conversely, the wood can be burned in 10 modest fires or all at once in a gigantic bonfire.

In the simplest thermodynamic description of building construction, a selection of materials are prepared, transported, and assembled into a building using human labor, the energetic potential of fuels and electricity, and a variety of "services" from tools to information (see Figure 3.2). All of that expended energetic potential is said to be "embodied" in the substance of the building, although only the energetic potential of the materials is physically embodied, while the fuels and services are sacrificed in construction. The stored potential of the work and resources used along the way is dissipated to the local environment, whose entropy increases, while the building achieves greater order.

Building-as-shelter

Buildings themselves can be burned to produce heat, but that would return only a small fraction of the work expended in their construction. So, the value of construction cannot be measured by its immediate energy content or its utility bills, but must include its many upstream costs and downstream effects. The real value of building design is the ability to direct and amplify flows of energetic potential to the advantage of its occupants; the thermodynamic diagram helps identify the ways the building is organized to maximize power, how it adapts (or not) to new costs and potentials, and what insight this provides for design. The choice explored in the many varieties of contemporary building is between the different uses of lower intensity materials and the more highly concentrated fuels or electricity. Determining the relative degrees of concentration, the e[m]ergy intensity of different building materials and power sources, reveals the underlying organization.

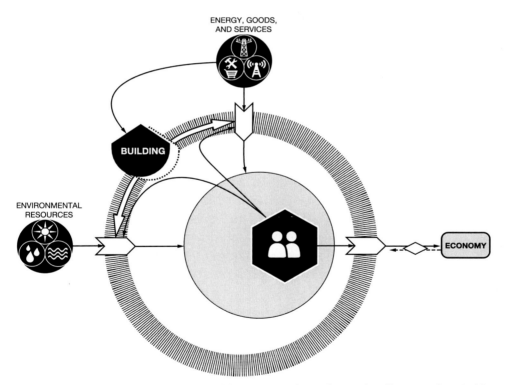

Figure 3.2: Thermodynamic diagram of building construction and operation. Resources invested in the substance of the building regulate the flows of environmental and purchased resources

Building-as-shelter

Accounting

The first step in assessing the value of construction is to determine its longevity, which dictates the amount of services that can be delivered. The duration of buildings can be extended by design and careful maintenance (albeit at a cost of additional work and resources) and it can be shortened by any number of factors, including lack of maintenance, to social or climactic changes. The real life span of a project can only be assigned a statistical probability based on past experience, and contemporary buildings are composed of multiple components, products, and subsystems, each of which has its own typical life span. A great deal of research has been done in this area, both for determining investment depreciation and for optimizing the utility of products. It makes little sense, for example, to use long-lived components in a product designed for a shorter life, or to intermingle elements whose utility may change at different rates.

Including the effect of the different longevities of building elements, or the different rates at which they need to be replaced, demands a more complex thermodynamic diagram, one that accounts for rates of change as well as the interactions between them. For commercial buildings, this principle has been followed for decades. Interior partitions are moved every few years, while structural elements are expected to endure for the life of the building. Pre-technological forms of construction had to accommodate only a few such differences—buildings and furnishings—but with the standardization of construction in the nineteenth and early twentieth century, buildings are now almost entirely constructed with interchangeable components. The full arrival of standardized construction was heralded by the classification of US building products in *Sweet's Catalog* (1906), and the "mechanization" of construction became an explicit preoccupation of the historical avant-garde in architecture. Giedion identified the period between the wars (1918–1939) as the period of "full mechanization"; he called his efforts to theorize the historical process "typological," opposing it to stylistic categorization, implicitly invoking the classification methods of evolutionary biologists (1948).

In 1920, the Purists, Amédée Ozenfant and Le Corbusier, lauded the development of "typical products," such as office furniture, as a process of "natural selection" according to principles of "maximum economy" (372). They called it "mechanical selection," which "began with the earliest times and from those times provided objects whose general laws have endured; only the means of making them changed." By 1939 Kiesler was prepared to chart the "twelve progressive stages" through which new products were selected and developed from variations in existing products, identifying the characteristic time from "invention" to "quantity production" as "approx ... 30 years" (64). Many designers since that particular period of intensity have considered the evolutionary aspects of the built environment, which can all be traced back to Samuel Butler's speculations in his book *Erewhon* (1872) about whether the rules of natural selection also applied to machines, which he wrote after reading Darwin's *Origin of Species* (1859).

The problem of accommodating mechanical evolution in buildings had already appeared in an 1869 book on domestic life by Catharine Beecher and Harriet Beecher Stowe, the *American Woman's Home*, which contained Catharine's proposal for a discrete "core" to accommodate the pipes and chimney, which has since become a characteristic feature of higher powered buildings of all kinds. The differentiation of parts of the building based on different rates of replacement (or servicing or sequencing of construction) can be traced through the rich history of mechanical cores and curtain wall construction, but explicit theories about classes or layers of change seems to begin with the "office landscape" systems (*Bürolandschaft*) developed in the 1950s by the Quickborner Team in Hamburg to help companies adapt their operations more quickly (Gottschalk 1968) (see Figure 3.3). The British architect Frank Duffy extended those methods in the 1960s, describing four layers of commercial construction based on their longevity: "shell, services, scenery, and sets" (Duffy 1964), which were generalized and popularized by Stewart Brand in the 1990s with his diagram of six "shearing layers" of buildings: "site, skin, structure, services, space plan, stuff" (Brand 1994). In a further adaptation, the Dutch group, Smart Architecture, added a seventh layer, "access, circulation," and explained the basic principle: "Be careful when mixing systems together" (Hinte and Neelen 2003, 24).

The specific layers of building construction will vary depending on the type of building. To test the hypothesis about different layers in the Ellis House, we prepared a general diagram using the six layers proposed by Brand, with the addition of a seventh for software or information systems (see Figure 3.4). In the language of US construction industry, the layers are site, structure, external envelope, systems, interiors, furniture, fixtures, and equipment (FF&E), and software. Structure includes all the weight-bearing elements, with an expected life span of 75 to 200 years. The external envelope includes the roof, walls, windows, and

Building-as-shelter

Figure 3.3: One of the early *bürolandschaft* (office landscape) experiments by the Quickborner consulting group in the 1950s, including one of the earliest office plants

© 1968 O. Gottschalk

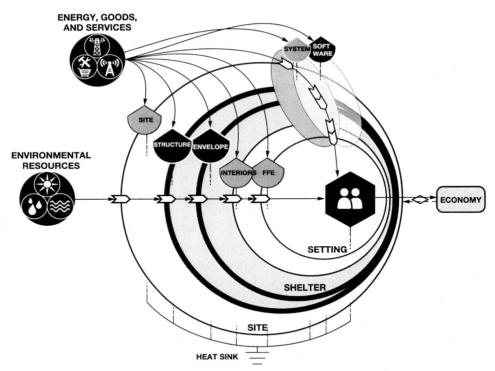

Figure 3.4: Thermodynamic diagram of seven layers of building construction based on longevity and purpose: site, envelope, structure, interiors, FF&E, systems, and software

so on, which can last from 25 to 75 years. Systems are the most intermingled of the layers and are comprised of all the elements of the building that manage the resource flows of heating and cooling, fresh air, water, and electricity. They typically remain useful for five to 25 years. Interiors include all the partitions, ceilings, finishes, and lighting that are fixed in place, and can last anywhere from three to 30 years, while FF&E include all the furnishings, fixtures, and equipment that accommodate the activities of the occupants in their daily, weekly, and seasonal movements. The software that controls contemporary systems, which is infiltrating nearly every level of contemporary buildings, introduces a seventh category that changes even more quickly, hours to months, though accounting for its upstream costs is challenging.

Examining the thermodynamic diagram helps reveal the seven layers' different roles, as well as the effect of their different rates of change. Structure supports all the other layers, while the envelope serves as the primary agent of climate modification. The interiors and FF&E are almost entirely dedicated to accommodating the occupants' activities, while the systems and software contribute equally to climate modification and the occupants' work, channeling concentrated power in different forms. In each case, the diagram indicates the total embodied work and resources invested in each layer and the flows of resources they regulate. It is relatively easy to imagine the increased separation of the more material layers—structure, envelope, interiors, and FF&E—and the characteristic elements of contemporary construction, such as suspended ceilings, curtain walls, and cubicles, illustrate techniques for that separation. However, the power and information systems present a different architectural challenge because they so explicitly cross the boundaries between layers. One example of the architectural "face" of this condition is the electric outlet, which facilitates adaptation at the point that the electric system literally crosses between layers, from concealed, more permanent wiring to the mobile devices.

Once we identify the longevity of each component, annual costs can be evaluated using depreciation accounting. The practice of allowing an annual expense for the estimated loss in asset value due to wear and tear began in the 1830s, with the growth of industries such as the railroads, based on expensive, long-lived assets. The US Tax Code only accepted the practice in 1909 and, in the 1930s, began preparing "depreciation studies," which provided official schedules of "probable, useful lives" for nearly 2,700 types of asset (Brazell et al. 1989). The services provided by building components (as a fund-of-services) are

Building-as-shelter

counted as a steady release of the work originally expended on them. Of course, the different elements of buildings wear out in different ways and their performance may degrade slowly over that time, but the decision about replacement is ultimately a judgment about their continued utility. When the furnace stops delivering heat, the decision is straightforward, while determining the useful life of paint on a wall may be less clear cut. For the thermodynamic accounting, the work and resources embodied in a building component are considered to be expended equally over that useful life. Assuming that the elements of the envelope are replaced in kind, the annual contribution would continue for as long as the building was maintained.

To determine the work and resources expended for a specific building material, the calculations rely on the e[m]ergy intensities (sej/kg) reported in the research literature, which summarize their total costs (see Appendix B). Like other life cycle kinds of calculation, there can be significant variability and uncertainties in the data, which is why they are referred to as estimates throughout this book and used primarily for comparative value to identify design principles. Mark Brown and Sergio Ulgiati, who helped develop these methods with Odum, have been working to reconcile e[m]ergy calculations with those used for conventional life cycle databases, which would greatly deepen the information available for building analysis (Brown et al. 2012). But even with the uncertainties in the data, the scope of systems ecology provides insights that are not possible with life cycle methods based only on first-law energy accounting within the human economy.

Disposal and recycling

A complete account of building construction also has to include the downstream costs of building materials, after their useful life is over. Srinivasan et al. recently compared four life cycle assessment methods, illustrating the different boundaries of analysis involved (2012) (see Figure 3.5). As his diagram explains, construction components and materials end up in landfills, are recycled for their materials, or, occasionally, are adapted for other uses. In 2003 the Environmental Protection Agency (EPA) estimated that the US generated about 170 million tons of building-related construction and demolition materials, with up to 48% recovered for some form of recycling (US EPA 2009). Whether materials are recovered or sent to a landfill, it requires more work to disassemble, sort, and transport them

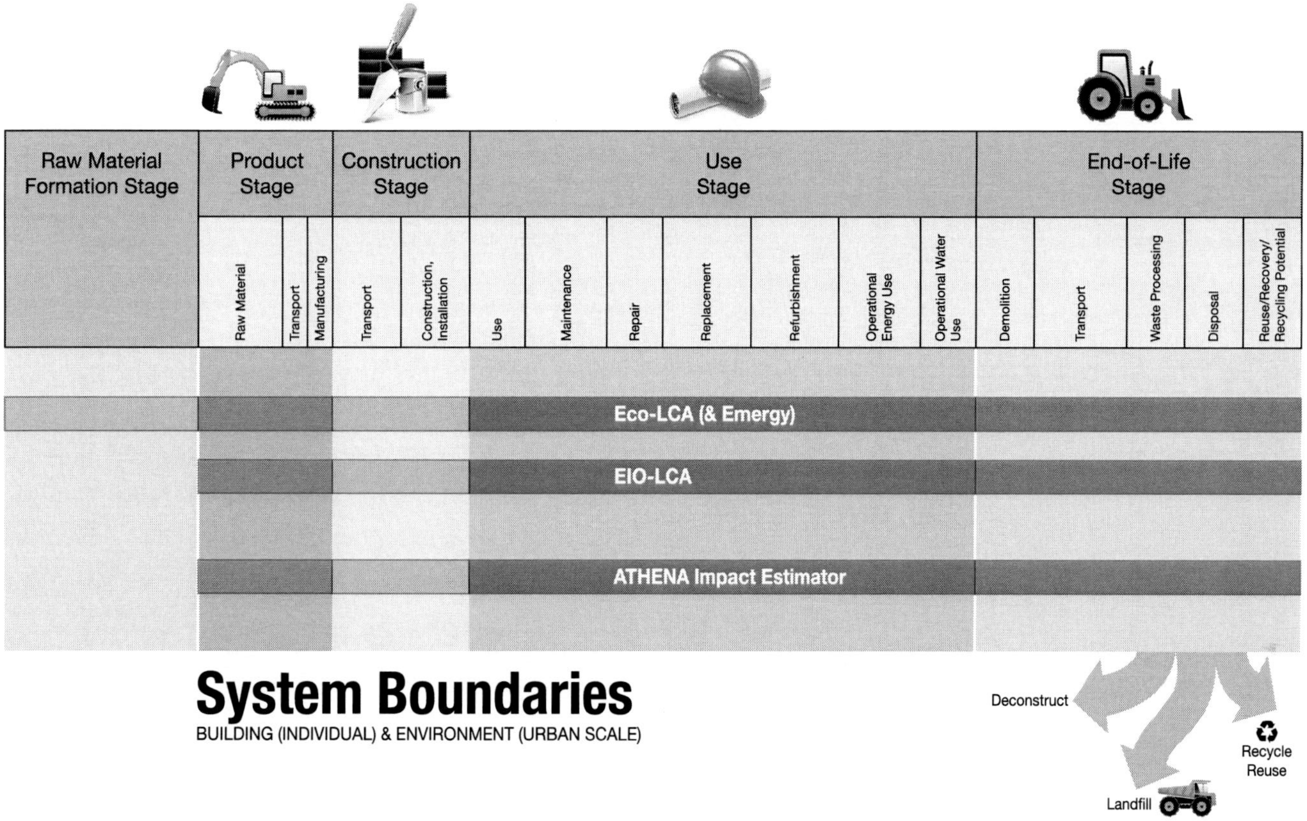

Figure 3.5: System boundaries for four life cycle inventory and impact assessment methods used to evaluate the built environment

Srinivasan 2014

to their destination. When Mark T. Brown and Vorasun Buranakarn (2003) examined construction material recycling in Florida, they evaluated the total thermodynamic cost of recycling different materials; on average, they discovered that demolition, collection, and landfilling added 182,000 sej/kg to the cost of materials, while more careful demolition, sorting, and processing added further costs that ranged from 194,000 sej/kg for steel to 305,000 sej/kg for aluminum.

There are different forms of recycling, which are dictated by the nature of the material involved. Brown and Buranakarn identified three alternate processes, with the most common identified as direct material recycling. Demolition materials diverted from the landfill or waste materials recovered at earlier stages in the manufacturing process simply replace supplies of raw materials. However, many materials cannot be recycled directly. Concrete and most plastics, for example, cannot be returned to their "plastic" state, so they can only be ground up and used as filler in other products. This is called adaptive reuse or "downcycling," and cannot be repeated. Finally, waste or by-products can be substituted for raw materials in a different process, with the most common example being the use of fly ash from coal-fired power plants as a substitute for some components of Portland cement.

The value invested in construction materials can be recovered in other ways, including direct reuse of components, although each step requires additional work or energy. Mature ecosystems achieve nearly complete material recycling, but dissipate energy with every cycle. In imitation of natural ecosystems, William McDonough and Michael Braungart proposed total material recycling as the goal for the built environment, which demands a deeper understanding of material cycles and of design for disassembly (McDonough and Braungart 2002). One of the most powerful results of Buranakarn's work was the identification of the hierarchies of e[m]ergy intensity among construction materials. As we might expect, simpler materials such as wood, concrete, and brick have lower intensities, ranging from 800,000 to 3,000,000 sej/kg, while more highly refined materials including steel, aluminum, plastics, and glass have intensities an order of magnitude higher, up to 13,000,000 sej/kg. Organic materials such as wood can biologically decompose, but their lower intensity makes industrial recycling more expensive. Conversely, technical materials such as aluminum, steel, and glass can be readily remelted and reformed. Their higher intensity becomes a measure of their value or quality.

Layers and longevities of construction

To complete the estimates of the e[m]ergy required to build the Ellis House, we determined the quantity of each material, its specific energy intensity, and its anticipated replacement time (see Appendix B). For the original construction, the house and all its contents weighed 535 metric tonnes, had a total e[m]ergy cost of 6.83×10^{17} sej, and an annual depreciated cost of 1.38×10^{16} sej/yr. The improved and *Passivhaus* NZE versions of the Ellis House both require incrementally higher investments than the original, reflecting the better windows and increased amounts of insulation. The quantities by themselves tell us very little, except to describe the tremendous upstream investment in contemporary construction. Like other consumption measures, they can be compared to the total usage of other buildings and as more systemic efficiency measures. But the more ambitious goal of systems ecology is to understand the hierarchies of quality between different elements, longevities, or classes of construction, to reveal the thermodynamic logic of its organization.

In a fully adapted system, we would expect the quantities of materials in a building to reflect their e[m]ergy intensity. The more expensive and valuable a material, the more discretely it should be used. Charting the materials in the structure and envelope of the Ellis House reveals a rough correspondence between the amount (kg) and intensity (sej/kg) of materials used in its construction, but the statistical correlation is low (see Figure 3.6). That may reflect the difference between economic and e[m]ergy costs for the specific case study and suggests a valuable area of additional research. Conversely, the calculations reveal the expected hierarchy between the longevity of the structure (80 years), envelope (70 years), systems (61 years), interiors (38 years), and FF&E (24 years). But the variations within the layers seem as important as those between layers (see Appendix B). For example, the life span of much of the envelope is about 70 years, though the paint has to be replaced every 10 years, while the longevity of the systems layer is about 61 years, even though the HVAC systems themselves only last 20 to 30 years. The longer duration of the ducts and wiring built into the fabric of the building extend the average but, as will become evident in the next section, the e[m]ergy of the utility energies that are channeled by those systems dwarf those of its physical infrastructure. Ultimately, the value of building construction can only be understood by evaluating its role in the system as a whole, including the channeling of both environmental energies and more highly concentrated power.

Building-as-shelter

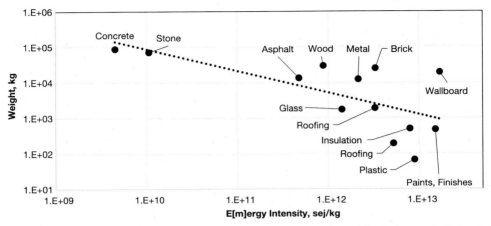

Figure 3.6: Materials of building structure and envelope plotted by weight and annual e[m]ergy cost: the Ellis House, normative version

After reviewing the tables of e[m]ergy calculations for the different components and resource flows in the Ellis House, we decided to organize them according to the three scales of purpose—site, shelter, and setting—apportioning the layers of construction between them. The investments in the structure and envelope are considered with the climate modifying systems in the next section. The costs of interiors and FF&E are examined as part of the activities of working and living in buildings, while the systems are apportioned between the two.

Climate modification

The fundamental service provided by the building-as-shelter is the modification of the climate for human comfort. Building envelopes selectively filter the climate—adjusting temperature, humidity, moisture, wind, and sun by their formal configuration and material properties, and by using concentrated power in specialized mechanical and electrical systems. Throughout the modern period, remarkable advances have been made in the capabilities of construction materials and devices to move heat and techniques to generate light. The understanding of building physics has advanced in parallel, leading to new thermodynamic design strategies—from super-insulated, passive houses to net zero commercial buildings. Systems ecology can help describe the differences among the many specialized forms of buildings, but it starts with comfort.

Thermal comfort has been the subject of tremendous research, which began with the recognition in the mid-nineteenth century that the human body was a kind of heat engine, transforming food into work and releasing heat that has to be dissipated to the environment. Comfort became the subject of scientific research in subsequent decades, resulting in increasingly precise descriptions of the conditions that would make (most) people comfortable. The development of mechanical chillers in the early twentieth century demanded more precision; unlike heating, cooling requires the control of humidity as well. Willis Carrier, the father of air-conditioning, developed a chart of thermodynamic states of air and used it to identify a zone of comfortable conditions. However, the description of comfort that penetrated the architectural community was the bioclimatic chart developed by the Olgyay brothers in the 1950s, which illustrated the connection between comfort and the ambient conditions of sun, wind, and air temperature. Although both charts describe similar conditions of comfort, they represent the two different approaches to climate modification described by Banham: the power-operated and the structural solution. The bioclimatic chart by the Olgyay brothers is configured to show the kinds and degrees of environmental change that would be required to achieve that comfort—more or less sun, more or less ventilation. The psychrometric chart attributed to Carrier is a tool for ready calculation of the energy required to make warm, moist air comfortable. The bioclimatic chart is a tool for thinking about the modification of building envelopes, while the psychrometric chart is a tool for sizing mechanical equipment. Banham charted the opposition between these two approaches in the 1950s and 1960s, and his account records the development of the radically new types of building that became possible with the "full control" of HVAC equipment (Banham 1969).

That opposition may seem irreconcilable, pitting architects against engineers and building envelopes against HVAC. But in the decades since power-operated buildings became the norm, the two approaches have largely converged. The conventional elements of architecture—walls, windows, floors, etc.—have been hybridized with power delivery technologies in all kinds of new configurations: plenum floors, active glass walls, conditioned atria, suspended ceilings. The elements of bioclimatic design—thermal insulation, operable windows, shading and reflecting devices, seasonally adjusted walls—have become more efficient and effective with the refinements of feedback-based building automation systems, which use modest amounts of power and information to regulate and amplify lower quality environmental flows. We might call it the "cybernetic reconciliation of the mechanical approach, as it infiltrates the bioclimatic." For the buildings of the twenty-first century, we have to move beyond Banham's richly rhetorical opposition between bioclimatic and mechanical.

The matter of comfort also exemplifies the degree to which technologies change those who use them, even for a "need" as fundamental as thermal regulation. Environmental conditioning epitomizes the coevolving escalation of needs and technologies, as the luxuries of one generation become the necessities of the next. Central heating was a technical innovation of the late nineteenth century that used one of the original feedback devices, the thermostat, to allow small amounts of electric power and information to replace the human work of regulating the furnace. Central heating was developed to save labor and increase productivity, but it quickly became a regular service and is now mandated by law (in cold climates), with the comfort zone written into regulations. The building-as-shelter can never be wholly reduced to the energy exchanges of heating and cooling, but requires an account of the social, cultural, and economic hierarchies in which central heating obtains its value.

A powerful dependency has developed between the "bodies" of contemporary buildings and the technologies that have so enhanced their power to modify climates. Most large buildings, and even many smaller ones, are literally uninhabitable without the active support of their power-operated systems, and for some environmentalists it can seem compelling to dismiss this dependency in favor of simpler, human-powered approaches. The effectiveness of different systems has to be established on thermodynamic grounds, comparing the work of construction, the flows of environmental resources and concentrated power, and the value of replacing human work with coded information. Tracking total costs and e[m]ergy intensities in the built environment reveals the constant tradeoff between power and efficiency. The selection for maximum power offers a compelling explanation for the emergence of high-powered buildings over the last 100 years, and the hierarchy of intensities helps identify design strategies for navigating the transition to renewable power over the next 100 years.

Bioclimatic approach

Understanding the conditioning of buildings for comfort is probably the most intuitive and straightforward use of thermodynamics in this book, because the energy exchanges are largely concerned with temperature differences and draw on the basic formulations of heat transfer. Thermal conditioning can also be confusing because heat, which is the primary "service" provided by climate-modifying devices, is the unavoidable by-product of any energy transformation. In other words, the second law requires a clarification: there can be no perfect conversions of energy into work, unless that work is low-temperature heating. Heat can be produced in many different ways, with greater or lesser environmental costs, so our concern is not with the efficiency of conversion by itself but with the e[m]ergy intensity of different fuels and methods. Burning a high-quality fuel, for example, natural gas or converting electricity generated by burning coal represents a significant upstream cost, even if the final conversion to heat can be nearly perfect.

Keeping in mind the unique status of heat, we start with the simplest thermodynamic diagram of the bioclimatic effects of a building envelope: an enclosure with no power-operated or feedback technologies. As research into human comfort has established, the basic thermal service of a building is the dissipation of the heat generated by human metabolisms as they convert food to work. Our bodies accomplish this through a variety of physical mechanisms—conduction, convection, radiation, evaporation—which work best in room temperatures of about 10 to 15 degrees (C) below their core temperature. To keep interiors in that range, the building envelope has two basic routes of energy exchange:

1 heat transfer through the many components of the building envelope, driven by the temperature difference between the interior and exterior;
2 penetration of sunlight through windows, which converts to heat when it strikes interior surfaces.

Both mechanisms vary according to the location, season, weather, and time of day. In effect, the building skin is a filter that mediates the highly variable, local environmental conditions to maintain a relatively constant interior temperature suitably below the body temperature of its occupants (see Figure 3.7).

This basic diagram helps reveal a couple of critical points about bioclimatic strategies. The first has to do with the fundamental difference between hot and cold climates or seasons. Put simply, it is easier to keep a building warm than it is to cool it off. A building envelope can be sufficiently well insulated to mostly

Building-as-shelter

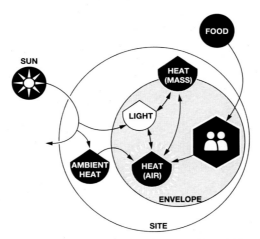

Figure 3.7: Thermodynamic diagram of basic thermal regulation of a building

maintain its interior temperature using the heat from the sun (and from its occupants) and, when that falls short, converting stored energy to heat. In the opposite condition, when it is hot outside, someplace cooler has to be located or a heat engine has to operate backwards to move heat "uphill" to the hotter conditions outside (a chiller). For both heating and cooling, it is necessary to identify the temperature of all the heat sources and sinks available in the immediate environment, both physically in space and over time. There are a variety of ambient temperatures available to buildings at different times, or by different mechanisms—ground temperatures to high and low air temperatures, the wet-bulb evaporative temperature, and even the temperature that sunlight can produce on a surface. The range of available temperatures establishes the maximum rate and efficiency of different strategies.

Because ambient conditions are so variable, the task of the building envelope is fundamentally dynamic, modifying and stabilizing the available energy flows. The thermodynamic diagram can be used to simulate the dynamic characteristics of the building envelope as a filter of climate. These kinds of simple, lumped-parameter models have been used for decades to analyze the thermal behavior of buildings, and they can be remarkably accurate at simulating the temperatures and heat exchanges of quite complex buildings, especially when they are developed through the inverse modeling of real building data (Sonderegger 1977). The charts in Figure 3.8 show an hour-by-hour simulation of the temperatures in the

Building-as-shelter

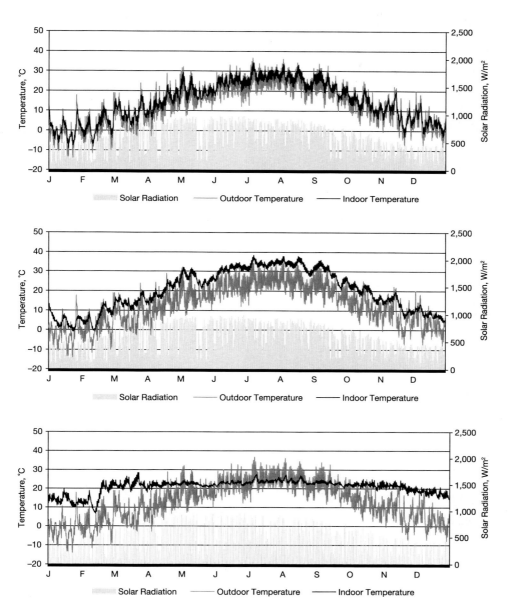

Figure 3.8: (a) Temperature simulation of the original, normative, unconditioned version of Ellis House, full-year, hour-by-hour; (b) Temperature simulation of the improved, insulated, unconditioned version of the Ellis House, full-year, hour-by-hour; (c) Temperature simulation of the responsive, unconditioned, Passivhaus version of the Ellis House, full-year, hour-by-hour

three versions of the Ellis House over a year of typical Philadelphia weather. It is a simple shelter—an insulated box with fixed windows and thermal mass in its interior—but even so, it reveals the ability of a building enclosure to moderate the climate by its form and material properties alone. The original house was uncomfortable 86% of the time mostly because it was too cold. The improved, insulated version is only uncomfortable 77% of the time, but the temperature proportions have nearly been reversed and it is more often too warm. The original house closely tracks the outdoor temperature in winter and summer, while the insulated house is generally warmer in both seasons, which accounts for the shift in proportion between too cold and too warm. The behavior of the third, responsive version will be explained shortly, but first we examine the three important relationships that explain the behavior of the dynamic building: time constant, gain-to-mass, and gain-to-loss.

Three relationships to explain dynamic building behavior

In the heating and cooling seasons, the interior temperature of both the original and the improved versions mostly remain above the outdoor temperature, though their oscillations between high and low are significantly dampened by the internal mass of the building. Neither building is exactly comfortable, although in winter the improved one is notably warmer than outdoors, while in summer the original, leakier building does better. Examining the relation between sunshine and indoor and outdoor temperatures makes the interaction apparent. The sun warms the building up during the day, and it then cools overnight and through cloudy days. The rate at which it cools, in winter or summer, is determined by the insulation values of the building envelope—the "lossiness," to use the term coined by the early researchers—and the amount of thermal mass. The ratio between the two is known as the thermal time constant (τ) and describes the amount of time it takes the building to cool most of the way to the outdoor temperature ($1/e = 63\%$). For the original Ellis House, the time constant is about 22 hours, which increases to 77 hours for the more insulated version. The time constant also determines how quickly the building warms up, whether from sunlight, the heat given off by people, or other sources. A larger thermal mass and lower lossiness stabilizes the interior temperature. It is important to note that time constants are nearly independent of size. Large and small buildings can have the same rates of response to temperature changes, although larger buildings often have a number of thermally distinct zones with their own characteristic time constants.

There are two other size-independent ratios revealed by this simple model that complete the description of the response of the building to heat. The second is between the thermal mass and heat sources or gain-to-mass. In this simple model, the sun is the primary heat source, whose magnitude is a direct function of the window area. The basic relationship modulating its effect is the ratio between the amount of thermal mass and the area of glass or mass-to-glass. The ratio describes how rapidly the sun will heat the interior (Mazria 1980; Balcomb 1982).

The third dynamic relationship called gain-to-loss is the ratio between heat gain and the lossiness, which in this model determines how much warmer the indoors will be than the outdoors as a result of sunlight coming in through the windows. In the more complex models explored in the next sections, other sources of heat gain are added, including heat from people, lights, equipment, and furnaces. In its more complete form, the ratio of internal heat gains to lossiness can be used to understand the distinction between buildings driven by the exterior climate and buildings preoccupied with their internal activities.

These three ratios—time constant, gain-to-mass, and gain-to-loss—determine the underlying, natural response of the building envelope to its climate. The interaction with sunlight coming in through the windows distinguishes the envelope design strategies for winter from those for summer. As the temperature charts indicate, the Ellis House basically needs more heat in the winter and as little heat as possible in the summer. This means that there is no fixed combination of lossiness, thermal mass, and glass area that will produce comfortable conditions in both hot and cold seasons. A compromise design could have a huge amount of thermal mass to dampen the indoor temperature to the average temperature of the climate, which in most climates would still be uncomfortable (about 13°C in Philadelphia).

The classically effective strategy for buildings that experience both hot and cold climates is to alter their properties between the seasons. In summer the windows are shaded during the day and opened at night when it is cooler, while in winter the windows are configured to capture sunlight, with the envelope sealed tightly to retain the heat. The temperature chart in Figure 3.8 (c) shows the responsive version, which is insulated to *Passivhaus* standards and switches between the two strategies depending on the indoor and outdoor temperatures. In cold conditions it is heavily insulated with larger south-facing glass. As the indoor temperature becomes too hot, the windows are shaded, and if the outdoor air is comfortable, the windows are opened. As a result, the responsive version is uncomfortable only 8% of the time, roughly 10 times better than the other versions. This is how most buildings were managed before central heating and air-conditioning.

Of course, contemporary buildings have many other sources of heat, which will elevate temperatures and require even more responsive strategies to manage hot weather. But the general principle should be clear. Using information to adjust the ratios between the basic thermal parameters of a building envelope, a building can be made to heat itself in cool weather, and keep itself at or near the average outdoor temperature during hot weather. This is the essence of the *Passivhaus* approach, whose performance is limited only by the amounts of unavoidable internal gains and the average outdoor temperatures in summer. To achieve colder temperatures in hot weather requires one of two conditions: either access to a colder ambient heat sink like the ground, the evaporative potential of dry air, and some longer term storage of "coolth" (ice kept from winter, for example), or the use of some other energy source to run a heat engine to remove heat (a chiller).

Evaluating the building envelope

This simple thermodynamic model sets the basis for evaluating the building as shelter over the next few sections. Incorporating the e[m]ergy costs of the building envelope can help us answer questions about the value of more insulation or better glazing. From the previous section, we know that the annual depreciation cost of the original building structure and envelope is 3.9×10^{15} sej/yr. Adding insulation to the envelope and improving the windows added 1.82×10^{14} sej/yr (about 5%) to the cost, but how do we determine the value of the improvement? The physical changes in the envelope improved the number of comfortable hours in winter, although it decreased them in summer, making insulation appear a questionable investment. The real improvement occurred by adjusting the properties of the envelope in response to the climate.

We typically evaluate such improvements based on the amount of energy that is not expended on furnaces or chillers. With that approach, each additional layer of insulation has less effect than the previous one, since there is progressively less energy to save, so the choice becomes a balance between the cost of fuels and the cost of insulation. But this gives us no way to evaluate more ambitious,

Passivhaus-type buildings that have no furnaces. Instead, we need to determine the positive contribution of the envelope to sustain comfort, rather than its negative effect on utility bills. We can do that by considering the thermodynamics of Banham's bubble, which keeps a volume of air comfortable by containing it and adding or removing heat as needed. Without the bubble, the air would be at the outdoor temperatures. We can simply calculate the energy required to keep it comfortable. In an unconditioned building, any positive difference between inside and outside temperatures can count as a contribution of the envelope.

The Ellis House contains 833 m^3 of air. By counting the hours and temperatures that the climate is uncomfortable, we determine that it would require 1.47×10^{12} J to keep a completely open shelter at 20°C through a typical Philadelphia year. It would feel even more magical than an all-glass room, but at many, many times the energy cost. Even the simplest enclosure has the power to replace some of that energy, moderating the temperature through its configuration. The original, leaky Ellis House is more comfortable than being outside by about 14%, and adding insulation increases that to 23%, meaning that the work and resources invested in the improved version effectively contribute 3.45×10^{11} J/yr to maintain the interior temperature simply by their material properties and configuration. With that approach, we can develop an intensity measurement of the improvements, calculating the amount of e[m]ergy dissipated for each unit of energy delivered to maintain comfort. For the original Ellis envelope, the intensity is 3,840 sej/J of thermal regulation, while the intensity of the improved version is 924 sej/J. The combined selection pressures of the construction industry, real estate markets, architectural fashions, and the human economy generally interact to produce these kinds of intensity hierarchy within buildings.

The responsive version of the Ellis House demonstrates that the real power of the enclosure was only realized when someone walked around and changed its properties to match the ambient conditions, when the shades were drawn or the windows were opened at the right time. Evaluating the work involved in making those adjustments gets a bit ahead of this model, because it involves estimates of the time and value of human labor that we will take up later. By a conservative estimate, it takes an additional 1.04×10^{15} sej/yr of human work to manage the windows and shades. But even with that additional cost, the intensity of the responsive model is lower because of the much greater thermal comfort it provides, which translates to about 306 sej/J. We will put this in more perspective in the following sections, but as a point of comparison, the e[m]ergy intensity of natural gas is about 178,000 sej/J. Viewed as a matter of efficiency, the thermal comfort provided by a well-regulated building enclosure is clearly superior, providing comfort at a much lower cost. However, understanding e[m]ergy intensity as a measure of quality in a system self-organizing to enhance its power changes the argument. For instance, natural gas is an expensive resource, but it has a high energy density, it retains its energy content until needed, and it can be used in any number of ways. Its higher intensity indicates precisely that flexibility and concentration, which is a suitable introduction to the mechanical approach that is largely based on the power of such concentrated fuels.

Mechanical approach

The use of fire probably preceded the construction of shelters, but regardless of which came first, the two have coevolved since the beginning of architecture. Building envelopes contain and amplify the heat of fires, which supplement the climate-modifying effects of shelters. The power-operated, mechanical approach of the modern era began as an intensification of the fire in the hearth. New fuels and more efficient techniques of combustion advanced heating through the nineteenth century, enhanced the capacity of fireplaces, stoves, and then central furnaces, and simultaneously raised the standards of comfort and the dependence of building enclosures on the heat they provided. But the introduction of mechanical chilling, with its ability to remove heat and control humidity, completed the establishment of contemporary levels of comfort. Combined with the advances in artificial lighting, the new levels of thermal control released buildings from the reliance on windows for cooling and illumination, facilitating the development of radically new sizes, shapes, and types of buildings.

Authors from Banham (1969) to Fitch (1972), Ternoey et al. (1985), and Hawkes (1996) have examined the details of that transformation, but the general outline is clear. The availability of new sources of power and new technologies of climate modification increasingly freed building envelopes from their role in climate modification, allowing myriad experiments with buildings of different thermodynamic characteristics and rates of energy consumption. A recent account by Philip Oldfield et al. about the "five energy generations" of tall buildings in New York summarizes the historical interaction between envelopes and systems (Oldfield et al. 2009). In that account, the first generation began with the construction boom after the Civil War and experiments with greater height from 1865 to the passage of the 1916 zoning law, which regulated the proportions of buildings to guarantee the penetration of daylight to street level. The second generation continued to about 1950 and, like the first generation, still relied on windows for daylighting and cooling, although the more slender forms of the second generation increased the exterior surface area and so required greater amounts of heating. The third generation began with the arrival of all-glass walls, air-conditioning, and fluorescent lighting in the early 1950s, which paradoxically freed the curtain wall from almost any positive environmental role except views. Although precise figures are difficult to establish, the first two generations had energy use intensities (EUI) up to 315 kWh/m^2, while the intensity of the third generation increased to about 800 kWh/m^2 until the energy supply crises of the 1970s. Higher fuel costs and new regulatory standards brought the intensity of new buildings back down to around 315 kWh/m^2 over the following decade, even though the buildings of the fourth generation had added air-conditioning to the other services.

The fourth energy generation continues to the present day and is characterized by buildings that satisfy the minimum regulatory requirements with more efficient assemblies and equipment, but otherwise continue the relationship between building envelopes and HVAC systems established in the post-war period. Oldfield et al. mark the beginning of a fifth generation in the late 1990s, with the "rise of environmental consciousness." The category includes the more ambitious buildings that intentionally exceed regulatory requirements, exploring new forms of construction, new sources of power, and new interactions between building envelopes and systems. The specific stages and dates will be different for other cities and building types, but the broad pattern is similar. New types and scales of building became possible with the integration of higher powered systems within building enclosures in the post-war period. Those new formats of integration were made more efficient after the energy supply crisis of the 1970s, while new arrangements and environmental performance standards have been explored since the 1990s.

The coevolution between buildings and mechanical systems can be understood as an exploratory process, enhancing the power of buildings and testing tradeoffs between efficiency and power as new energy sources and innovations appear. With that historical trajectory in mind, we can begin to elaborate the thermodynamic diagram of the Ellis House with power-operated, climate-modifying technologies (see Figure 3.9). The basic thermal task of the building

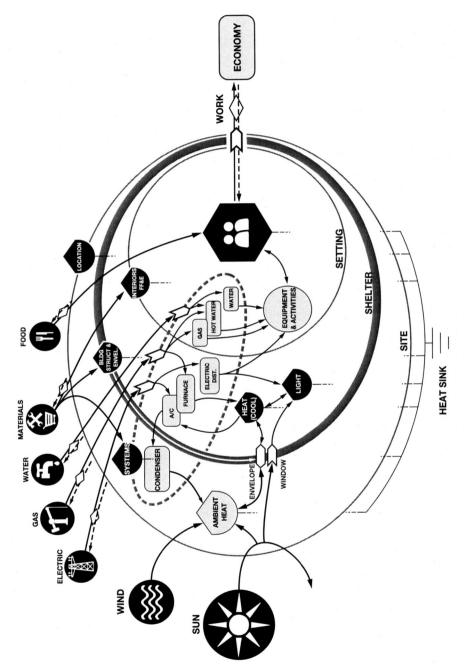

Figure 3.9: Thermodynamic diagram of the building-as-shelter, the Ellis House, original, normative version

is unchanged and the distinction between heating and cooling remains fundamental. Mechanical and electrical devices use fuels and electricity to add or remove heat from the building, adjusting and compensating for the natural, bioclimatic behavior of the envelope.

Heating and cooling

Heating is almost always easier than cooling. Any available fuel can be converted to heat, now at very high (first-law) efficiencies, while the waste from other energy-consuming activities—people, lighting, and equipment—will produce waste heat that offsets the need for explicit heat (a concept discussed further in the next sections). The heat delivered from furnaces or boilers is effectively added to the heat already in the building structure and air, compensating for any that is lost through the envelope to the colder outdoors, with some additional heat required to warm outdoor air introduced through infiltration, ventilation, or for combustion. As a basic comparison to the thermal contribution of the envelope, the e[m]ergy intensity of natural gas burned in a high-efficiency (96%) furnace is about 185,000 sej/J, while a resistance heater (100% efficient) using electricity from the US grid has an intensity of about 397,000 sej/J (see Figure 3.10). The *Passivhaus* version achieves its net zero status by using photovoltaic panels to replace the grid electricity, but it is not free and only reduces the intensity of the power to 145,000 sej/J, because of the high-tech materials of the panels (Brown et al. 2012).

Cooling a building to below the ambient outdoor air temperature is a less intuitive process than heating, since heat has to be induced to flow "uphill" from a cool interior to a warmer outdoors. But it basically mimics the evaporative effect of sweating. As described by the second law, heat can only be moved against a temperature gradient by putting some other form of energy to work, increasing the entropy and waste heat elsewhere in order to decrease the entropy and heat inside of the building. That is accomplished by forcing a material (for instance, water or Freon) to evaporate, which reduces its temperature so it can absorb heat from the interior, and then condensing it elsewhere so it warms up and can lose heat to the environment. Clever builders over the centuries have used the simple technique of evaporating water in dry air, largely tapping the work of the wind to provide the dry air; the process does result in more humid, less comfortable air, so its effectiveness for cooling is limited to very dry climates.

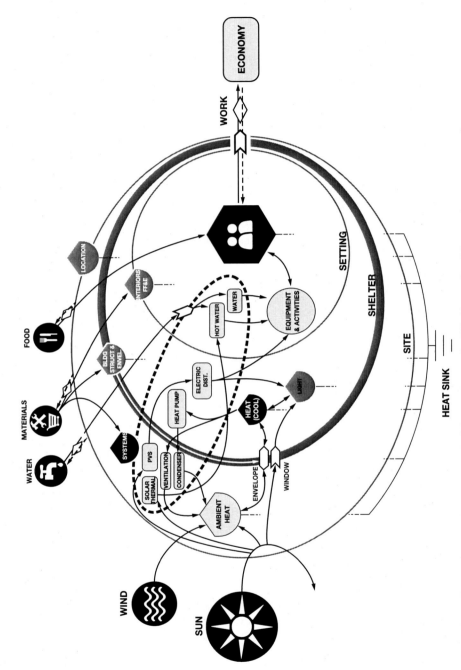

Figure 3.10: Thermodynamic diagram of the building-as-shelter, the Ellis House, Passivhaus net zero energy version

Other builders through the nineteenth century experimented with fan-powered and indirect variations of that technique, which are still used in the "economizer" cycles of contemporary cooling towers or the "swamp coolers" common in the American southwest. Mechanical refrigeration cycles are conceptually similar, but produce even colder temperatures by using closed cycles of evaporation and condensation driven by engines of different kinds.

Those experiments with evaporation converged in the early twentieth century when Willis Carrier began to apply mechanical refrigeration to cool (and dehumidify) air at rates that could be useful in buildings (Cooper 1998). He combined the power of Carnot's heat engines with his own research into the thermodynamics of moist air, determining the minimum energy expenditures required to cool and dry the muggy summer air of American cities. From Frank Lloyd Wright's Larkin building in 1906, to William Lescaze and George Howe's PSFS building in 1932, to the widespread adoption of air-conditioning in the post-war period, architects tested the effect of the new conditioning technology on buildings and their occupants. Air-conditioning was initially offered as a tool to enhance worker productivity, but quickly became an item of luxury as exemplified by its early adoption by movie theaters. However, the acceptance of air-conditioning in homes lagged its use in commercial settings by decades, and underscores the very different nature of homes and workplaces.

The third energy generation of commercial buildings, which so intrigued Banham, increased the power and reach of climate control, while the fourth and fifth generations have made that control more effective and efficient. Heat pumps, chillers, refrigerators, and heat engines of all kinds represent an elegant refinement of Carnot's initial insight, leveraging controlled cycles of evaporation and condensation to move environmental heat. Banham would have appreciated the current popularity of ground-source heat pumps (confusingly called geothermal), which move large amounts of heat into and out of the mass of the ground around buildings using much smaller amounts of electricity to drive the pumps and compressors. A well-designed system can move three to five (even seven) units of heat for every unit of electricity used by the motors; in many locations, the ground effectively stores excess summer heat for use in winter and winter cold for use in summer. Recording the principal mechanisms and pathways of the mechanical approach in the diagram of the Ellis House adds to its complexity, but makes visible the degree to which the thermodynamics of climate modification have been explored over the last 75 years. There are shelves of books and journals that describe the many variations and refinements in mechanical systems, but our goal is to keep the system diagrams clear enough to articulate their environmental purpose.

We can list many reasons to reduce or eliminate the use of high-quality power for conditioning buildings: fuel costs, air pollution, heat island effects, climate change, and a host of other environmental impacts. The analysis in the previous section confirms the much greater efficiency of regulating the climate with a well-designed building enclosure, but the particular power of mechanical and electrical systems made them successful, not their efficiency. Efficiency can be a technique for reducing impacts related to consumption, but ultimately we use or trade efficiency for increased power. Which brings us back to the matter of quality. We accept the much greater environmental cost of high-quality fuels, and especially of electric power, because of their greater flexibility and quality. Even the responsively managed model of the Ellis House envelope was only comfortable 92% of the time, and the work required to address the last 5 to 10% has almost always demanded a more concentrated and controllable form of heat delivery—wood burned in a fireplace, gas in a central furnace, or heat moved out of the ground by an electric-powered heat engine. For a building to be completely conditioned by the low-density flows of sun or wind, some portion of those energies must be concentrated and stored, whether as heat, electricity, or some other readily tapped potential, which can only be accomplished by investing additional work, resources, and time, and increasing their cost and e[m]ergy intensity.

It is precisely this kind of tradeoff between cost and quality that leads to the hierarchies of power usage described by Odum in all manner of self-organizing systems—ones that we see being worked out in different configurations between building enclosures and high-powered mechanical systems. Continuing the analysis of intensities in the Ellis House outlined previously, we can compare the thermal contribution of heating and cooling using actual utility data (instead of the simple model). For the original Ellis House, with consumption levels that are typical of contemporary houses, the furnace contributed only 5.2% of the heat required through the year, while the air-conditioner removed about as much heat as the envelope, again highlighting the differences between heating and cooling. To evaluate the intensity of that contribution, we estimate the amount of work and resources invested in the furnace, air-conditioner, wiring, and so on, which came to 1.97×10^{14} sej/yr, while the total upstream costs of the power were 1.64×10^{16} sej/yr for the natural gas and 7.67×10^{15} sej/yr for the electricity. So the total intensity of providing heat from the furnace is 56,500 sej/J and of providing cooling from the air-conditioner is 136,000 sej/J, compared with an overall intensity of 4,700 sej/J by the envelope for heating and 113,000 sej/J for cooling.

The improved Ellis House, which followed contemporary, economically determined improvement strategies, cut its utility usage by over 60%. However, the intensity of the contribution by the furnace and air-conditioner actually increases, because of the fixed costs of the equipment, ducts, and wiring. This illustrates the tradeoff between the costs of a fixed, depreciating device and the particular resources or services it channels. Over the last 200 years, we have adjusted the interaction between buildings and devices that use high-quality fuels and electricity, changing the proportions as their costs have risen and fallen. After we have reviewed the additional climate-modifying devices of the contemporary building, what become visible are the surprisingly precise hierarchies that develop, reflecting the different environmental costs that have been internalized over time. These hierarchies offer a powerful design principle that can be used to imagine the buildings of the next energy generation, in an economy based on renewable resource flows.

People (again)

The success of Carrier's inventions, and their dramatic effect on contemporary buildings, can distract us from the actual goal of climate modification, which is to allow the occupants to dissipate their internal heat. The reduction of humidity is important because evaporation is one of the principal methods by which human bodies cool themselves when ambient temperatures increase. The HVAC systems of the third and fourth energy generations are typically designed to condition the interior of the building to a uniform standard, but many of the innovative approaches deployed for buildings of the fifth generation have focused instead on heating or cooling the occupants more directly. For example, underfloor air distribution systems (UFAD) allow conditioned air to simply displace warm air as it rises, making only the air around the occupants comfortable. Radiant heating and cooling of floors, walls, or ceilings permits greater variation in the air temperatures, a condition that is

Building-as-shelter

easier to maintain with passive envelope strategies. Recent efforts have even experimented with heating and cooling the more intimate surfaces of furniture, further targeting delivery and allowing for even more individual control of comfort. It is worth remembering that for most of human history, the last, most difficult "delivery" of comfort was achieved by adjusting clothing.

Ventilation and waste processing

Indoor air pollution began with the first fire in a cave or dwelling. Unlike the other aspects of shelter provided by buildings, air quality was probably worse indoors than outdoors for most of human history (Mosley 2014). The general leakiness of building construction and the development of chimneys mitigated the buildup of pollutants. But air conditions actually worsened in the early modern period, which witnessed the greater use of coal for heating, the burning of gas for indoor illumination, and the general tightening of construction. Banham called the 1800s a "dark, satanic century," and recorded a host of medical innovators who designed improved radiators and specially ventilated houses and hospitals to stem the epidemic of pollution-related ailments (Campbell 2005). Through the second half of the century, the complex nature of "stuffiness" was investigated, and the contributing factors were nicely summarized in a text from 1905: "An excessive amount of vapour or water, sickly odours from respiratory organs, unclean teeth, perspiration, untidy clothing, the presence of microbes due to various conditions, stuffy air from dusty carpets and drapes, and many other factors" (Banham 1969, 42).

As cities grew in size throughout the nineteenth century, the severity of outdoor pollution combined with the density and crowding of the poor inspired the "clean air and sunlight" ethic of urban reform. Of course, ventilation can only diminish indoor pollution to the degree that outdoor air is clean, and determining the amount of ventilation is further complicated by the social nature of "freshness." The standards that are still largely used today were developed in the 1920s and based on a very human question: At what rate of ventilation does the room stop smelling stuffy? The critical threshold occurs when the subjects no longer "smell" their neighbors, a threshold that can differ between individuals, classes, and cultures (Janssen 1994, 1999). In contemporary buildings, the apparent flexibility of ventilation rates makes them a tempting target for building operators faced with higher energy costs, who can decrease ventilation and save on both fan power and the energy required to heat or cool the outdoor air. The health tradeoffs became starkly evident in the late 1970s when building ventilation standards were dramatically reduced in response to the energy supply crises. Over the following decade, a host of buildings began exhibiting "sick building syndrome," in which large numbers of occupants reported headaches, nausea, and other symptoms (Lundin 1992). Not all the reports could be attributed directly to ventilation, but the symptoms diminished when ventilation rates were increased.

Like other aspects of building operation, ventilation involves multiple forms of work, energy, and resources. "Natural" ventilation draws on the power of the wind or buoyancy from temperature differences between inside and outside, while mechanical ventilation uses the power of motors and fans to circulate air. In either case, the outdoor air has to be conditioned to match the indoor conditions, which can be accomplished indirectly as it mixes with room air or directly by heating, cooling, and dehumidification. In older residences like the Ellis House, ventilation is mostly achieved with the leaky infiltration of air through the joints and cracks in construction, which compensates for the air exhausted by the fans used in bathrooms and kitchens to control smells and humidity. For commercial buildings with tighter methods of construction and larger volume-to-surface ratios, explicit means of ventilation are mandatory and are commonly incorporated in the air-based heating and cooling systems. In 2010, for example, ventilation fans in commercial buildings accounted for about 9% of the operating energy and the fresh air itself for 15% of the heating load (US DOE 2012).

As the energy efficiency of residential construction is improved, the use of weather stripping, caulking, and carefully layered construction details can dramatically reduce leakiness and heat loss, which then exacerbates the accumulation of indoor pollutants. Once buildings reach *Passivhaus* standards of tightness, dedicated ventilation systems similar to those used in commercial buildings have to be introduced. In buildings with air-based systems that operate frequently to meet heating and cooling loads, ventilation is simply blended into the return air, conditioned, and then distributed with the supply air. However, in water-based systems or high-performance buildings whose conditioning systems rarely have to operate, ventilation air has to be introduced independently, either through controlled openings in the envelope or dedicated fan-powered systems. For example, the *Passivhaus* version of the Ellis House is ventilated with a low-volume system that runs continuously (33 l/s of air, drawing 40 w of power).

Ventilation is normally viewed as a simple tradeoff. Fresh air makes people healthier and happier, but requires more energy. Fifth-generation projects, designed for ventilation rates two or three times greater than the required minimum, use heat-exchange techniques to reduce extra conditioning costs. Since the air being exhausted is still nearly comfortable, its heat or coolth can be used to temper the incoming outdoor air. These kinds of heat recovery ventilators (HRV) require some additional fan power, but can achieve exchange efficiencies of 50 to 80%, meaning that ventilation rates can be doubled with no increase in conditioning cost. By transferring humidity through filtering membranes in energy recovery ventilators (ERV), efficiencies up to 95% can be realized. In effect, the ERV ventilation system in the *Passivhaus* version reduces the amount of air that has to be conditioned to about 1.6 l/s, making freshness more affordable.

But what actually makes the air fresh? If we shift the focus from the costs of delivering outdoor air to its actual effect, it becomes clear that ventilation is a form of waste processing, which draws on the chemical and biological activities of the biosphere to remove pollutants and restore the balance of gases. Human consumption of oxygen is a miniscule part of the global carbon cycle, in which plants (mostly trees) release oxygen as a waste product of photosynthesis, while their decay reverses the process with the respiration of carbon dioxide. The real issue in buildings is the accumulation of pollutants: dusts, mists, bioaerosols, gases, especially volatile organic compounds, and the buildup of carbon dioxide from human respiration (or open combustion). In sealed environments, such as submarines and spaceships, energy has to be expended to "scrub" carbon dioxide and other gases from the air, filter particulates, and even produce some make-up oxygen. The biosphere provides an equivalent amount of work, so ventilation adds two paths to the thermodynamic diagram of the building—one for the work of moving and conditioning the air, the other for processing the wastes.

Since the beginning of space exploration, organic systems of air processing have been explored, from Gerard O'Neill's rotating colonies of 1976 to the spectacular experiment of Biosphere II and continuing research. But, as one NASA researcher noted about the international space station, "the chemical-mechanical systems are much more compact, less labor intensive, and more reliable than a plant-based system" (Perry 2000). Compared to space stations,

Building-as-shelter

terrestrial buildings are actually quite difficult to seal as completely, but the lessons are instructive. Plant-based filtration systems require more space because they operate with low-power density light, not high-density fuels, but that is precisely what should make their total cost of operation lower than chemical-mechanical systems. The limiting factor for sealed environments has been the knowledge and experience to engineer stable, isolated ecosystems. Plant-based systems in terrestrial buildings are more like gardens that are periodically reinvigorated by inputs from the biosphere.

Although greenhouses have existed in various forms for millennia, as have windowsill plants, the widespread deployment of interior plants seems to parallel the rise of the deep floor-plate commercial buildings. Among the first contemporary buildings to incorporate a partially plant-based ventilation system was in 1968 at the Ford Foundation in New York, whose air-conditioning system circulated return air through its tree-filled atrium (see Figure 3.11). Subsequent regulation of air movement through atria to control the spread of smoke in fires now complicates such configurations, although the enthusiasm for organic

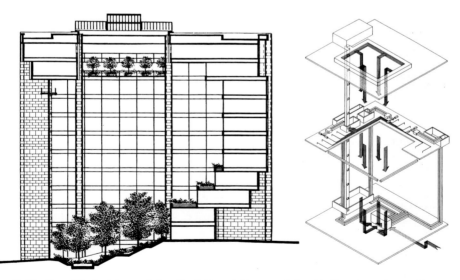

Figure 3.11: Tree-filled atrium of the Ford Foundation used for biofiltration of conditioned return air

© 1968 Roche Dinkeloo Associates

Building-as-shelter

filtration only intensified with the appearance of sick building syndrome. The Department of Defense and NASA investigated the filtration properties of healthy plants over the subsequent decades, and through the 1980s the market for indoor office plants grew exponentially. Over the last decade vertical indoor planting systems have been developed that reduce the space required and can be integrated with mechanical ventilation in numerous configurations. But how do they compare with the use of outdoor air?

A full accounting includes the work and resources for the plants, equipment, installation, maintenance, and nutrients. In effect, we are comparing the costs of an engineered, indoor garden with the ecosystem services of the biosphere delivered by a mechanical ventilation system. Tilley prepared an analysis for an

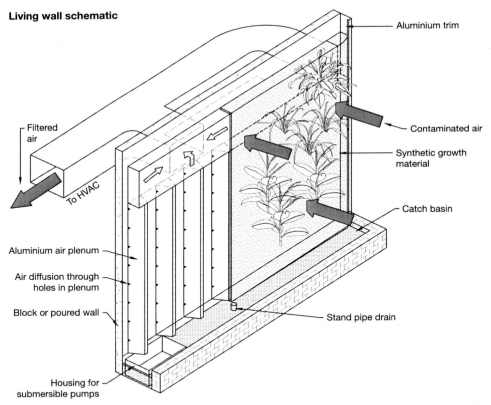

Figure 3.12: A biofilter living wall combining biofiltration and phytoremediation in a hydroponic plant wall, Nedlaw Living Walls

Building-as-shelter

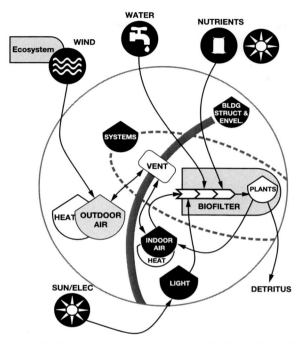

Figure 3.13: Thermodynamic diagram of ventilation with biofilter

exterior planted wall (2006), whose "services" cost about 8.27×10^{12} sej/ m² yr, of which the most intense inputs were from the human economy. It is unlikely that an engineered wall could outperform the biosphere. Campbell's work determined that a mature forest is about 10 times more efficient at processing such wastes, but the limiting factor for biofiltration is the electricity (Campbell 2014). Data from a commercial living wall product show that the pumps, lights, and fans to support enough living wall to clean the air in the Ellis House (about 1 m²) would require 100 watts of electricity, whose upstream costs dramatically outweigh the biofiltering aspects. In contrast, it takes 40 watts to power the ERV and six watts to heat and cool the air it introduces. However, the largest power draw for the living wall is lighting for the plants, so if it was naturally illuminated, the power demand would drop to about 20 watts, offsetting the other costs of the indoor ecosystem (see Figure 3.12).

The thermodynamic diagram reminds us that outdoor air only becomes fresh as it cycles through the metabolism of plants (mostly trees) in the biosphere, which processes wastes and balances the mix of gases. However,

103

Building-as-shelter

the real value of an engineered, biofiltration system is in comparison with air in a metropolitan area, where buildings and people in dense concentrations exhaust pollutants that overwhelm the capacity of local ecosystems. In other words, most buildings in dense, urban environments have no access to truly fresh air, relying on wind-driven circulation to dilute the accumulated wastes and using various degrees of mechanical and chemical filtration to clean ventilation air (see Figure 3.13). In these contexts, internalizing the processing of pollution can improve the operation of the building and the quality of urban air.

Illumination: windows and lamps

Light cannot be stored (as light). It has to be used as it arrives, and it turns into heat once it is absorbed by the materials of the building. Light and heat have different uses, but they form an inseparable cascade of energy transformations, which affects the design of windows and artificial lighting alike. For the thermodynamic diagram of the building, we add the competing pathways by which light from the sun arrives and converts to heat: one direct pathway through windows when it is available, and the other indirect pathway as concentrated power (mostly electricity) that can be released as needed. In both paths, material infrastructures have to be built and energies have to be channeled to provide the light, each of which has different upstream costs. As with high-powered heating systems, the value of "artificial" light is the ability to store the potential until it is needed (in darkness), and to deliver it with precision.

It is difficult to understand how gloomy the interiors of most buildings were before the development of inexpensive sources of light. Until the modern period, transparent materials and artificial sources of power were generally so expensive that nighttime illumination was a sign of real wealth, or the particular value of the activity. Over the last 200 years, ready illumination has become one of the regular services of contemporary buildings—equivalent to protection from weather and provision of comfort—and cheap light is intimately bound up with the new sizes, shapes, and specializations of buildings. The transformation facilitated by the ready delivery of light in human civilization cannot be overstated: it extended the day, increased productivity, and fundamentally altered buildings.

For most of human history the controlled generation of light involved the combustion of organic fuels in fireplaces, candles, or lamps, which released the stored potential of the sunlight fixed by plants in organic molecules or further concentrated by animals (and insects) in waxes, fats, and oils. As an initial point of comparison, the ratio of light to heat (in lumens of visible light) for candles and oil lamps is between 0.1 and 0.3 lumens/watt, while daylighting provides 90 to 110 lumens/watt. In other words, the light that comes through windows is 1,000 times cooler than the light from traditional sources. Through the nineteenth century, better performance was initially achieved with more concentrated fuels, along with a better grasp of combustion (Schivelbusch 1988). For example, lamps burning kerosene and natural gas began to deliver up to 1 lumen/watt, roughly 10 times the output of traditional sources, but they still contained 100 times more heat than daylight. The heat bound up in the delivery of light can be welcome in cold weather, but open forms of combustion are basically a messy way to make light, producing much more heat and pollutants than illumination.

Through the early twentieth century, lighting from combustion became cleaner and more efficacious, but the real improvements came with the development of electric lighting in the late nineteenth century: carbon-arc lights and Thomas Edison's incandescent lamp. Electric lamps are virtually free from indoor pollutants except heat, although that cleanliness is achieved by outsourcing the combustion and release of pollutants to electric power plants (where roughly three times as much fuel is burned to produce a unit of electricity). Edison's original bamboo filament bulb produced a clean, 1.4 lumens/watt, but efficacy of conversion is not the only factor to consider. The transition to electric light increases the upstream costs, which are already considerable for the organic fuels, but even higher because of the waste of converting them to electricity. If we compare an original Edison lamp and a gas lamp of equivalent efficacy, the total e[m]ergy intensity (measured in sej/lumen) of the cleaner electric light is five times greater than that of the gas burned in a lamp. The higher quality light is achieved with a lower total efficiency.

The nineteenth century also heralded the development of more sophisticated architectural techniques for capturing and distributing daylight, which characterize the great public buildings of the period. Beginning with the "invention" of toplighting in the first museums at the end of the eighteenth century, the configurations for capturing and distributing daylight became increasingly effective and precise (Gloag 1965; Connely 1972). In this respect, the coevolution of artificial sources of illumination and building envelopes

Building-as-shelter

differs from the development of central heating, where the power-consuming technology rapidly eclipsed the bioclimatic capacity of building envelopes. In part, this simply reflects the dirtiness of using combustion to make light. The real dominance of artificial illumination was delayed until electricity became less expensive and light sources more efficacious in the mid-twentieth century.

The delay also reflects the sensitivity of occupants to the specific qualities of illumination and the effectiveness of daylighting, made possible by less expensive glass, higher ceilings, and the light wells, skylights, atria, and other techniques that transformed the buildings of the nineteenth century. In museums in which sophisticated forms of toplighting and theories of the appropriate illumination for display had coevolved, galleries resisted artificial lighting until long after it was common in other public settings. In homes, the candle remained the standard of quality for illumination well into the twentieth century and, like the open fireplace, is still preferred on formal or ritual occasions (Schivelbusch 1988). The investments in the material infrastructures of building envelopes or lighting technologies involve more than physical costs to be minimized. They are configurations that resist physical change and accumulate social and cultural expectations as well. As Kiesler observed in 1939, changes in the construction industry take 20 to 30 years to be fully realized, matching also the cultural shifts of human generations.

The success of Luxfer prism glass in the early twentieth century illustrates the complex interaction between buildings and new sources of illumination. Using prismatic optics, Luxfer glass redirects daylight horizontally into rooms, extending and sometimes doubling the depth of space that receives useful illumination (see Figure 3.14). It was targeted at commercial buildings, and helped increase the amount of floor space that could be built on tight urban sites by extending the workable depth of floor plates. Luxfer was launched in 1896 and used widely in projects until the 1930s, even as Edison's electric light was being adopted and refined. The convenience of electric lamps was mitigated by low efficacy and high cost. The Edison lamp had been improved to about 4.5 lumens/watt by 1910, but the average cost of residential electricity was still over 100¢/kWh and did not reach contemporary prices, around 15¢/kWh, until the post-war period (Ayres and Warr 2009). So although the natural light delivered by Luxfer glass was only available during the day, it remained strongly competitive with electric lighting until the perfection of linear fluorescent lamps in the late 1930s, when efficacies had reached 50 lumens/watt in 1939.

Building-as-shelter

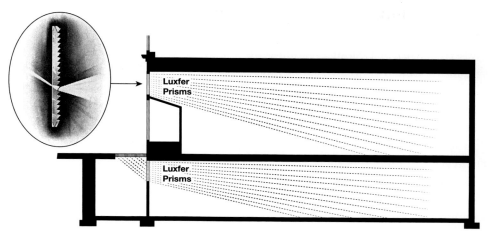

Figure 3.14: Luxfer prism glass redirects incident daylight into the interior, extending the effective depth of the building, 1909

Combined with declining electricity prices, newer fluorescent lamps finally matched the efficacy of daylighting in the post-war period, nearly freeing buildings from the need for the light provided by windows. It allowed them to expand to the limits of their sites, eventually making the floor plates of the Luxfer era seem tiny. As these bulked-up buildings of the third and fourth energy generations became the norm and eventually the symbol of modern cities, the interaction between building envelopes and artificial illumination shifted. The physical size and configuration of contemporary commercial buildings dramatically restricts the amounts of daylight possible; most interior space is simply too far from a window. Even contemporary residential buildings, which are still required by code to have windows in habitable rooms, rarely provide enough daylight to meet current expectations. In effect, most contemporary buildings so reduce the penetration of daylight that modern light sources are virtually the only choice. The contrast between the high cost of fundamentally altering existing buildings to admit more daylight and the lower cost of replacing lighting technologies illustrates the differences among the layers of longevity in buildings. The coevolution between the slower, more substantial envelope and the quicker, more dematerialized components such as lighting involves not only their upstream costs but the inertia of construction cycles and social expectations.

For example, just as candles and open fireplaces were retained in nineteenth-century homes despite the power of gas lighting, a strong social attachment to incandescent lamps developed in the twentieth century. It appeared in dramatic (and partisan) resistance to the rollout of the 2007 energy conservation law that was passed to phase out incandescents by 2014 (US Congress). Some of the reactions were a simple objection to regulation of any kind, but most revolved around the visual quality, flicker, and warm-up time of compact fluorescent lamps, even though they dramatically surpass incandescent lamps in performance. The transition from incandescent to fluorescent lamps occurred over 60 years earlier in commercial settings, where economic productivity is the primary concern. The difference between home and office reminds us of the complex social and cultural factors involved in the adoption of new technologies. Technically, the choice is straightforward: a contemporary incandescent lamp has an efficacy of about 11 lumens/watt and lasts for 1,000 hours, compared to an efficacy of about 70 lumens/watt for a compact fluorescent that lasts about 12,000 hours. Even if the compact fluorescent cost $100 (currently more like $5), it would still cost less over time, and yet people dislike them.

The compact fluorescent has become something of a symbol of the premise that sustainability requires some form of sacrifice, specifically that the fluorescent's lousy color and warm-up time are necessary for greater efficiency. The nostalgia for the 60-watt incandescent lamp relies partly on the kind of technological optimism that commonly stands in opposition to environmentally motivated sacrifice, expressed as the confidence that a better incandescent-like bulb will be developed when it is needed. A more evolutionary version of that optimism is based on the argument that innovations are abundant, and simply need the correct market conditions to "select" them. The recent refinements in LEDs seem to vindicate some of that optimism. The latest LED replacement for the 60-watt lamp outperforms the compact fluorescent on almost every count, including the color of the light.

Determining the full costs of lighting—whether through the building envelope or in lamps—is similar to the evaluation of air-conditioning. We have to establish the investment in the material infrastructure, the upstream costs of the energy, and the efficacy of its conversion to light. Although heat is a by-product of light, it is ultimately an inseparable co-product of windows and lamps, meaning that the investment of work and resources in the envelope is counted toward the delivery of light and heat. But considering the proportion of costs, the two paths could not be more different. There is a large investment of work and resources in the building envelope, while the e[m]ergy intensity of the daylight itself is 1 sej/J (by definition). Conversely, the investment in the lamps and wiring is small relative to the intensity of electricity, 3.97×10^5 sej/J. Adding them together, the intensity of e[m]ergy light from windows is 1.65×10^{10} sej/lumen, compared with 65.4×10^{10} sej/lumen for the light from the original incandescent lamps. The improved Ellis House was relamped with compact fluorescents, reducing the power consumption and the intensity of artificial light to 10.1×10^{10} sej/lumen. In the *Passivhaus* version, fluorescents were replaced with LEDs, whose intensity was slightly lower, 9.16×10^{10}.

With the installation of higher performance lamps, we see the emergence of the same kind of hierarchy that appeared between the thermal contribution of the envelope and of the systems. The envelope provides more lumens of light at lower intensity, while the higher intensity light from the lamps is used more frugally. Since the price of electricity has remained low and does not reflect the full environmental costs, there is little economic pressure to further reduce the use of higher intensity lighting. In fact, even though the incandescent lamps in the original Ellis House used 10 times as much electricity to deliver the same amount of light, they were still being used in 2005. For the original Ellis House, the windows over the year contribute roughly twice as much light at a much lower intensity as the incandescent lamps, illustrating the basic proportionality between energy and intensity that we have seen for other sources. In the improved and *Passivhaus* versions, the more efficient lamps use less than half the energy at the same intensity, making the hierarchy even more pronounced.

Improved lighting is one of the most common strategies for reducing energy consumption, which involves replacing older, inefficient lamps with more efficacious ones that are operated with some form of automated controls. The cost of new lamps and fixtures is low, can be accomplished quickly, and the decrease in consumption can be substantial. The contrast between daylighting and electric lighting makes even clearer the logic of e[m]ergy intensity hierarchies in buildings. The investment in a durable, long-lived envelope can deliver substantial amounts of lower intensity illumination, although that lighting is limited by the rhythm of the sun and weather and the necessity of making the floor plates "thin" enough for daylight to penetrate. For existing buildings with deeper floors, it requires dramatic renovations to open up the configuration, if it is possible at all. Conversely, artificial lighting uses lightweight, short-lived devices that convert very high-intensity power into light, though the cost of the power can be mitigated by using lower intensity power. In the *Passivhaus* version, the electricity from photovoltaics has an e[m]ergy intensity about 40% lower, further enhancing the effectiveness of the LEDs but still at many times the cost of daylighting.

The thermodynamic diagram reminds us that building envelopes serve many purposes, so they cannot be optimized just for lighting or anything else. Windows and other apertures are among the most dynamic environmental aspects of the building skin, selectively channeling light, heat, air, and views, each of which connect to other processes and criteria. This book began by describing the luxurious appeals of the all-glass high-rise building that now symbolizes the power of the contemporary metropolis. The inseparable connection between work and waste heat complicates the design and analysis of lighting, and applies to every other form of work in buildings. The effect of that heat forms the subject of the next section.

Wasting waste heat

> The deeper the building, the more it depends on artifice for its servicing.
> (Koolhaas et al. 1995, 663)

In the previous sections, we presented system characteristics like the thermal time constant to understand the interactions that temper interior temperatures, and to show how the elements of the building work together. Because we take this so much for granted, the point cannot be overstated. As the various versions of the Ellis House have helped demonstrate, the right configuration, proportions, and adjustments of building materials can perform the very real work of modifying the climate over time. The description of that dynamic system is not complete until we include the other sources of heat in buildings, especially the waste heat released by other forms of work. Using the energy systems language to place "waste" within the sequence of energy exchanges helps temper the moralizing assumptions about waste and shifts the evaluation of performance from narrow definitions of efficiency to more comprehensive descriptions of power.

I keep returning to Banham's parable about the wood in the clearing because it captures something fundamental about the restless process of development and self-organization in buildings, not the stark choice between shelter and fuel but the many tradeoffs between efficiency and power. The lower intensity of the services contributed by building envelopes makes them a far more economical choice, but the question is really a matter of proportion. How much wood to invest in shelters and how much wood to burn in the fires that are needed for cooking and lighting anyway? The imperative to maximize power appears again and again, at multiple scales, in the interaction between long-term, harder-to-change investments that regulate local flows of available power or the imported, concentrated forms of power, all of which end up as heat.

The amount of residual heat released inside contemporary buildings has grown dramatically through the last century. Combined with the increases in volume-to-surface ratio of commercial and institutional buildings, this increase in residual heat has produced a new thermodynamic type that engineers call "internal load dominated." The Ellis House, and most other smaller, thinner, lower occupancy buildings, simply respond to the immediate demands of the climate, heating in cool weather and cooling in hot. But bigger buildings, with higher occupancies and larger amounts of lighting and equipment, become preoccupied with removing their excess heat. We only have to think about the windowless core of any large commercial building, which is only connected to the outdoor climate through its systems and has to be air-conditioned year round. In its normative configuration, the Ellis House is a climate-dominated building but it could eventually become internal load dominated as its envelope is tightened, illustrating the point at which a by-product becomes a problematic form of waste.

The transition from climate to internal load dominated is determined by the ratio between internal gains and the lossiness of the envelope. The balance between them dictates how much warmer the inside will be or how much heat has to be removed to keep it comfortable. For smaller buildings with conventional envelopes and modest internal gains, this will only be a few degrees. But for buildings with very tight envelopes (e.g. *Passivhaus* standard), large amounts of internal gains (typical commercial buildings), or both, the effect on interior temperatures can be dramatic. The temperature increase from internal gains in the original Ellis House is a modest 4°C. If we kept the internal gains at the same normative level, the improved version would have an increase of 15°C, while an envelope raised to *Passivhaus* standards with those same gains would have an increase of 25°C. Temperature charts of the normative and *Passivhaus* versions show the transition from climate to internal load dominated (see Figure 3.15).

Building-as-shelter

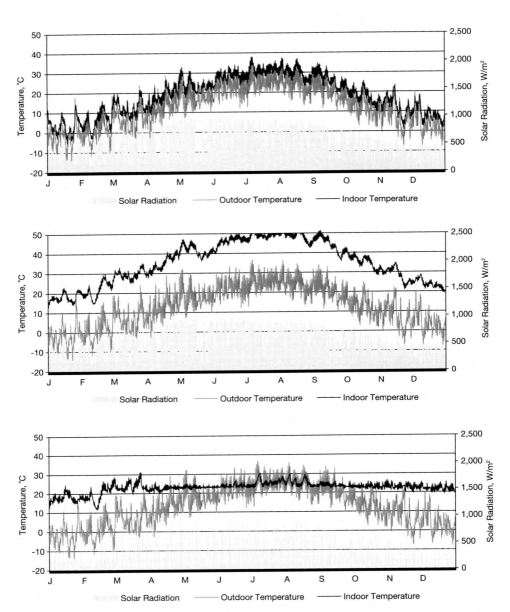

Figure 3.15: (a) Temperature simulation of climate-dominated building. Original, normative version of the Ellis House with normative internal gains; (b) Temperature simulation of internal load-dominated building. Improved version of the Ellis House with normative internal gains; (c) Temperature simulation of balanced loads and gains. Responsively managed, Passivhaus version of the Ellis House with reduced internal gains

Because these kinds of calculation were first used to determine the size of heating equipment, this ratio has most commonly been presented in the opposite way, as the "balance point," the outdoor temperature at which no heating or cooling is required. It is calculated by subtracting the temperature increase from the desired indoor temperature. The balance points of the three versions of the Ellis House with the same internal gains are 16°C (original), 5°C (improved), and −6°C (*Passivhaus*). The lower the balance point, the less heat the furnace will have to provide—but for outdoor temperatures above that point, the building will need to get rid of heat. The transition from climate dominated to internal load dominated occurs roughly when the balance point is below the average outdoor temperature for the climate (about 13°C in Philadelphia). This is directly analogous to the thermodynamics of the human body, whose "balance point temperature" for comfort is between 20 and 24°C, though with higher levels of exertion (more internal gains) or more clothing (more insulation) the temperature at which we are comfortable drops. If the temperature is not low enough, we have to reduce our level of activity, remove some clothing, begin sweating to increase the rate of heat loss, or find some other way to remove heat.

The picture is even more dramatic if we include the average amount of solar gains through the windows. The original Ellis House is nearly unchanged, but the combined balance point temperature of the improved version is −3°C, while it is −24°C for the *Passivhaus* version. In reality, the increased efficiency of lights and equipment is an integral aspect of efficiency improvements, as is the control of solar gain, so the internal gains in both the improved and *Passivhaus* versions are reduced proportionally, keeping the balance points between 14 and 15°C. On the one hand, the dynamic balance between gains and losses illustrates the central principle of the super-insulated, *Passivhaus* approach; on the other, it explains the wastefulness of internal load-dominated buildings.

The third temperature chart (c) in Figure 3.15 shows the responsive version of the Ellis House with proportionally reduced internal gains, adjusted by opening and shading the windows as needed to keep the interior comfortable. It shifts between a balance point of −1°C with a time constant of 125 hours when the windows are sealed, to a balance point of 19°C with a time constant of 20 hours when the windows are shaded and opened. By keeping the internal gains in proportion to the lossiness of the envelope, the *Passivhaus* version is able to adapt to the changing conditions of the climate with small amounts of work and information about the state of the building.

Building-as-shelter

The interaction among building properties reinforces the point that buildings behave as a dynamic thermal system. Any single performance strategy—increasing insulation values, installing better windows, installing better lights or equipment—reaches some threshold beyond which its effect diminishes (decreasing comfort or increasing cost), and needs to be countered by a compensating strategy. Among the clearest examples of indirect self-organization are the productive uses of "waste" heat, which are only wasteful when they exceed the capacity of the building to use them. As the transition from climate to internal load dominated makes evident, residual heat constitutes a critical aspect of building thermodynamics. The practical point of Odum's fifth principle is that the e[m]ergy intensity of different sources can be used to reveal the hierarchical cascades that emerge as buildings are configured to maximize power. One question is whether contemporary buildings have had time to become optimal in this way, or can adjust quickly enough to reflect changing prices and technologies. As the theory suggests, higher intensity sources are more flexible and so can be used to adapt to market changes more quickly.

We complete the thermal analysis by determining the intensity of the different sources summarized in Figure 3.16. For the internal heat released by people, lights, and equipment, we combine the upstream costs of their different power

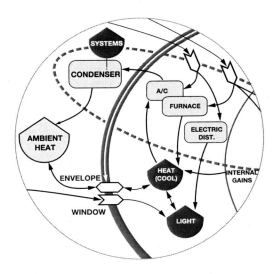

Figure 3.16: Detail, heat gains and losses in the Ellis House, original version

sources and the infrastructure that channels them. The equipment that produces heat gains in the Ellis House can be divided into devices that use natural gas and electricity, both of which have very high-energy intensities but involve modest investments in infrastructure. The metabolic energy given off by people involves no infrastructure cost (unless we count clothing or kitchen equipment), and has an even higher energy intensity, reflecting the very high upstream costs of contemporary food production, packaging, and delivery.

When we add the e[m]ergy intensities determined for these heat sources to the ones previously calculated for the envelope and the conditioning systems, it produces a full spectrum of energy quantities and e[m]ergy intensities for the thermal exchanges in the Ellis House. The original and *Passivhaus* versions are plotted on log-log charts, revealing a surprisingly precise hierarchy (with a good statistical fit for the original version) (see Figure 3.17). In each case, the building envelope provides the most heat at the lowest intensity (~1,000 sej/J), while the various forms of residual gains provide the least amount of heat at the highest intensity (750,000 sej/J). The hierarchy remains relatively constant as the utility usage of the versions decreases, reflecting the distribution of improvements across all the categories (lighting, equipment, etc.) to keep the building in balance. The hierarchy reflects both the degree to which upstream environmental costs are present in economic prices and the relative independence of higher intensity sources, which facilitates their adjustment as costs shift over time.

We have collectively been extending the spectrum since the beginning of the modern period, developing higher quality, more e[m]ergy intensive products and services, translating them into new forms of building, and encoding them in new devices to amplify their power. The fact that larger commercial and institutional buildings of the third and fourth energy generations are generally internal load dominated has long been accepted as a natural condition of these new building types, but the productive uses of waste heat in more balanced buildings indicate that those buildings are simply wasting their waste heat. Like the mature ecosystems they seek to imitate, buildings of the fourth and fifth energy generations enhance their power with hierarchical cascades of energy transformation.

A thermodynamic minimum

In the restless back and forth between the structural and power-operated solutions, between the slower, weighty influence of the building envelope and

Building-as-shelter

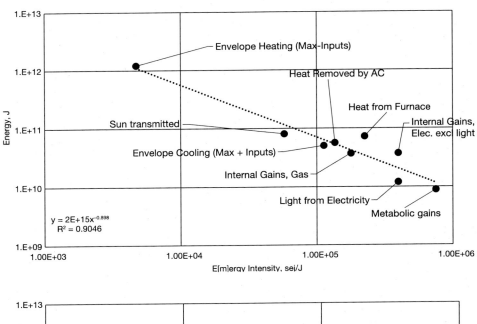

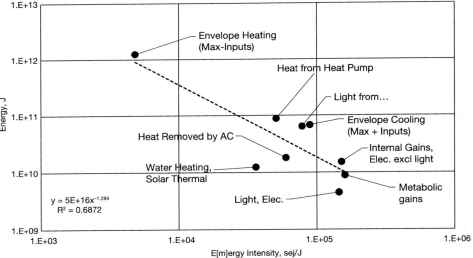

Figure 3.17: (a) Energy–E[m]ergy intensity chart of thermal exchanges in the Ellis House, original, normative version; (b) Energy–E[m]ergy intensity chart of thermal exchanges in the Ellis House, Passivhaus net zero energy version

the more nimble effects of concentrated power, a challenging performance goal emerges: to achieve a thermodynamic minimum of their combined e[m]ergy costs while delivering the services of a contemporary building. Minimizing the e[m]ergy footprint of a building reduces its imposition on the biosphere, but there are many paths to that goal. Throughout this chapter, the historical developments of the different aspects of the building-as-shelter—insulation, central heating, comfort standards, light sources, ventilation—were introduced to understand some of the many formats that have been tested to achieve that minimum. As we reviewed the radical transformations over the last 200 years, we discerned a pattern that is consistent with the theory of maximum power and that also highlights the provisional, searching nature of the process in which competing arrangements are developed and tested over time.

Buildings are both the outcome of considered, individual design decisions and equally the product of complex social, economic, and cultural enterprises with their different goals and historical trajectories. Patrick Geddes and Lewis Mumford identified progressive stages of technological evolution—eotechnic, paleotechnic, and neotechnic—and attributed them to the interaction between new sources of power, new technologies for exploiting those sources, and new social arrangements for managing and accommodating them (Geddes 1915; Mumford 1934). The buildings of the first, second, and third energy generations leveraged the new levels of power to explore more effective forms of environmental control. As fuels became more costly in the energy price spikes of the 1970s, the efficiency improvements of the fourth generation, largely imposed by regulation, enhanced the overall climate-modifying power of buildings. The more ambitious buildings of the fifth generation continue to test new arrangements to enhance power and reduce impacts. The vast space of "adjacent possible" variations that has been explored through this period can be described with the simple thermodynamic diagram introduced at the beginning of this chapter and the spectrum that develops from the constant adjustments between the more and less intense elements of buildings (Kauffman 2000, 142) (see Figure 3.2).

The tables in Appendix B show the total e[m]ergy costs for the three versions of the Ellis House, with each subsequent version further reducing the total. The efficiency improvements of the second version dramatically reduced the amounts of electricity and natural gas expended on heating, cooling, and lighting, marginally increased the cost of the building envelope, and shifted the proportion between the two, so that the annual cost of the utilities is nearly equivalent to the cost of the envelope. The third *Passivhaus* NZE version required an even greater investment in the envelope, systems, and photovoltaics, which has reduced the utilities of conditioning by nearly two-thirds, leaving the annual cost of the envelope somewhat greater than the cost of the utilities. At this point, the design priority shifts from the efficiency of power-operated equipment to the intensities of the materials in the envelope.

The e[m]ergy intensity spectra can also be used to visualize the evolution of contemporary buildings and design strategies for the transition to a renewable economy. Compared to pre-industrial forms of construction and living, the spectrum of intensities in contemporary buildings has steadily been increased and extended, with everything from building materials to power sources increasing in their e[m]ergy intensity. One path to the all-renewable building is to return to the mix of materials, power sources, and intensities of pre-industrial buildings. In the intensity–quantity plot, that would mean shifting the spectrum down radically, using local, renewable materials and fuels, effectively returning to the agricultural economy that preceded the current hydrocarbon-based economy (see see Figure 3.18). Those buildings have much to teach us, but the spectrum of intensities helps us see other possibilities. The increased understanding of building science and new information technologies have been used to reduce consumption and enhance power since the development of the thermostat, extending the spectrum by using small amounts of even higher intensity sources to amplify the effect of lower intensity environmental energies.

The table of e[m]ergy costs (see Appendix B, Tables B.2 and B.3) summarizes the different categories used to evaluate the performance of the building-as-shelter. Minimizing e[m]ergy for the same building and services provides a kind of efficiency measure assessed on a life cycle scale, revealing the full costs and systemic limitations of well-intentioned practices such as more efficient envelopes and systems, "passive-before-active," and "long-life-loose-fit." However, the principle of maximum power is a long-term selection principle that operates simultaneously at the scale of the building and of the overall system. When we adopt it as an approach to building design, we must remember that the building-as-shelter also contributes (or not) to the productivity and health of the larger economy and ecosystem in which it is built. Even a building with the lowest thermodynamic costs must enhance the power and resilience of the larger system for which it is built, and for this we need to examine the activities they house and the larger purposes they serve.

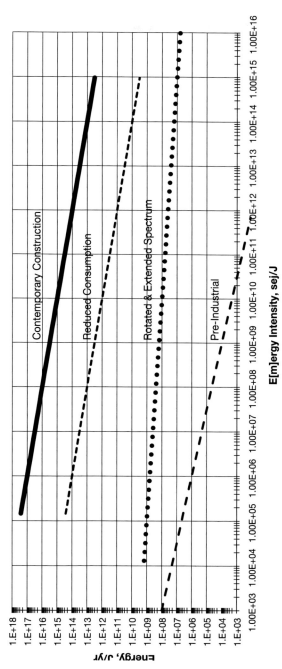

Figure 3.18: Illustration of energy–e[m]ergy intensity spectra for different energy regimes

After Tilley

Bibliography

1906. *Sweet's Indexed Catalogue of Building Construction*, edited by The Architectural Record Co., New York.

Ayres, Robert U., & Benjamin Warr. 2009. *The Economic Growth Engine: How Energy and Work Drive Material Prosperity*. Cheltenham: Edward Elgar.

Balcomb, J. Douglas. 1982. *Passive Solar Design Handbook*. Washington, DC: US Department of Energy.

Banham, Reyner. 1969. *The Architecture of the Well-Tempered Environment*. Chicago, IL: University of Chicago Press.

Brand, Stewart. 1994. *How Buildings Learn: What Happens After They're Built*. New York: Viking.

Brazell, David W., Lowell Dworin, & Michael Walsh. 1989. *A History of Federal Tax Depreciation Policy*. Washington, DC: Department of Treasury, Office of Tax Analysis.

Brown, M. T., & Vorasun Buranakarn. 2003. "Emergy Indices and Ratios for Sustainable Material Cycles and Recycle Options." *Resources, Conservation and Recycling* 38: 1–22.

Brown, Mark T., Marco Raugei, & Sergio Ulgiati. 2012. "On Boundaries and 'Investments' in Emergy Synthesis and LCA: A Case Study on Thermal vs. Photovoltaic Electricity." *Ecological Indicators* 15: 227–235.

Butler, Samuel. 1863. "Darwin among the Machines." *The Press Newspaper*. Christchurch, New Zealand, June 13.

Butler, Samuel. 1872. *Erewhon, or, Over the Range*. London: Trubner & Co.

Campbell, Elliott T. 2014. "Valuing Ecosystem Services from Maryland Forests using Environmental Accounting." *Ecosystem Services* 7: 141–151.

Campbell, Margaret. 2005. "What Tuberculosis did for Modernism: The Influence of a Curative Environment on Modernist Design and Architecture." *Medical History* 49: 463–488.

Connely, James L. 1972. "The Grand Gallery of the Louvre and the Museum Project: Architectural Problems." *Journal of the Society of Architectural Historians* 31: 120–132.

Cooper, Gail. 1998. *Air-Conditioning America: Engineers and the Controlled Environment, 1900–1960*. Baltimore, MD: Johns Hopkins Press.

Darwin, Charles. 1859. *The Origin of Species by Means of Natural Selection, or, the Preservation of Favored Races in the Struggle for Life*. Philadelphia, PA: John Wanamaker.

Duffy, Frank. 1964. "Bürolandschaft." *Architectural Review* (September 1987): 31–39.

Fitch, James Marston. 1972. *American Building: The Environmental Forces That Shaped It*, 2nd ed. New York: Schoecken Books.

Geddes, Patrick. 1915. *Cities in Evolution: An Introduction to the Town Planning Movement and to the Study of Cities*. London: Williams & Norgate.

Georgescu-Roegen, Nicholas. 1971. *The Entropy Law and the Economic Process*. Cambridge, MA: Harvard University Press.

Giedion, Siegfried. 1948. *Mechanization Takes Command: A Contribution to Anonymous History*. New York: W. W. Norton.

Gloag, H. L. 1965. *Museum and Art Gallery Design, a Short History of the Daylighting of Art Galleries*. Garston: Building Research Station.

Gottschalk, Ottomar. 1968. *Flexible Verwaltungsbauten: Planung, Funktion, Flächen, Ausbau, Einrichtung, Kosten, Beispiele*. Quickborn: Verlag Schnelle.

Hawkes, Dean. 1996. *The Environmental Tradition: Studies in the Architecture of Environment*. London: Taylor & Francis.

Hinte, Ed van and Marc Neelen. 2003. *Smart Architecture*. Rotterdam: 010 Publishers.

Janssen, John E. 1994. "The Centennial Series – The V in ASHRAE, an Historical Perspective." *ASHRAE Journal* 36(8): 126–132.

Janssen, John E. 1999. "The History of Ventilation and Temperature Control." *ASHRAE Journal* 41(10): 47–52.

Kauffman, Stuart. 2000. *Investigations*: Oxford University Press.

Koolhaas, Rem, Office for Metropolitan Architecture, & Bruce Mau. 1995. *Small, Medium, Large, Extra-large*. New York: Monacelli Press.

Lundin, Lena. 1992. *On Building: Related Causes of the Sick Building Syndrome*. Stockholm: Almqvist & Wiksell International.

Mazria, Ed. 1980. *The Passive Solar Energy Book*. Emmaus, PA: Rodale Press.

McDonough, William, & Michael Braungart. 2002. *Cradle to Cradle: Remaking the Way We Make Things*. New York: North Point Press.

Mosley, Stephen. 2014. "Environmental History of Air Pollution." In *Encyclopedia of Life Support Systems*. Paris: Eolss Publishers.

Mumford, Lewis. 1934. *Technics and Civilization*. New York: Harcourt Brace & World.

Oldfield, Philip, Dario Trabucco, & Antony Wood. 2009. "Five Energy Generations of Tall Buildings: An Historical Analysis of Energy Consumption in High-Rise Buildings." *Journal of Architecture* 14(5): 591–613.

Ozenfant, Amédée, and Le Corbusier (Charles-Edouard Jeanneret). 1921. "Le Purisme." *L'Esprit Nouveau* 4:369–386.

Perry, Jay. 2000. NASA Environmental Control and Life Support Systems (ECLSS) project.

Schivelbusch, Wolfgang. 1988. *Disenchanted Night: The Industrialization of Light in the Nineteenth Century.* Berkeley, CA: University of California Press.

Sonderegger, Robert. 1977. *Dynamic Models of House Heating Based on Equivalent Thermal Parameters.* PhD dissertation, Princeton University.

Srinivasan, Ravi S., Wesley Ingwersen, Christian Trucco, Robert Ries, and Daniel E. Campbell. 2014. "Comparison of energy-based indicators used in life cycle assessment tools for buildings." *Building and Environment* 79:138–151.

Srinivasan, Ravi S., William W. Braham, Daniel E. Campbell, & Charlie D. Curcija. 2012. "Re(De)fining Net Zero Energy: Renewable Emergy Balance in Environmental Building Design." *Building and Environment* 47: 300–315.

Ternoey, Steven, Larry Bickle, Claude L. Robbins, Robert Busch, & Kit McCord. 1985. *The Design of Energy Responsive Commercial Buildings.* New York: Solar Energy Research Institute/Wiley-Interscience.

Tilley, David R. 2006. "National Metabolism and Communications Technology Development in the United States, 1790–2000." *Environment and History* 12: 165–190.

US Congress. 2007. *Energy Independence and Security Act.* In *Public Law* 110–140.

US DOE. 2012. *2011 Buildings Energy Data Book*: Buildings Technologies Program. US Department of Energy.

US EPA. 2009. *Estimating 2003 Building-Related Construction and Demolition Materials Amounts*, edited by Office of Resource Conservation and Recovery. US Environmental Protection Agency.

Figure 4.1: Fred McNabb's visionary *House of the Future* (1956) predicted almost everything available in the contemporary US household, from microwave ovens to video phones (skype), though personal helicopters are not yet common and he didn't anticipate the mobile, handheld "screens"

Chapter Four

Building-as-setting for the work of living

I once lived in a tremendously efficient "single resident occupancy" apartment, which was so small I could watch the living room television from the bathtub. Unfortunately, the apartment's only sink was also in the bathroom, and I used to speculate about how much work it would take to add another one in the kitchenette to hide the dishes. But while it was easy to "add" a TV to the apartment, sinks are simply more complicated. Water is heavy, corrosive, and has to be removed once it is "dirty." It took over 50 years for bathtubs and toilets to reach the majority of US households, while TVs reached that many in under a decade. The contrast illustrates the different amounts of material involved and the different kinds of "work" for which they are used. The *House of the Future* of 1956 (see Figure 4.1) was already replete with screens, and with the increases in productivity through the twentieth century, most of the US population now elects to spend their increased leisure time watching screens in their various forms. As we consider the activities that are enabled and supported by buildings, the environmental imperative to reduce consumption and mitigate pollution quickly becomes a question about what people do with their time, and about the different costs of working, bathing, eating, and watching TV.

Activities within buildings draw on a tremendous variety of resources, which can be organized along a spectrum of dematerialization—from the weighty management of dirty water to the seemingly effortless sampling of media, now transmitted by Wi-Fi. That spectrum of resource flows supports the work of living in all its messiness, using more concentrated resources like electric power and information to amplify and regulate the delivery of water, food, and supplies.

Building-as-setting for the work of living

To begin elaborating, the thermodynamic diagram of the activities in buildings, the flows of work and resources are organized into two classes: "material services" and "concentrated power." The two classes are never wholly separate; each material service involves degrees of concentrated power and even the most dematerialized form of power or information requires some material carrier. They can be distinguished by their e[m]ergy intensity and the residue they leave behind once they have been used. In general, material services result in degraded substances and pollutants that must be managed and removed, while the concentrated flows of power and information are cleaner and more flexible because they shed their weight and pollutants in the process of concentration.

For households and workplaces alike, material services, concentrated power, and information replace human labor, reduce work time, and amplify human capacities (Cowan 1983). For example, new forms of cooking have been developed following the introduction of each new source of power, from wood fireplaces to gas ranges, electric toasters, microwave ovens, and induction stoves, each more efficient and cleaner than the form they replaced but requiring higher qualities of power. The ice box, with its seasonally harvested ice delivered by cart, replaced the spring house or cold cabinet, and was, in its turn, replaced by the electric refrigerator. The advances in kitchen equipment reduced the need for actual labor or servants, increasingly transforming the kitchen from a room of production to one of consumption. The labor of washing clothes or cleaning floors was similarly reduced by washing machines, tumble driers, and vacuum cleaners, each with its own history of innovation and development while requiring more power and different kinds of space in buildings.

The work in commercial buildings has been reshaped even more quickly and completely than in houses. The transformation of workshops into factories and offices was made possible by more concentrated forms of power and information, which enhanced productivity by facilitating more specialized forms of work and hierarchical management structures. Commercial buildings increased in size, made from more refined materials and divided into highly specialized types and configurations. The emergence of the internal load-dominated building illustrates one unintended consequence of those transformations, which have otherwise reduced waste and increased economic productivity by concentrating people and power in contemporary workplaces. Establishing the thermodynamic role of currency completes the spectrum of concentrated power.

Buildings provide settings for the work that makes the wheel of the economy turn, where production and consumption are linked in the endless cycle of supply and demand. Commercial, industrial, and residential buildings are now wholly distinct types but, as anthropologist Thomas Abel has argued, they are occupied by the same people who appear as producers one moment and consumers the next (Abel 2004). The roles are never really separate, and exist largely as an abstraction for economic analysis. Examining the building-as-setting, and its support of human activities, puts the many different acts of production or consumption in their full environmental context.

Material services

The delivery of fresh water to buildings exemplifies the "free" environmental work expended to obtain any useful resource, and also the deeply intertwined social and technological activities for which buildings provide a setting. Since water is so palpable (and heavy), it offers a more concrete example of e[m]ergy intensity than the energy-rich fuels. It is also more intimately involved with daily activities—washing, cooking, cleaning, and the transport of sewage—and so makes apparent the coevolution of consumption, technologies, and social conventions.

For most of human history, people could be divided into two classes: those who carried their daily water, and a minority who had someone else carry it for them. In periods of particular wealth, water was occasionally delivered directly to people where they used it. During the time of the Roman Empire, water was piped to neighborhood fountains, apartment buildings, bathhouses, and wealthy residences. In another example of Jevon's paradox, reducing the work of carrying water markedly increased the amounts used each day. People who carry their water typically use about one to three gallons a day for drinking, cooking, bathing, cleaning—an amount that increased to somewhere between 15 and 150 gallons per person in Rome when water was piped in (Hansen 2014). Charles Dickens noted the same effect in 1842 when he visited the first modern water supply system in Philadelphia:

> Philadelphia is most bountifully provided with fresh water, which is showered and jerked about, and turned on, and poured off, everywhere. The Water Works, which are on a height near the city, are no less ornamental than useful,

being tastefully laid out as a public garden, and kept in the best and neatest order. The river is dammed at this point, and forced by its own power into certain high tanks or reservoirs, whence the whole city, to the top stories of the houses, is supplied at a very trifling expense.

(Dickens 1874, 142)

Built 30 years prior to Dickens' visit, the Water Works (officially known as Fairmount Water Works) had rapidly become a model for metropolitan water systems around the world, where similar increases of water use followed the installation of pressured and piped supply systems. Some of that usage was lost in the leaky systems of distribution as pipes were extended into households and business. Water was rarely metered until the twentieth century, so the population was largely free to explore uses of water that had not even been imagined by even the wealthiest bathers of previous generations.

This transformation exemplifies the classic account of technological innovation, in which human labor is replaced by mechanical (or hydraulic) ingenuity and the amounts of work (or water) that can be accomplished are dramatically increased. It is fitting that the steam engines of the eighteenth century, which heralded the first Industrial Revolution, were developed to pump water from mines that were being dug below the water table. The ingenious technology developed to help satisfy the growing demands for coal both required more coal to operate it and enabled the more rapid use of other resources like fresh water.

The first water works in Philadelphia was powered by a steam engine and only relocated when demand exceeded its capacity. As water use continued to strain the ability of local ecosystems to simultaneously provide fresh water and absorb waste, water intakes were extended upstream and distribution made more efficient, but consumption continued to increase (Lewis 1924). A report from 1900 noted that "the average daily consumption in Philadelphia has risen from 36 gallons per capita in 1860, to 215 gallons in 1897," so municipal engineers began seeking the installation of meters to help moderate rates of use (Beardsley 1900, 119). These dramatic increases in consumption can seem quite abstract in the engineering reports, but it is important to understand the dramatic change in personal habits that corresponded to the hundreds of gallons of water suddenly flowing into households and businesses.

At its most fundamental, this cultural change involves a transformed concept of cleanliness, both of the water and of those that used it. In the final chapter of *Mechanization Takes Command*, Siegfried Giedion examined this change through the history of the modern bathtub, contrasting it with the public bathing habits of the ancient world (Giedion 1948). An illustration of the depth of the shift to modern forms of cleanliness can be discerned in a late eighteenth-century diary entry, penned just as Philadelphia was beginning its experiments with readily available water:

> In the summer of 1798 Henry Drinker, a well-to-do Quaker merchant, installed a shower box for his family in the backyard of his Philadelphia town house. A year later on July 1, his wife Elizabeth, then sixty-five years old, went in for the first time. "I bore it better than I expected," she wrote in her diary, "not having been wet all over all at once, for 28 years past."
>
> (Bushman and Bushman 1988, 1214)

It can be hard to imagine such a different regime of cleanliness from our own, in which total immersion prevails. The change did not happen all at once or everywhere at the same rate. But when we consider the role of resources like water use in environmental buildings of the twenty-first century, it is imperative to understand the moist evolution of habits, habitats, and inhabitants that are involved in the new technologies of water use.

A particular technical alignment and public health regulation marks a critical threshold in this evolution. The installation of the first water supply systems typically preceded the construction of sewage systems, sometimes by decades. Dirty water was simply dumped into existing yards, privies, and drains until they overflowed, causing a host of health problems. The installation of closed sewers completes the modern system, which uses one set of pipes for clean water and another for dirty. The final acceleration in water use begins once the two systems are aligned, when the drain for dirty water is located below the faucet that delivers clean water. Public health officials quickly learned about the dangers of letting the systems connect, with dirty water unintentionally siphoning back into supply pipes, and so legislated a minimum "air gap" between the bottom of the faucet and the top of the tub or sink. This alignment between faucet and drain, with its hygienic gap, announces the realization of a powerful new technology for maximizing the conversion of clean water into dirty: all you have to do is turn it on.

Water supply

The fresh water delivered through modern pipes requires two basic kinds of work. The first is the mostly physical work of lifting and delivering it, while the second is the largely biochemical work of distilling and cleaning it. The primary work of most municipal water systems is moving water that is already fresh, drawing it from lakes, rivers, and underground aquifers, filtering it for particulates, and then pumping it through the massive water supply infrastructure under pressure. The economic cost of the water supply, whether paid through taxes or individual meters, covers the work of building and operating that hydraulic enterprise, but the value of "freshness" becomes starkly apparent in regions where fresh water is scarce. Salt water, by comparison, can be distilled by boiling and condensing it using large amounts of heat, or by reverse osmosis under very high pressure using pumps that use more than 10 times the electricity needed just to move fresh water.

Granted, municipal engineers can purify seawater to augment or even replace fresh water supplies, but the higher costs make evident the tremendous work the biosphere does to deliver fresh water to lakes and rivers. As with the refined materials used in building construction, the freshness of water is purchased with work, whether by the biosphere or the technosphere. Andres Buenfil prepared a comparative analysis of fresh water supply systems in Florida, from municipal delivery of surface water to desalination, home filtration, and the water in plastic bottles (Buenfil 2001). A generic diagram of a water supply system distinguishes the work of the biosphere from that of the human economy (see Figure 4.2). Water succinctly illustrates the limitations of market pricing for valuing environmental resources. In regions where the biosphere has done less work, providing less fresh water, the costs are higher.

In Buenfil's study, the least costly water supply was a municipal system drawing fresh water from a lake, which required about 1×10^{12} sej/m^3 of water. Using reverse osmosis with brackish water doubled the cost, while a system using seawater as a source requires over seven times as much work. This largely confirms the conventional engineering ranking of economic costs, but highlights the contribution of ecosystem services and the value of maintaining the health of existing watersheds. More surprising was Buenfil's analysis of the costs of individual domestic water treatment, from the filtering and boiling of ground water to backyard solar distillation; the individual treatments were 25 to 100 times as

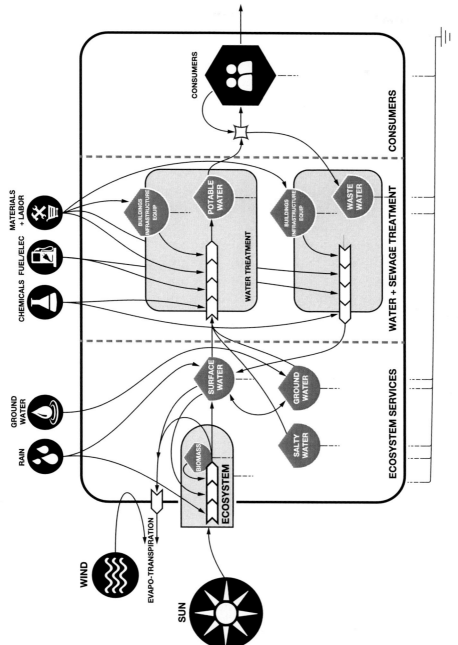

Figure 4.2: Water supply and wastewater treatment, distinguishing ecosystem work from work of economy

After Buenfil

costly as larger systems, due primarily to the economies of scale realized in municipal facilities. Not surprisingly, the most expensive method of delivering fresh water is in plastic bottles, which required over 150 times as much total work and materials per liter, even when the water had been drawn from a local, fresh water source. It turns out to be much, much more expensive to deliver water in a diesel-powered truck than to pump it through pipes.

Bottled water is the most luxurious, inefficient form of fresh water available. Its use can only be understood at the larger scales of social and economic organization (see Chapter 5), where symbols of wealth obtain their meaning and the perception of purity is assigned a value. The cleanliness of water exemplifies the way in which biological necessities and real environmental costs take on additional social values. Once water has been used for any purpose, however lightly, it is considered dirty (although there are degrees of dirtiness) and cannot be used until it has been made clean again. Water carrying organic matter and bacteria from food or human waste is considered "black," while water from clothes washers, bathtubs, showers, or lavatories is called "gray." Even the recycling of gray water for flushing the lavatory is only possible once the organic materials have been filtered. In other words, the work and resources invested in producing fresh water are all dissipated once it enters a drain and becomes dirty.

Wastewater treatment

The costs of water are only complete once it is sufficiently clean to return to local waterways. For example, reverse osmosis can also be applied to sewage water, in a process called "toilet-to-tap." This requires somewhat less work than desalination, although as a county official in San Diego remarked, it is still "one of the most expensive kinds of water you can create" (Archibold 2007). Filtration is really just the final step in the project of water recycling, a process engendered in 1948 when the first Federal Water Pollution Control Act created an epic shift in American municipal practices by regulating the effluents that could be dumped into waterways. Strengthened by revisions in 1972, this legislation, now commonly known as the Clean Water Act, makes it illegal to dump raw sewage or any pollutant into water systems and navigable waters and required effluents to meet new treatment standards, primarily the elimination of biodegradable organics.

Most wastewater treatment is performed in the tanks of conventional treatment plants, using microbes similar to those found in natural waterways that consume the organic material as food. They neutralize the wastes before they are returned to waterways, where the water is often extracted. A common urban saying allows that the river water of major cities is "drunk seven times between the source and the sea," but the anxieties associated with cleanliness and completing the last step from sewage to drinking water are profound (Foundation for Water Research 2008). San Diego ultimately decided to pump its osmotically filtered sewage water into local aquifers, where it actually becomes somewhat less pure before it is subsequently withdrawn as drinking water. However, "laundering" it in this way more adequately satisfies public beliefs about cleanliness.

It is a fascinating perception-one where we trust the natural processes of the hydrologic cycle to deliver cleanliness while we count their services as "free," and yet we distrust the engineered services for which we have to pay. Impartial nature versus imperfect people perhaps, but the distinction highlights the difference between common-sense perceptions and the economic exchange value of natural resources. As long as the human uses of a river are within the capacity of the waterway to clean itself, the exchange value more or less reflects the work of obtaining and delivering it. But once renewal capacity is exceeded, when consumption rates exceed those limits, the real costs of purifying and delivering the water become evident in the work and energy required to reproduce the natural processes.

Adding wastewater treatment to the thermodynamic diagram completes the accounting of costs associated with fresh water, and it involves the dissipation of considerable untapped energetic potential in the organic waste (see Figure 4.2). In a study of conventional sewage treatment plants, experts estimated that the processing required from 1.25 to 8×10^{12} sej/m^3 of wastewater, matching the scale of the work required to clean the water in the first place (Vassallo et al. 2009). Almost all of that remaining potential is a residue from the food cycle, either from kitchen wastes or after human digestion. In the conventional arrangement, the two cycles are linked, with fresh water being used as a vehicle to carry kitchen and toilet waste to sewage treatment plants. In one estimate, standard sewage contains about 56×10^6 J/m^3 of residual energy that can be converted to gas or electricity, or used as a food or fertilizer for other biological processes. If the food and water cycles are separated, with the organic wastes removed and composted, the cost of cleaning the remaining water is considerably lower. In improved and *Passivhaus* versions of the Ellis House, part of the reduction in e[m]ergy costs of the kitchen is from the composting of solid food wastes, although a separate infrastructure like composting toilets or a "living machine" would have to be introduced to handle the dirtier wastes.

Water is a powerful agent of chemical transformation and of heat and mass transfer. It is integral to most biological activities and is deeply entwined in social and symbolic ones as well. As water supply and wastewater infrastructures were developed through the nineteenth and twentieth centuries, the rates of water use increased dramatically and the accommodation of water flow in buildings expanded proportionally. From plumbing fixtures and piping to the specialized rooms and finishes necessitated by the moisture, the provision of water has become an integral aspect of contemporary buildings and epitomizes the difference between the building-as-setting and the building-as-shelter. Shelter and setting cannot really be separated, but the thermodynamic evaluation of water supply and disposal belongs to the activities of work and living that they support, where environmental work is exchanged for human work.

The standards for water use are bound up with the value of human work and the socially negotiated perceptions of cleanliness and luxury. The thermodynamic evaluation provides a measure of the real cost of fresh water, but not of its value to those who turn on the tap. With the alignment of faucet and drain, and the low economic cost of water, conditions were established for the easy overshooting of watershed capacity. Fixtures such as lavatories, dishwashers, and washing machines have steadily become more efficient, using less water for the same service. An alternate approach is to redesign the fixtures and the practices with which they are used. A simple example would be to interrupt the alignment of faucet and tap, like the pasta pot faucets in high-end kitchens. A filled pot has to be carried to a sink with a drain in order to empty it, requiring labor but slowing the use of water to a series of pot-sized increments.

Making the thermodynamic exchanges explicit allows us to evaluate the real costs of the ready supply of fresh water and visualize new approaches, ranging from new forms of efficiency to new kinds of recycling to new technical arrangements. In the original Ellis House, the e[m]ergy cost of water and its disposal is about 1% of the building total, and its use is divided among the different water-based activities of the kitchen, bathroom, and laundry. The costs of processing wastewater are notably higher than the cost of heating it, reinforcing the point that the utility of water is the removal of wastes.

Food supply

The supply of food appears less integral to the operation of most kinds of building, but, as the previous sections demonstrate, the food that "fuels" people is linked to all the other thermodynamic flows in buildings. The most basic form of internal heat that buildings must manage comes from the conversion of food consumed by people, while some of the largest flows of water are used to transport the organic waste remaining after the food has been converted to human work and heat. Certain types of building—residences, food stores, and restaurants—have explicit capacities for storing and processing food, but some amount of food moves through virtually every building occupied by people. In the Ellis House, the e[m]ergy cost of the food is about 9% of the total; when we include all the other resources used to prepare and serve it, the cost is about 20% of the work and resources used in the household.

An item of food in a kitchen literally sits at the top of an industrial food chain, which exemplifies the hierarchical dissipation and concentration of energy. As George Bataille observed about the French population during the Second World War, when food is scarce, you can simply eat lower on the food chain (Bataille 1988). Meat is a luxury. With modern methods of fuel and fertilizer intensive agriculture, the amount of energy and resources embodied in each level of the pyramid increases. The expenses associated with transportation, warehousing, and distribution add to those costs, making contemporary processed foods among the most highly refined fuels available. In a study of food production in Sweden, the average e[m]ergy intensity of consumed food was estimated to be 160,000 sej/J at the farm and 750,000 sej/J at the point of consumption, reflecting the costs of packaging and distribution. Among different foods, the intensity ranges from 200,000 sej/J for commercially produced vegetables to 1,730,000 sej/J for meat from fattened cattle (Johansson et al. 1999).

In the thermodynamic diagram, the flow of foods of various intensities are consumed and transformed by the occupants into work, heat, organic waste, and trash. Depending on the type of building, foods may be stored and prepared in the building, requiring additional work and fuels, or they may be processed and packaged for direct consumption. A central aspect of this material flow is the matter of time and convenience which, like the issue of cleanliness, is driven by social and economic organization rather than single-resource efficiency. The candy bar in a vending machine represents one of the most intensive forms of

Building-as-setting for the work of living

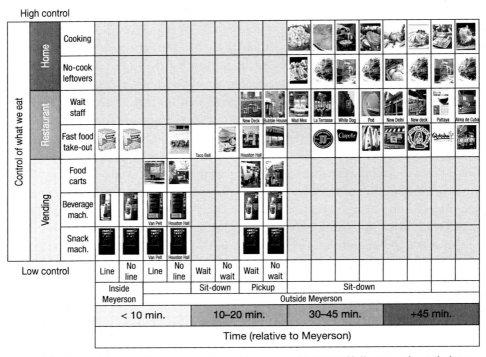

Figure 4.3: Time analysis and taxonomy of food delivery near Meyerson Hall, comparing calories per minute

Blomeier et al. (2009)

food, but it also delivers among the fastest calories available. A different hierarchy of food quality can be elaborated based on the time of preparation—a hierarchy that spans from a meal prepared at home from low-intensity foodstuffs to prepared food delivered in cafés, concession stands, or street trucks and all the way up to the high-speed meal from a vending machine (see Figure 4.3).

Supplies and solid waste

Supplies and solid waste, which represent the final category of material flows, include everything from clothing, books, and media to materials for commercial or industrial processes. They can be difficult to track in detail, especially as the quantities of stuff consumed by households and businesses have swelled over the last two centuries and become largely disposable. Most of the materials and products that move through buildings involve some form of furniture, fixture, or equipment in their use, and in thermodynamic terms the building-as-setting can be understood as an arrangement for extracting the useful potential from a complex flow of materials. If the water supply system can be called a "technology" for turning clean water into dirty water, buildings can be described as "machines" for turning useful material into trash.

For some kinds of building, it may be possible to use regular accounting procedures to track these flows, although even with exact quantities of materials or products it can be daunting to determine the work and resources involved in the long chains of production. We are organizing more and more of these data to facilitate carbon accounting, embodied energy calculations, and life cycle assessment, but the simplest approach is the form of input–output analysis described earlier, determining the amounts of money spent on supplies of different kinds. Monetary flows can be converted to thermodynamic intensities by using the average e[m]ergy intensity per dollar for the economy in which the project operates. The proportion of income that US households spend on these kinds of supply has decreased over the last decade, in favor of longer lasting products. However, for the Ellis House versions, the "non-durable" supplies consumed in a year still constitute almost one-third of the e[m]ergy cost of the building as setting (Department of Labor).

Items from every source and process are blended together in the waste stream. This simple disordering represents the first stage in the dissipation of the work and resources invested in the products and materials that stream through buildings. The second stage is the loss of concentration in the materials through decomposition or corrosion. For both stages, William McDonough and Michael Braungart's simple proposal helps cut through much of the complexity. In their book *Cradle to Cradle*, they distinguish between "biological" and "technical" materials, arguing that they belong to two different "metabolisms" (McDonough and Braungart 2002). Biological materials, they write, can be "consumed by microorganisms in the soil and by other animals" in the biosphere, while technical materials are all those substances that are indigestible or toxic, but serve as "nutrients" to the technosphere. Keeping the two metabolisms separate would preserve some of the value embodied in the waste.

That proposal to separate biological and technical flows is part of the authors' larger argument to eliminate "the concept of waste" by analogy with the recycling of nutrients in well-established ecosystems, where "waste equals food"

(McDonough and Braungart 2002, 92). It is true that materials are almost perfectly recycled in mature ecosystems, but not the work required for their use and reuse. As apt as the analogy may be, it overlooks the irreversible dissipation of potential that occurs with each act of consumption and excretion. For every energy conversion, some potential ends up as low-level heat, unavailable for any further use, so some strategies of recycling or reuse will be more effective than others. In the conventional form of solid waste disposal, all wastes are combined and deposited in sealed landfills where they degrade slowly over time. In these anaerobic conditions, the organic materials produce methane, which can be burned for heat or used to drive some other process. However, the technical materials remain distributed through the landfill. An alternate disposal strategy is incineration, which is typically combined with the generation of steam ("trash-to-steam") to recover more of the energetic potential in the waste and reduce the volume. It releases the heat potential of the technical materials and, with very high temperatures of combustion, has the added advantage of neutralizing many toxic materials.

A recent study comparing landfill with methane recovery to incineration highlights the differences in the two approaches (Cherubini et al. 2008). Even after burning the methane to produce electricity, the landfill is largely a method of dissipating the physical potential in the waste, while the incinerator recovers substantially more energy than is invested in the process. In terms of the net e[m]ergy outcome, the work and resources invested in the process minus the energy recovered, the landfill resulted in a net loss of 4.21×10^8 sej/g, while the incinerator yielded a net gain of 384 million sej/g. However, those comparisons do not include the original work and resources embodied in the production of materials in the waste stream, which are considerable. For the Ellis House, the original thermodynamic cost of a modest annual flow of supplies is 14 times the amount of heat recovered through incineration, meaning that all the value of those materials and products was converted to a small amount of heat. Incineration may be a better choice than landfills for municipalities facing mountains of solid waste. However, the further upstream that materials are separated and diverted, the greater the thermodynamic potential that is retained.

Useful separation of materials can occur at many stages in the flow and has formed a significant design challenge over the last few decades, specifically as environmentalists and building managers have sought ways to accommodate the proliferation of containers for different materials and products. Separating biological materials that can be composted from technical materials that can be recycled is a fundamental step, and one which must distinguish among forms of dirtiness currently combined in a broad category that anthropologist Mary Douglas called "matter out of place" (Douglas 1966). There is a difference between a disordered mixture of materials that can be considered clean (you would stick your hand into it), and a mixture that involves moisture, decay, and odors. The deeply ingrained avoidance of feces readily attaches to every form of waste. Most current approaches to material separation involve some coded or labeled multiplying of waste containers, which all retain some of the stigma of mixed and decaying waste.

The transformative power of organic recycling, like the final "laundering" of sewage effluent in waterways mentioned earlier, suggests some ways in which that might be accomplished. When biological materials are composted, there is a critical point after the microorganisms have completed their initial work and the results become recognizable as a kind of soil. That process is almost theological in its conversion of a dangerous form of dirtiness into a useful and accepted substance, not clean enough to put on a table but subject to a very different form of social regulation (Hillman 2000; Greer 2008). As McDonough and Braumgart demonstrated through their work, redesigning the products and processes themselves can yield dramatic improvements by altogether eliminating classes of waste and facilitating their recycling. Separating the components of buildings by life span, and allowing for more efficient maintenance and renovation, also applies to many of the products and materials that flow through buildings.

The e[m]ergy accounting of the material flows in the Ellis House quantifies the tremendous throughput of high-quality "stuff" in contemporary buildings, which is converted into waste and dissipates the work invested in its production. Some loss of energy is necessary to support the work conducted in buildings, even if every bit of material is recycled or reused. Adding the flows of supplies and solid waste to the thermodynamic diagram makes visible the many opportunities to "close the loops" in material services, but their role in the larger process of concentrating higher quality forms of power will become evident in the next section.

Concentrated power

According to the Energy Information Agency (EIA), roughly 42% of the primary energy in the US is used by or inside buildings (EIA 2012). About 60% of that energy is used for climate modification—heating, cooling, ventilation, and lighting. The remaining 40% is used for some activity inside buildings. These statistics have been widely disseminated, cited regularly to convey the importance of buildings in energy policy. But as the previous sections have demonstrated, there is tremendous energetic potential delivered in many other resources and services. The energy systems language and e[m]ergy accounting connect the well-documented flows of concentrated, primary energy to the many other forms of work and resources that they support and mobilize. The process of concentration is itself the key to understanding the hierarchies of energy quality that develop over time and to understanding the particular success of our technological and economic activities in producing more refined, concentrated forms of power.

The concentrated power delivered in high-quality fuels and electricity has transformed virtually every aspect of building construction and operation, at once both highly valued and useful because their high-energy density (J/kg) makes them portable and flexible. But these virtues have very large upstream costs and correspondingly high e[m]ergy intensities. With water, food, or other supplies, the energetic potential is wholly bound up with the delivery and condition of materials. The concentration of power reduces the immediate amounts of material that have to be handled and wastes removed, but even the most concentrated form of power is ultimately used to rearrange other materials. The role of concentrated (or dematerialized) power becomes clearer when we organize its use according to the different kinds of work it facilitates, and when we recognize that every activity requires a combination of materials, concentrated power, and information.

The organization of this book is largely based on that approach. We identified the three broad categories of work provided by buildings—shelter, setting, site—and this chapter's focus on building-as-setting describes how to divide and analyze the work of the setting according to activity. But the overwhelming attention to primary energy supplies has obscured the many other forms of concentrated energy used in the human economy. The distinction between production and consumption is something of an artifice, useful to economists for distinguishing between the work in businesses that create "supply" from the work of living that creates "demand." When viewed thermodynamically, those two kinds of work appear as stages in the progressive concentration of energy that makes the economic wheel spin (see Figure 4.4). It is easy to understand the work of distilling gasoline or growing crops as a concentration of solar

Building-as-setting for the work of living

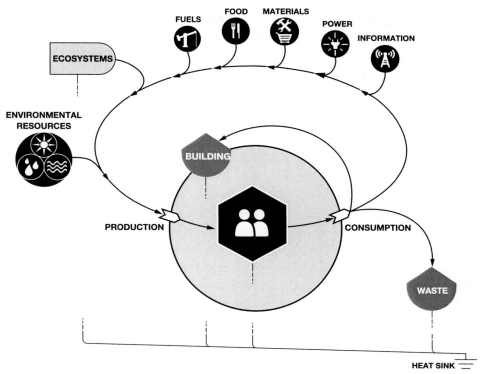

Figure 4.4: Thermodynamic diagram of production and consumption showing linked cycle of environmental and extracted resources, after Odum

energy, but even the most literal forms of "consumption," burning gasoline or eating food, are a further concentration of energetic potential into human work and movement. Energy is lost at every step in the process of concentration, increasing the e[m]ergy intensity of each product. Put the other way around, concentrated power is achieved with the dissipation (or waste) of energetic potential, and the forms and amounts of waste identify the quality of that power.

Fuels

It is often observed that fossil fuels are merely stored solar energy, but the energy density of fuels dramatically exceeds that of raw sunlight and that makes them powerful and valuable. Coal has an energy density of around 24 MJ/kg, gasoline and diesel have roughly 46, while compressed hydrogen weighs in at 123. The same is true of renewable fuels. Dry wood has an energy density of about 16 MJ/kg, carbohydrates about 17, while animal and vegetable fats can be as high as 37. The energy density of fats helps explain the value of whale oil, and underscores why kerosene was first developed from petroleum as a substitute when whale populations were hunted to the point of scarcity in the mid-nineteenth century. That historical transition between fuels illustrates the temporal dimension of the process. Whale fats are a concentration of the solar energy captured in the oceanic food chain, and take time to accumulate. Coal, oil, and natural gas took millions of years to develop, and any effort to produce equivalent biofuels has to speed up the work of millennia. The costs of the acceleration can be evaluated with the upstream costs inherent in e[m]ergy accounting. Recent studies have estimated the e[m]ergy intensity of the fossil fuels to be about 132,000 sej/J for hard coal, 156,000 sej/J for crude oil, and 178,000 sej/J for natural gas, with each increase corresponding to higher energy density and lower carbon content (Brown et al. 2011; 2012). The intensity for a basic biofuel such as plantation pine is about 700 sej/J, while that for a refined biofuel such as ethanol ranges from 170,000 to 270,000 sej/J because of the greater investments needed to accelerate the process.

In addition to being captured slowly and long ago, fossil fuels were also captured by gathering sunlight over very large areas, which means they also represent a spatial concentration of energy. For this reason, Vaclav Smil has favored the power density per unit of area as a metric of comparison (W/m^2), which combines the land area involved and the rate at which power can be delivered (Smil 2008). He determined that coal has a power density of 100 to 2,000 W/m^2 depending on the mine and technique, while oil and natural gas have densities of 200 to 500 W/m^2 for wells, distilleries, and delivery networks. A fuel-fired electric generating station, not including its mines or wells, has a remarkable density of 1,000 to 3,000 W/m^2, and can be taken as another measure of quality. In contrast, the power densities of renewable sources rarely surpass the 100 W/m^2 for solar thermal collectors, with lower densities of 5 to 5 W/m^2 for high-head hydrogeneration, wind turbines, and geothermal sources. Low-head hydro-generation is down at about 1 W/m^2, and biomass (agriculture) is even more diffuse. Renewable sources can be gathered and concentrated to competitive levels, but it simply requires more land that will, in turn, demand new infrastructures and even patterns of settlement. Europe's Roadmap 2050 outlines the extensive

Building-as-setting for the work of living

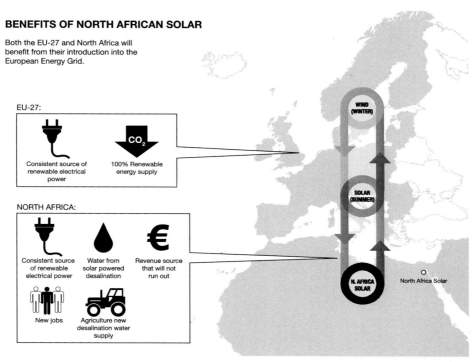

Figure 4.5: "Benefits of North African Solar" demonstrarting the land area required to capture sufficient renewable resources to supply a contemporary economy. OMA/AMO Roadmap 2050, European Climate Foundation

new infrastructure that would have to be assembled to "unplug" fuel-based power plants and "plug in" the more diffuse renewable sources (see Figure 4.5).

Concentrated fuels include both the biogeosphere's work of gathering and concentrating the solar energy and the human work of extracting, refining, and delivering it. In the 1970s C. A. S. Hall and his colleagues first recognized that the ratio between the energy content of a fuel and the energy that had to be expended to obtain it (the net energy) was an indicator of its value (Hall et al. 1986). He called it the energy return on investment (EROI); the value of a fuel decreases as the ratio approaches one, when it takes as much energy to obtain the fuel as it provides. At the beginning of the twentieth century, the EROI for oil deposits close to the surface was around 100, but it has fallen steadily as reservoirs have become harder to reach and is currently in the range of 10 to 20 for conventional wells (Hall et al. 2009). There is a continuing debate about

Building-as-setting for the work of living

whether the EROI of oil from shale formations or tar sands is actually greater than one. The EROI provides an economic measure of the value extracted from an environmental resource, and the declining EROI in recent decades indicates the urgency of more comprehensive environmental measures that help us evaluate the transition to the use of low-density, environmental energies (Hall and Klitgaard 2012).

Expanding the EROI approach to use full e[m]ergy accounting provides an estimate of the total work that would actually have to be replaced, which includes the spatial and temporal costs of concentrating energy into equivalent forms. The equivalent metric is the e[m]ergy yield ratio (EYR: see Figure 4.6); like the EROI, it compares the work and resources invested to obtain the fuel to the total e[m]ergy content delivered. For the oil in the pipeline from the Alaska North Slope , the net e[m]ergy yield is about 11, while oil purchased from the Mideast is at about 8, and Texas crude is at about 3.2. Comparatively, harvested spruce wood has a yield of about 5.4 and Swedish willow plantations manage a net yield of 1.11 when processed and delivered as chips to the final user (Odum 1996, 2007). EROI and EYR are measurements of economic efficiency, valuable for comparing one energy resource to another, but we also have to consider their

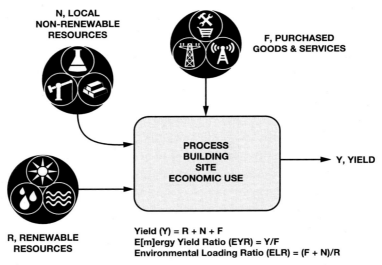

Figure 4.6: "Three-arm diagram" of renewable, non-renewable, and purchased resources

role in the whole hierarchical system of concentrating energies up through the human economy. Higher e[m]ergy intensities represent greater amounts of waste but also indicate higher quality, so they should be matched to the value of the activity for which they are used.

For the building-as-setting, fuels are typically used for heating water, cooking food, and other forms of process heat. Most hot water is used at relatively low temperatures, which can be provided by waste heat or slightly concentrated sunlight, so it is a mismatch with high-quality fuels. For cooking, by way of contrast, concentrated fuels are largely used to transform foods, making them more edible, digestible, and even increasing the available energy content. In the original Ellis House, the e[m]ergy content and intensity of the food overshadows the modest amounts of fuels used to prepare it, and so seems better matched to the task. Other fuels are used for industrial processes requiring heat, and occasionally to drive mechanical processes directly. But for most of the mechanical work performed in buildings, fuels are converted into electric power, which exemplifies the power of concentration.

Electricity

Most electricity is produced in centralized plants by thermal processes, burning hydrocarbon fuels or using nuclear fission at high temperature to produce steam and drive generators. The unavoidable wastes in that conversion, even for very large power plants, increase the cost substantially. Average first-law efficiencies for fossil fuel and nuclear plants in the US range from 32% for coal, nuclear, and oil-fired plants to 41% for natural gas generators (US DOE 2012). This means that the total e[m]ergy intensity of electricity is roughly three times higher than for the fuels, averaging 300,000 to 700,000 sej/J depending on the fuel and process, while the e[m]ergy yield ratio (EYR) is about one-third of the yield for the fuel itself, averaging 2.5 to 5 (Brown et al. 2012). That process stands as a prime example of the principle that maximum power occurs at intermediate levels of efficiency. The maximum Carnot efficiency of thermal plants is 60 to 70%, but the processes have to operate at lower efficiencies to deliver power at useful rates. The higher e[m]ergy of electricity reflects the time and work required to concentrate the original fuel and the rate at which it can be converted to electricity. The cleanliness and versatility of electricity exemplifies the value obtained with the greater costs and wastes.

Like the capture of waste heat inside buildings, the waste steam from electric generation is still hot enough for many other uses, including the heating of buildings. Utilizing the steam for secondary purposes is called cogeneration or combined heat and power (CHP), and is used for the district heating arrangements in denser settlements. As an almost equal co-product of electric generation, the steam has about the same e[m]ergy intensity as the electricity, because the same work and resources have to be degraded to produce it. However, since about 40% of original heat content can be usefully recovered, the net yield is effectively doubled. An electrochemical version of cogeneration is achieved using fuel cells that convert hydrogen (or natural gas) directly to electricity and heat without combustion. Their first-law efficiency is about the same as thermal power plants—roughly 40% depending on the temperature of that catalyst—but because of their clean exhaust (water and CO_2), they can be used directly in buildings. In both cases, the recycling of waste heat doubles the yield of the content of the fuel.

Electricity can also be generated without combustion by a couple of other means, including direct mechanical conversion in turbines and by solid-state effects such as thermoelectric and photovoltaic conversions. Direct mechanical conversion is used to extract the gravitational potential from water flows and the kinetic energy of wind, both lower density environmental flows. Recent studies have shown that the e[m]ergy intensity of wind and hydrogenerated electricity is roughly 60,000 sej/J, reflecting the much lower environmental intensity of the flows, with net yields of about 7 (Brown and Ulgiati 2002). Except in unique settings, both wind and water flows are difficult to capture at building scales. The installation of photovoltaic panels (PVs) on building envelopes has become one of the most recognized symbols of environmental building design, and is the basis for most formulations of net zero energy design.

Over the last few decades, the conversion efficiency of photovoltaics has steadily improved. Their use on building envelopes connects the work of gathering and concentrating sunlight with its use inside the buildings, making the elements of concentration visible. The amount of sunlight that can be gathered is a simple function of area—more space yields more power—while the conversion to electricity is accomplished with very high-intensity solid-state materials. Early e[m]ergy studies suggested that the higher manufacturing costs combined with low conversion efficiencies resulted in an EYR below 1 (Odum 1996). As the manufacturing techniques have been improved, EYRs now appear to exceed 2 with promises of further refinements, but the electricity is far from free (Brown et al. 2011). The most recent evaluation of the e[m]ergy intensity of power from photovoltaics is 145,000 sej/J, meaning its environmental cost is less than half of that generated by central thermal plants, but it still remains a very high-quality form of power that should be matched to the value of its use.

In the *Passivhaus* net zero energy version of the Ellis House, the roof is covered with PVs to meet the (reduced) electrical load of the building. The PVs significantly decrease the total e[m]ergy expended for the home's electricity (which is used to power a heat pump for cooling and heating), effectively reducing by one-third the intensity of the heat being transferred. The domestic hot water is heated by an evacuated-tube solar thermal collector made from less intensive materials, giving it an even lower e[m]ergy intensity (around 36,200 sej/J). The connection between the increased quality gained by concentration and the increased costs is evident. One compelling aspect of the net zero energy formula is that it makes the limits of renewable power visible in the area of the panels themselves, whose configuration and display becomes a form of information regulating the use of the concentrated power they provide.

Information

The value of information is illustrated by the calculation that every survivalist or pioneer has had to make. In the absence of industrial society, how many tools and how big a library would it take to hold all the information required to maintain a contemporary lifestyle? It is staggering to think how much information is needed to make even the simplest part of a building, as well as the knowledge embodied in specialized tools, machines, and concentrated power. The question escalates further as you include all the skills and knowledge needed to understand the material in a library—from reading to physics, math, and coding—and it becomes even more discouraging when you assess the tremendous amount of time and work expended across the economy for every widget. The task of replacing a photovoltaic panel or cell phone would quickly become impossible unless you had already perfected a "replicator" smart enough to make anything (and repair itself).

There are four kinds of cost involved with information: the work of its original development, the work of maintaining it, the work of extracting and condensing it, and the work of making copies. The whole point of information is that the cost of copies is so much lower than doing it all over again each time.

Information can be conveyed with varying degrees of material intensity, from the physical arrangement of buildings to signals transmitted by radio waves. It takes considerably more work to build a physical copy of a building from another building than to convey those plans electronically. The cost of design services is small relative to the cost of construction, but it provides the critical information to guide the process. The original cost of design services would include the societal resources invested in the designer's education and the value placed on the results. In effect, a portion of the work embodied in every artifact is information about its design or operation. Like other forms of stored potential, it depreciates over time, but unlike the storage potential of fuels, for example, it can be maintained at low cost from its copies.

David Tilley estimated the work and resources invested in developing and maintaining five modern US communications technologies—mail delivery, telephone, radio, television, and communication satellites—and his work illustrates the conceptual difficulties in performing such calculations (Tilley 2006). Every invention depends on the knowledge and support of the society in which it is hatched, and all the previous inventions that it incorporates. Tilley focused the analysis on the US economy since the beginning of the Industrial Revolution (1790), charting the declining intensities as each technology matured and was widely adopted. In his calculations, the current e[m]ergy intensities ranged from 4.8×10^{12} sej/J for communications satellites to 2.5×10^{6} sej/J for postal mail delivery, with television weighing in at 7.2×10^{10} sej/J. At that rate, the information delivered by the LED TV in the Ellis House would involve more e[m]ergy than all the other activities of the household, unless we included the information embodied in them as well. Unlike the life cycle analysis of concentrated power, there is no simple boundary of analysis for evaluating the cost of information, which has to be detected by its effects.

The estimate of the labor necessary to maintain the Ellis House was based on the e[m]ergy content of metabolic energy spent on household chores and the average wage that would be paid, which together total about 2% of the e[m]ergy demand of the household (Brandt-Williams 2002). To account for the knowledge actually contained in the labor, we could do the calculation the other way around, using the education level to determine the value that society places on the work (Brown et al. 2012). Both wages and education levels change steadily and differ from country to country, so their use is also approximate. In schools and universities, we find systems for producing more concentrated (and mobile) forms of information, with each level of education and experience involving an additional expenditure of society's resources, concentrated in fewer and fewer individuals at each level of attainment. In 1996 Odum used this approach to estimate the average e[m]ergy intensity for each level of education in the US, an approach that was elaborated in greater detail in 2009 by Daniel Campbell and Honfang Lu to both improve the estimates of intensity and chart the evolving distribution of knowledge in the US. If the labor on the Ellis House were performed by someone with a high school education, whose intensity is 1.9×10^8 sej/J, it would involve about 10% of the household e[m]ergy; if the homeowner had a PhD, it would involve about 22% of the total.

Examining the building as a setting for work involves just this kind of tradeoff between human time and the expenditure of available resources. When we recognize educational attainment as an investment made by society and not merely as an individual achievement, it becomes another concentrated resource that should be matched with the task. In thermodynamic terms, there are really two forms of work performed by people. The first are primary forms of obtaining, concentrating, and storing energetic potential, which range from farming and mining to the preparation and delivery of fuels, power, and food. The second are all the forms of ordering and the processing of material, energy, and information that we call work in everyday language—everything from moving people and material around to arranging files and abstracting information in more concentrated forms. The primary work largely takes place in industrial settings that can be engineered to optimize the efficiency of processes, and everywhere that food is processed and prepared. Almost all the rest of the work in buildings is processing work of one kind or another and occurs in both commercial and residential buildings.

The office as a separate setting for managing the information related to industries and business only emerged as a distinct building type in the mid-nineteenth century, with the rise in energy use and increasing specialization of the economy. The office setting became almost entirely focused on the gathering, ordering, and transmission of information. From ledgers, newspapers, and filing cabinets to calculators, typewriters, computers, and now networked information services, people use offices to regulate and amplify the flow of resources from more primary forms of production. The rapid adoption by businesses of the telegraph, telephone, computer, networking, and the internet when they were still innovative, expensive technologies illustrates the social and economic power that is leveraged by timely delivery of information. But the singular focus on efficiency and productivity leads to fruitless questions, such as whether it is wasteful for someone with a PhD to perform household or office maintenance.

Unlike commercial buildings, modern residences are conceived as sites of labor saving and leisure, whose characteristic technology is the signature television, which is now a networked multiscreen, media delivery service. The contrast with work measured by productivity is striking: the many time-use studies conducted over the last century have confirmed that most of the time people have "saved" through productivity gains and advances like the 40-hour work week has been used to watch television in its various forms (Robinson and Godbey 1997). The estimates for the value of labor and the information concentrated in education assume that there is an even balance between productive work, leisure, and sleep, eight hours a day for each in the average life. This may be another example that maximum power occurs at intermediate levels of efficiency, and that we are most productive when we only spend part of our time working. That, too, is part of the calculation made by our imagined survivalist. If we had to start over, what would we spend our time doing?

Currency

Since the physiocrats of the eighteenth century, and especially since the development of thermodynamics in the mid-nineteenth century, there have been repeated efforts to establish a biological or energetic value for money. As Luis Fernández-Galiano observed about energy accounting in the 1970s, it has been "held by many to be at once the basis of a new theory of value, the fundamental concept by which to supersede monetary fetishism, the essential tool for econometrics, social forecasting, and economic planning, and the philosopher's stone that would make it possible to reconcile technology and nature, economics and ecology" (Fernández-Galiano 2000, 181). Money is a flexible form of symbolic information that circulates as a medium of exchange and a measure of value, but as previous sections have argued, it is notoriously bad at valuing natural resources. Nevertheless, establishing the connections between energy and money is fundamental for environmental building, because real wealth derives from the control of useful power in all its forms.

Without reaching for a completely unified theory of value, we developed the approach of this book from the field of ecological economics, which holds that the global ecosystem is the ultimate source of economic wealth. As the economist

Nicholas Georgescu-Roegen argued, "Our whole economic life feeds on low-entropy," meaning the available energy expended to create refined materials, manufactured products, and the fuels and electric power of modern life (Georgescu-Roegen 1971, 276). The difference between the real costs of providing goods and services and their exchange values illustrates the difference between currency and other forms of energetic potential. It can be used both to amplify human technological innovation and to transfer real wealth, but as repeated economic cycles have demonstrated, it can also disappear without a trace. Herman Daly and Joshua Farley explained that the confusion arises from the premise of mainstream economics that the material causes (energy, resources) and efficient causes (capital, labor) of economic wealth are simply interchangeable, and that labor or capital can simply be substituted for low-entropy resources (Daly and Farley 2011).

The belief in the interchangeability between the two was supported by the declining energy intensity of the US and other economies, which have been steadily using less primary energy per dollar of GDP since the beginning of the Industrial Revolution. Most economists attributed that improvement to innovation or "technical progress." Energy intensity is cited as evidence that technological innovation can circumvent physical constraints, "dematerializing" the economy, which can continue to grow even as resource supply limits are reached. A number of economists have demonstrated that the specific form of progress involved was the efficiency of converting primary energy supplies to useful work (Kummel 1989; Ayres and Warr 2009). Technical progress is not itself a source of wealth, but another technique for extracting energetic potential from the biosphere through such activities as converting fuels, logging forests, farming land, and concentrating them in labor and capital. Technical inventiveness can improve energy efficiency and extend the utility of non-renewable sources, but it cannot serve as a substitute for the low-entropy, energetic potential that provides the basis for wealth.

Labor is regularly purchased with wages, and the ability to substitute capital for labor has given currency much of its power. Money can also purchase technologies that convert energetic potential to work, saving labor and increasing productivity. But just as money cannot serve as a substitute for food, neither can it be substituted for the energetic sources feeding industries. The underlying power of currency is its ability to facilitate the concentration and transfer of the potential to accomplish useful work. As the preceding sections have argued, every aspect of the construction and operation of buildings exemplifies these thermodynamic principles. The growth in size and capacity of buildings through the modern period corresponds to real increases in wealth, derived from the increased flow of resources, but every investment in buildings is subject to the inexorable increase in entropy. Maintenance and operation require real work, just as living creatures require food, and once the flow of energetic potential is dissipated, it cannot be reused.

In the thermodynamic diagrams, money flows in the opposite direction from energy and resources, facilitating their concentration and enhancing the development of more complex production hierarchies. The ratio of money to the total throughput of resources in the economy provides an index of its thermodynamic intensity (sej/$). It does not identify the useful work or value provided by the currency, but it serves as a tool for estimating the contribution of different services to the building. Odum and his colleagues have determined that thermodynamic intensity for a variety of national currencies, adding up all the renewable and non-renewable contributions to the economy in a year and dividing them by the gross economic product. In 2010 the intensity of the US economy was 1.73×10^{12} sej/$ (Odum 1996; Campbell & Lu 2009b). If we chart the e[m]ergy intensity for the US through the twentieth century, it shows a similar decrease of intensity as observed for primary energy supplies, which can be partly attributed to the increasing efficiency identified by Ayres and Warr. However, the e[m]ergy yield ratio (EYR) has been declining even more steeply through that period, which means that the improved efficiencies have been offsetting the declining quality of resources available for extraction and concentration (Brown and Ulgiati 2011).

The diagram of the building-as-setting is complete when it includes the transfers of work and resources through money, both in the income received by the occupants and the intensity of high-level products and services used within buildings (see Figure 4.7) These can overshadow the resources required for the building-as-a-shelter. In the Ellis House example, the "consumption" of high-level supplies has a thermodynamic cost larger than almost any other aspect of the building.

The work of living

The many blinking and beeping (and sometimes talking) devices in contemporary buildings compete for our attention, using tiny amounts of concentrated power to engage us in the activities for which they were designed. We are still early in

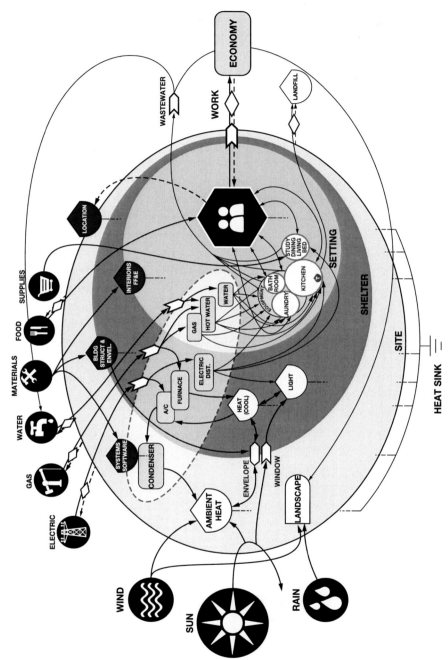

Figure 4.7: Thermodynamic diagram of the building-as-setting, the Ellis House, original, normative version

the evolution of "smarter" buildings, which seek to fulfill the promise of timely information to make buildings more effective and powerful, while reducing their resource throughput. When the refrigerator reminds us to close its door, we are following the directives of its designers (and programmers) to help it operate more efficiently. But what about the beckoning invitations from entertainment devices that distract us from productive work? The question of consumption is never just a matter of efficiency but of choices among activities. Ultimately, people have to do something with their time, so the thermodynamic diagram of the building-as-setting is a diagram of the work of living.

After organizing the diagram by function, it is possible to determine the environmental costs and intensity of each activity, which combine flows of materials, concentrated power, labor, and information. The e[m]ergy account of the kitchen in the Ellis House, for example, includes a full spectrum of resources, from water, food, and wastes to the power used to heat and cool them (see Table B.3 in Appendix B). The e[m]ergy intensity of processed, retail food dominates the activity, and even with greater efficiencies in every category, including more local food sourcing, the hierarchy of expenditures in the *Passivhaus* kitchen is similar: smaller amounts of concentrated power are used to transform and transport the weightier foodstuffs and remove their residues. The bathroom and laundry are almost wholly dedicated to cleaning and waste removal, but the largest category of "consumption" is leisurely entertainment, through activated screens in all their forms and the use of disposable stuff that moves through contemporary households.

The distinction between consumption and production, and its separation into different types of building, only confuses the matter. The history of architecture in the modern period is readily told through the increasing specialization of work, which demands specific types of building—from factories, supermarkets, and airports to high-rise office buildings. However, there are just as many types of building dedicated to activities of consumption or entertainment—restaurants, sports arenas, theaters, and resorts (not to mention churches, synagogues, and temples). Preparing the full thermodynamic diagram of the building as a setting for the different activities of living links environmental flows, extracted resources, concentrated power, and people in the dissipation of energy. From this perspective, consumption and production are just sequential stages in the progressive refinement and concentration of wealth. Greater productivity and more efficient consumption both help the wheel of the economy to spin faster.

Like the proliferation of niches in a developing ecosystem, new building types reflect the growing wealth and the increasing complexity of the economy that produces them. The diagram of the activities in the Ellis House illustrates how closely some forms of work, such as bathing and cooking, correspond to specific rooms such as bathrooms and kitchens, while other activities such as sleeping, typing, watching media are increasingly mobile and adaptable. The connection between space and function seems most permanent where the building has to handle greater amounts of material or power, while the equipment that channels smaller amounts of higher quality resources is less rigid. Granted, people have always adapted settings for different kinds of activity. A kitchen table can be used for dining at one moment, homework the next, and a meeting after that. But the transition from wired to wireless information technologies further loosens the connection between building typologies and activities: coffee shops become workplaces, offices become living rooms, and living rooms host conference calls, undermining existing spatial and social arrangements (Turkle 2010).

The broadly acknowledged goal of environmental building design is to eliminate polluting wastes and reduce resource throughput to match the available environmental flows, but neither achievement will reduce the amount of time people spend doing things. One paradoxical result of the maximum power principle is to allow people to be less "efficient," to balance productive work with the leisurely dissipation of the wealth accumulated by working.

Bibliography

Abel, Thomas. 2004. "Systems Diagrams for Visualizing Macroeconomics." *Ecological Modelling* 178(1–2): 189–194.

Archibold, Randal C. 2007. "From Sewage, Added Water for Drinking." *New York Times*. November 27.

Ayres, Robert U., & Benjamin Warr. 2009. *The Economic Growth Engine: How Energy and Work Drive Material Prosperity*. Cheltenham: Edward Elgar.

Bataille, Georges. 1988. *The Accursed Share: An Essay on General Economy*. New York: Zone Books.

Beardsley, Joseph. 1900. "Water Waste." *Municipal Engineering* 18: 117–121.

Blomeier, A., J. Evans, G. Feigon, N. Johnson, and C. McDonald. 2009. "Maximizing the Rate of Delivery in Vending Machines." Architecture 751: Ecology, Technology and Design.

Brandt-Williams, Sherry L. 2002. Folio #4, Emergy of Florida Agriculture. In *Handbook of Emergy Evaluation*. Gainseville, FL: Center for Environmental Policy, University of Florida.

Brown, Mark T., & Sergio Ulgiati. 2002. "Emergy Evaluations and Environmental Loading of Electricity Production Systems." *Journal of Cleaner Production* 10: 321–334.

Brown, Mark T., & Sergio Ulgiati. 2011. "Understanding the Global Economic Crisis: A Biophysical Perspective." *Ecological Modelling* 223: 4–13.

Brown, Mark T., & Sergio Ulgiati. 2012. "Labor and Services." *EMERGY SYNTHESIS 6: Theory and Applications of the Emergy Methodology*. The Center for Environmental Policy, University of Florida, Gainesville.

Brown, Mark T., Gaetano Protano, & Sergio Ulgiati. 2011. "Assessing Geobiosphere Work of Generating Global Reserves of Coal, Crude Oil, and Natural Gas." *Ecological Modelling* 222: 879–887.

Brown, Mark T., Marco Raugei, & Sergio Ulgiati. 2012. "On Boundaries and 'Investments' in Emergy Synthesis and LCA: A Case Study on Thermal vs. Photovoltaic Electricity." *Ecological Indicators* 15: 227–235.

Buenfil, Andres. 2001. "Emergy Evaluation of Water." PhD, Environmental Engineering Sciences, University of Florida.

Bushman, Richard L., & Claudia L. Bushman. 1988. "The Early History of Cleanliness in America." *Journal of American History* 74: 1213–1238.

Campbell, Daniel E., & Hongfang Lu. 2009a. "The Emergy to Money Ratio of the United States from 1900 to 2007." *EMERGY SYNTHESIS 5: Theory and Applications of the Emergy Methodology*. The Center for Environmental Policy, University of Florida, Gainesville.

Campbell, Daniel E., & HongFang Lu. 2009b. "The Emergy Basis for Formal Education in the United States." *EMERGY SYNTHESIS 5: Theory and Applications of the Emergy Methodology*. The Center for Environmental Policy, University of Florida, Gainesville.

Cherubini, Francesco, Silvia Bargigli, & Sergio Ulgiati. 2008. "Life Cycle Assessment of Urban Waste Management: Energy Performances and Environmental Impacts. The Case of Rome, Italy." *Waste Management* 28: 2552–2564.

Cowan, Ruth Schwartz. 1983. *More Work for Mother: The Ironies of Household Technology from the Open Hearth to the Microwave*. New York: Basic Books.

Daly, Herman E., & Joshua Farley. 2011. *Ecological Economics: Principles and Applications*, 2nd ed. New York: Island Press.

Dickens, Charles. 1874. "Philadelphia." *American Notes and Pictures from Italy.* London: Chapman & Hall.

Douglas, Mary. 1966. *Purity and Danger: An Analysis of Concepts of Pollution and Taboo.* New York: Praeger.

EIA. 2012. Table 8.1. Average Operating Heat Rate for Selected Energy Sources, 2002 through 2012 (Btu per Kilowatthour). US Energy Information Administration.

Fernández-Galiano, Luis. 2000. *Fire and Memory: On Architecture and Energy.* Cambridge, MA: MIT Press.

Foundation for Water Research (FWR). 2008. "Wastewater Forum Archive, Meeting 2nd July." *Foundation for Water Research.* http://www.fwr.org/wastewat/wransom12.htm.

Georgescu-Roegen, Nicholas. 1971. *The Entropy Law and the Economic Process.* Cambridge, MA: Harvard University Press.

Giedion, Siegfried. 1948. *Mechanization Takes Command: A Contribution to Anonymous History.* New York: W. W. Norton.

Greer, John Michael. 2008. "Title." *The Archdruid Report: Druid perspectives on nature, culture, and the future of industrial society.* http://thearchdruidreport.blogspot.com/ 2008/02/theology-of-compost.html.

Hall, Charles A. S., & Kent A. Klitgaard. 2012. *Energy and the Wealth of Nations: Understanding the Biophysical Economy.* New York: Springer.

Hall, Charles A. S., Stephen Balogh, & David J. R. Murphy. 2009. "What is the Minimum EROI that a Sustainable Society Must Have?" *Energies* 2: 25–47.

Hall, Charles A. S., C. J. Cleveland, & R. Kaufmann. 1986. *Energy and Resource Quality: The Ecology of the Economic Process.* New York: Wiley-Interscience.

Hansen, Roger D. 2014. "Water and Wastewater Systems in Imperial Rome." www.waterhistory.org.

Hillman, Chris. 2000. "A Theology of Compost," Sermon, July 23. Rochester, NY: First Unitarian Church.

Johansson, Susanne, Steven Doherty, & Torbjorn Rydberg. 1999. "Sweden Food System Analysis." *EMERGY SYNTHESIS 1: Theory and Applications of the Emergy Methodology.* The Center for Environmental Policy, University of Florida, Gainesville.

Kummel, R. 1989. "Energy as a Factor of Production and Entropy as a Pollution Indicator in Macroeconomic Modelling." *Ecological Economics* 1: 161–180.

Lewis, John Frederick. 1924. *The Redemption of the Lower Schuylkill: The River as it Was, the River as it Is, the River as it Should Be*. Philadelphia, PA: City Parks Association.

McDonough, William, & Michael Braungart. 2002. *Cradle to Cradle: Remaking the Way We Make Things*. New York: North Point Press.

Odum, Howard T. 1996. *Environmental Accounting: EMERGY and Environmental Decision Making*. New York: Joseph Wiley & Sons, Inc.

Odum, Howard T. 2007. *Environment, Power, and Society for the Twenty-First Century: The Hierarchy of Energy*. New York: Columbia University Press.

Robinson, John P., & Geoffrey Godbey. 1997. *Time for Life: The Surprising Ways Americans Use their Time*. University Park, PA: Pennsylvania State University Press.

Smil, Vaclav. 2008. *Energy in Nature and Society: General Energetics of Complex Systems*. Cambridge, MA: MIT Press.

Tilley, David R. 2006. "National Metabolism and Communications Technology Development in the United States, 1790–2000." *Environment and History* 12: 165–190.

Turkle, Sherry. 2010. *Alone Together: Why We Expect More from Technology and Less from Each Other*. New York: Basic Books.

US DOE. 2012. *Buildings Energy Data Book:* Buildings Technologies Program. US Department of Energy.

Vassallo, Paolo, Chiara Paoli, & Mauro Fabiano. 2009. "Emergy Required for the Complete Treatment of Municipal Wastewater." *Ecological Engineering* 35: 687–694.

Figure 5.1: A high-density city in a rural county, illustrating the land use patterns of twenty-first-century renewable economy

Butcher and Kurtz (2014)

Chapter Five

Building-as-site in urban and economic locations

> In the richer countries ... cities have survived the tumultuous end of the industrial age and are now wealthier, healthier, and more alluring than ever. In the world's poorer places, cities are expanding enormously because urban density provides the clearest path from poverty to prosperity.
>
> (Glaeser 2011, introduction)

In this chapter, we consider the thermodynamics of location. As information in previous chapters demonstrated, buildings themselves are not sustainable. They can only be more or less efficient in their consumption of resources and so moderate the environmental effects of the activities they house. Even a net zero energy building still requires a tremendous supply of materials, energy, and information, which it turns into various forms of waste, and can only do so as long as it belongs to a productive economy. The smallest meaningful unit of sustainable design is probably the city-state, or the city and its surrounding region, although with contemporary trade the boundaries of regions have literally become global. Romantic proposals for solitary, sustainable buildings in the landscape are dream-images or, at best, experimental laboratories for the work of reckoning with regional arrangements of production (and consumption).

The central role of energy in a global, industrial civilization is well established; fuels have largely replaced the laborers and slaves of agricultural civilization and wholly surpassed them in productive capacity. The portability and energy density of fossil fuels have increased wealth, expanded populations, and fueled growth in the number and size of cities. As Edward Glaeser argues, urban agglomerations are the engine of prosperity. Cities attract and concentrate wealth, talent, and productivity of all kinds. And the size, use, and quality of buildings is largely dictated by their location within these urban economies, fixed by the value of the land on which they are built and the economic value of the activities they can house. The two are wholly intertwined and coevolving; the spatial distributions of land use—rural, ex-urban, suburban, core—reflect and constrain the social and economic arrangements of human settlements.

The organization of cities and their economies can be detected by evaluating the e[m]ergy of different land uses, including the cost of structures and infrastructures, and the flow of resources. As described in earlier chapters, the weightier, more material investments adapt more slowly than the rapid responses of people and capital, but the economy can never be wholly dematerialized. Jobs and people still have to be in one location or another, with buildings to accommodate their work. Popular theories of the city in the mid-twentieth century viewed urban growth and adaptation as an ecological process of succession, with characteristic cycles of growth, decline, and recovery (Light 2009). However, people are not plants, and we have to account for their many modes of adaptation— technological, economic, and cultural—each with their scales of influence and different rates of change. The locational task of environmental building design is to conceive buildings appropriate to their locations in changing urban and economic arrangements, while accounting for both the inertia of the weightier elements and the de-territorializing effects of the quicker ones.

Admittedly, that task is as much a matter of social and cultural narratives as of resource efficiency. Since the beginning of the modern period, the idea of the "region" as location has served as a counterweight to the abundant appeals of universal, technological civilization, which has brought dramatic increases in wealth, power, longevity, and freedom. Narratives about regions offer local identities based on climate, geography, and longstanding cultural traditions of settlement. In its simplest form, this can be understood as a longing for the conventions of agricultural civilization even as they are overwritten by the mobile, media-based themes of liberation and globalization. In different degrees that has been the appeal of critical regionalism, bioregionalism, bioclimatic design, watershed politics, even ecotopia; they all offer methods by which social and aesthetic forms of identity can be negotiated for new environmental regimes.

Spatial hierarchies: urban self-organization

> [A]s the US population increased, a systematic hierarchical system of cities seems to have established itself. Nobody planned this development; it was a classic case of the self-organization of a complex system.
>
> (Fujita et al. 1999)

Through the second half of the twentieth century, the value of downtown land in many major US cities dropped dramatically in value. While Detroit with its desolate stretches of empty housing is the most often cited, patterns of manufacturing and settlement have shifted in cities across the US, rendering thousands of buildings suddenly less valuable. At the same time, stretches of land at the periphery of those cities increased in value as high-powered municipal services—highways, sewers, electric supply—were extended outward. It is the much studied phenomenon of urban sprawl, but it helps underline a point we often take for granted. Identical buildings can have radically different values according to their location, which depends not only on the qualities of the site itself but on its neighbors and its situation in the urban landscape. As Fujita et al. observed, nobody really plans the size or hierarchies of cities, which expand and shift according to larger economic dynamics (Fujita et al. 1999). Planners, designers, and politicians work to accommodate, mitigate, and occasionally direct that growth and development, but the value of location is largely determined by a collective process of self-organization that exceeds any individual plan or policy.

Building sites are a special category of thermodynamic asset. The land is first shaped by geology and through the uplift of plate tectonics, and then carved and redistributed by water moved by the hydrologic cycle. These processes also help form and concentrate economically valuable materials such as stone, gravel, clay, and mineral deposits, while biological activities generate the organic components of soils and establish ecosystems. Topography, geography, hydrology, climate, and ecosystems interact to determine a site's potential for mining, logging, agriculture, or settlement. The different ecological biomes present on sites—forest, grassland, desert, or swamp—are largely a function of local rainfall combined with climatic temperatures, both locational functions of longitude and elevation. Most of the terms we use to designate landscape locations are watershed terms—hilltops, valleys, lowlands, river, or wetland—and water has always established the first basis of locational value. Human settlements have to be situated near sources of

Building-as-site in urban/economic locations

drinkable water, and most larger cities have had to be situated near rivers or ports. Lewis Mumford even argued that water was the first limit to urban growth, although we have recently learned just how far a metropolis like Los Angeles or Beijing will reach for their water (Mumford 1956).

Patrick Geddes explained the interaction between the natural landscape and human settlements with his well-known "valley section" of 1909, developed as a reminder to the occupants of the new industrial landscape who were fueled by coal at the time and actively overwriting the earlier patterns of agricultural civilization (see Figure 5.2). The occupations and locations depicted in Geddes' valley emerged organically over the millennia of human development, and those pre-industrial relationships are still frequently offered as an antidote to the patterns of industrial and post-industrial growth. We have to read the section carefully to avoid the distractions of nostalgia for that earlier, less populous world. Geddes focused on occupations to make evident the economics and anthropology of "cities in evolution," specifically to locate leverage points "towards regional betterment and development, towards town improvement and city design" (1949, xxvi). In their *Doorn Manifesto* of 1954, Alison and Peter Smithson adopted Geddes' valley section to help articulate their criticism of the nostalgic resurrection of pre-modern city forms. They extended the sociological focus of his work to reveal the powerful urban dynamic latent in his analysis (see Figure 5.3). Their valley section shows the modern hierarchy of urban concentration, with the high-density core located along the river and progressively

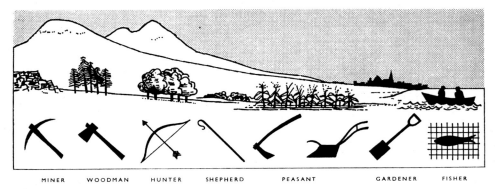

Figure 5.2: The occupations and locations depicted in Patrick Geddes' "valley section" emerged organically over the millennia of human development, and those pre-industrial relationships are still frequently offered as an antidote to the patterns of industrial and post-industrial growth

Building-as-site in urban/economic locations

Figure 5.3: "'Habitat' is concerned with the particular house in the particular type of community. Communities are the same everywhere. (1) Detached house-farm. (2) Village. (3) Towns of various sorts (industrial/admin./special). (4) Cities (multi-functional). They can be shown in relationship to their environment (habitat) in the Geddes valley section"

Smithson and Smithson (1954/1962)

less dense settlements—towns, villages, and house-farms—situated by height and slope. Higher powered cities increasingly overrun such topographic niceties as they grow, leveling hills and putting streams into underground channels. Beyond a certain scale, cities no longer draw their primary power from the land on which they are located, but depend instead on the regions and empires they control and tap for trade.

Economists make an important distinction between the resources on a site (wood, minerals, soils) and the underlying "Ricardian land," the physical extent that determines a site's capacity to receive sunlight, rain, or other inputs of value (Daly and Farley 2011). The first are stocks of energetic potential deposited on (or under) the site which can be depleted over time, while the extent of the site regulates the flows of resources, like sunlight, that can only be used as they arrive. Ricardian land is also the abstract entity to which the economic value of location is attached. It cannot be moved to another site or used up (except by submersion), and is distinct from the value of the resources it contains. Locational value is determined by land's proximity to other locations and resources; proximity to watershed features once ranked highest, but now locations obtain much of their value in relation to markets, infrastructures, and concentrations of population. Consider: the land in center city Philadelphia is many times more expensive than most of the suburban land in the periphery where the Ellis House is located. Its particular locational value derives from the train line and highways to the city, which reinforce the value of the center city, even though the decay of older city neighborhoods and the emergence of ex-urban business centers near highway intersections has altered any simple core–periphery model (Garreau 1991).

The evaluation of sites for construction is fundamental to architecture. In periods of slower growth, the difference between city and country or wealthy and poor neighborhoods is largely taken for granted. Internal change happens so slowly—or only episodically from disease, famine, or war—that locational value spanned generations. Formal theories of location economics only appeared after the population surges of the early modern period. Johann Heinrich von Thünen developed his "land-rent theory" in 1826 to explain the arrangement of productive activities around agricultural cities that were already beginning to change (von Thünen and Hall 1966). He recognized that the value of land in an agricultural economy was almost entirely locational, balancing the profits for the different activities that concentrate environmental energies in products against the transportation costs to bring them to the city market. The result is a series of concentric circles, with more profitable activities like intensive farming and dairying on high-rent land near the center while increasingly less profitable activities, such as field crops, forestry, and ranching, are located on less expensive land further out. The underlying source of wealth in pre-industrial economies was largely the control of land, followed by the control of markets where products and services are further concentrated with labor and expertise.

To expand the model of economic organization around a central market, the geographer Walter Christaller developed his "central place theory" in 1933 to describe the emergence of complex city patterns in more crowded landscapes (Christaller and Baskin 1966) (see Figure 5.4). Beginning with an even distribution of farms on a flat landscape, Christaller charted the hierarchical arrangement of market towns and administrative centers, which are differentiated when marketing, manufacturing, and administrative activities are concentrated to achieve economies of scale and minimize transportation costs. In the geometrically perfect form of his theory, the landscape is divided into a hexagonal lattice, with five levels of central places—hamlet, village, town, city, and regional capital—with each larger unit supplying and controlling increasing numbers of smaller units. August Lösch adapted the theory in the 1950s to describe the competition among retail centers within larger cities, and the population areas they serve (Lösch 1954). The underlying argument of both theories is based on the spatial efficiency of the hexagonal layout and the minimization of costs—but they offer little guidance for understanding the complexity of real cities, which over time exhibit dramatic

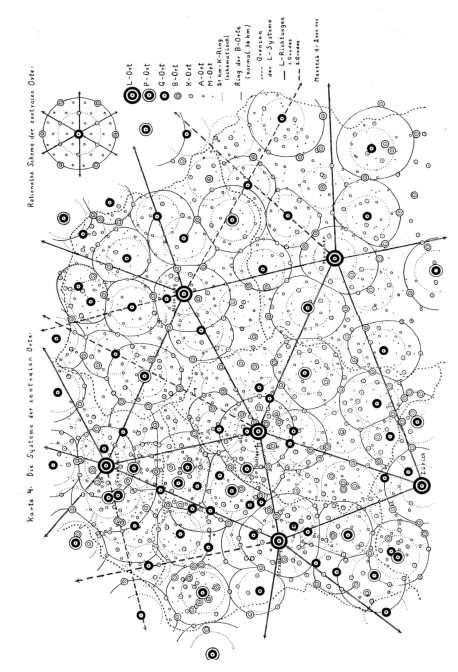

Figure 5.4: "Central place theory," showing the hierarchical self-organization of market towns and administrative centers in a largely agricultural economy

Christaller (1933)

variations in the simple hierarchies, influenced by different modes of transportation, variations in topography, competition with adjacent urban centers, unequal distribution of resources, and regional differences in costs and prices.

To understand how the location of factories differed from the location of land-based enterprises—farming, dairying, and logging—of von Thünen's agricultural city, new approaches had to be developed. The industrial economy largely derived from the extraction of power from high-quality fuels and minerals, whose portability and energy density overshadowed the locational constraints of the lower density environmental resources. Alfred Weber's *Theory of the Location of Industries* of 1929 incorporated the added complexity of sourcing multiple industrial materials, including fuels, and shifted the locational requirements from the control of land area almost entirely to transportation. Minimizing transportation costs between the factory, its suppliers, and its market led to Weber's famous triangle for determining the least cost location. Like von Thünen's model, his locational triangle assumed the economic advantages of agglomeration, but could not explain their mechanism. It was not until 1991 that economist Paul Krugman provided a model for an economic logic of urban agglomeration, one that explained the ability of urban concentrations to increase the returns on investment in a particular location. In his demonstration from first principles, Krugman showed how economies of scale interact with the concentration of manufacturing and consumer populations to increase the demand for its products and reduce transportation costs. The result is the emergence of the classic "core–periphery pattern" of urban growth (Krugman 1991).

Krugman's work initiated the "new economic geography," which offers more sophisticated models and further demonstrations that the concentration of population in larger urban centers can develop from rational decisions about measurable economic factors (Fujita et al. 1999). Even the emergence of spatial hierarchies among centers—first-, second-, and third-order cities—can be seen developing from the feedback amplification effects of urbanization with increasing populations. However, the economic theories still cannot explain the surprisingly precise hierarchy of sizes that occur among real cities. In different countries and across historical periods, the hierarchy of cities by population size frequently develops into what is known as the "Zipf distribution." G. K. Zipf was a linguist who first discovered the distribution in word usage, and then recognized that US city sizes also followed a simple, power series distribution where the population of a city is inversely proportional to its rank order (see

Building-as-site in urban/economic locations

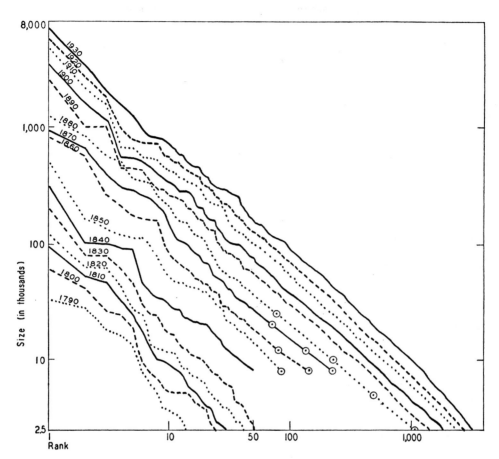

Figure 5.5: A logarithmic "rank-order" chart of US communities over 2,500 from 1790–1930, showing a power series distribution

Zipf (1949)

Figure 5.5). Many subsequent studies have confirmed (and debated) the result, which is typically illustrated with a log-log chart that shows a linear slope close to −1, which means that the second rank city would be half the size of the first rank city (1/2), the third rank would be one-third the size (1/3), and so on. It is a remarkable consistency, which has recently been shown to extend to megalopolitan regions as well (Berry and Okulicz-Kozaryn 2012).

Zipf adopted an efficiency explanation for the distribution, arguing that the distribution resulted from the principle of "least effort" in which individuals (and businesses) minimize the average amount of work required for their activities. He explained the tension this produced between forces concentrating the population into cities, and those pulling them apart, which included technological innovations and the competition among new products and services. Zipf's distribution of cities was first noted by physicist Felix Auerbach in 1913, and over the 100 years since it has attracted the attention of countless researchers. Glenn Carroll recorded five different forms of explanation for the distribution, each with its advantages and inadequacies (Carroll 1982). Stochastic models, which are based on random forces obeying a few simple laws, have been the most successful at reproducing the distribution, but not at explaining its causes. City growth and migration models, like Zipf's explanation, seek to describe the economic forces acting on individuals, while city hierarchy models, like central place theory, are more heuristic, offering descriptions of the resulting hierarchies. Finally, Carroll cited numerous models of "political, economic, cultural and historical" arguments, which make the key point that the rank-order distributions only emerge over time within relatively closed political or trade boundaries.

The enduring fascination of Zipf's distribution, and its relevance to our question, is the powerful dynamic of self-organization it suggests in the size, placement, and arrangement of the urban configurations that give building locations their value. If we can understand the actual mechanisms or goals of urban self-organization, they can help guide environmental design and policy. Most of the goals described in the literature reviewed by Carroll follow a micro-economic formulation, the minimization of costs, work, or "effort," but he failed to mention the arguments of system ecologists for whom rank-size distributions are a relatively common phenomenon. The distribution of species and individuals in food chains, the sizes of branches in trees or stream systems, and the relation of body mass to the territory of species all exhibit similar kinds of rank-order distribution. H. T. Odum and colleagues viewed the rank ordering of cities to be one among many examples of the energy exchange hierarchies that develop in open systems (Odum et al. 1995).

Recent work by Matthieu Cristelli et al. showed the importance of coherence among the cities being considered for a Zipf distribution, arguing that "we consider Zipf's Law to be the ultimate signature of an integrated system" (Cristelli et al. 2012, 7). Cities, regions, and nations are "integrated" economically, but in many different ways, and we would expect them to exhibit different signatures. When Cristelli et al. combined 16 countries in a rank-order plot, normalized to the size of their largest city, it revealed a number of variations in city-size distribution patterns, with first-rank cities in some countries dramatically larger than their secondary cities. Cristelli et al. argued that in countries such as the UK, Russia, Iran, and France, the capital cities achieve extreme concentration because of their centralized administrations or their role in larger trade networks or empires. It is something of a relief to find differences among urban rank order in different countries, suggesting a systemic selection principle and not a simple law. Cristelli et al. concluded with the hypothesis that guides the work of many ecologists: the coherence of rank-size distribution within an integrated system was "the result of some kind of optimization in growth processes or of an optimal self-organization mechanism of the system with respect to some (finite) resources" (Cristelli et al. 2012, 7).

Odum came to the same conclusion: urban hierarchies emerge over time to maximize the power of the larger political and economic systems within which they develop. These kinds of selection goals are difficult to verify, but much of complex systems behavior can only be explained with a teleological principle such as maximum power, in which urban concentrations succeed according to their ability to convert more energetic potential to useful work (Jorgensen 2007). The principle can be discerned in the many gradations of core–periphery relationships, and among the hierarchies of cities of different sizes, which over time select one largest city to reinforce. And it is not just a matter of size, but the intensity of the activities and the investment in elaborate structures to enhance the flows of power (Bettencourt and West 2010). Working with Odum in the 1970s, Robert Costanza and then M. T. Brown prepared evaluations of the total embodied energy for different kinds of landscape settlement in south Florida, confirming the intuitive result that the larger the settlement, the bigger its "footprint," while noting that larger settlements also had greater concentrations of infrastructure and used higher quality forms of power (Brown 1980). By measuring the embodied energy of the many resources used in cities, not just primary energy usage, the value of the many services that make cities effective becomes more visible. From the many specialized forms of work to the information that helps organize cities, urban land concentrates and intensifies the flows of power.

As that early work on embodied energy demonstrated, first-law energy accounting only tells part of the story, and can obscure both the costs and value of the concentrated resources used in cities. For decades, Peter Calthorpe has refined a compelling case he first made in 1982, when he showed that a suburban solar house would use more energy and resources than an urban apartment if transportation costs were included (Calthorpe and Benson 1979). That insight ultimately forms the basis of the *Vision California* plan he authored in 2011, which advocates more compact urban growth to reduce resource use and carbon emissions (Calthorpe Associates 2011). More rhetorical versions of his argument have been popularized in David Owen's *Green Metropolis* (2010) and in Edward Glaeser's *Triumph of the City* (2011), both of which offer Manhattan as the model for greener, more efficient settlements. The case makes sense when you examine the primary energy use of individual households. The higher cost of urban land dictates smaller residences, higher densities, and reduced travel distances. However, it is important to separate the criticism of suburban sprawl, which is a weedy, wasteful form of land use, from the idea of Manhattan as model for all urban settlements. The comparison neglects any embedded costs and effects other than transportation, largely overlooking the vast network of production and supply required for the very high-quality services that make the metropolis so productive.

The residents of contemporary urban cores may use fewer direct kilowatts of electricity or gallons of gasoline per person, but the reach of their many services is vast. The economic activity of twenty-first-century Manhattan includes the residents of the surrounding five boroughs (in less dense neighborhoods), the commuting suburbs beyond them, and considerable portions of the formerly independent cities of New Jersey, Connecticut, and Pennsylvania (even including Philadelphia). It is not simply that most individuals cannot afford to live in Manhattan; as von Thünen first pointed out, the intensity of the urban core requires corresponding regions of lower cost land to house activities that are not as economically or spatially intense. In countries that lack the wealth of the United States, those lower cost areas are dense "informal settlements," close enough to the core that residents can walk. Sprawl is not (just) a symptom of inefficient planning, but of the excess wealth of fuel-based civilization. If we mismanage the coming transition, the really low-energy alternative for all but the wealthiest citizens is not Manhattan but either an agricultural village or the urban slums that have characterized the surrounds of cities since the first urban concentrations.

Even though David Owen lives in rural Connecticut, he is still a citizen of Manhattan, working as a writer in part of the great metropolitan concentration of wealth and talent. His ability to live in a former farming village is another demonstration of the kind of paradox described by Jevons: the more efficient the enterprise, the more power is available to spend on other things like living in the country while doing city work. Owen himself recognized the paradox and wrestled with it in his next book, *Conundrum*, which explores the many forms of the rebound effect that appear to have undermined efforts to save energy with more efficient cars, houses, and shopping bags. Cities are the pinnacle and engine of human prosperity, but the useful comparison is not between the dense urban core and the leafy suburb but rather between cities in different energy regimes—especially between the megacities of the fossil-fuel economy and the agricultural cities that preceded them. Cities have to be understood in their entirety, including all their upstream and downstream costs, the different qualities of power they tap, and the many dimensions in which that power is expressed.

The simple question of city size illustrates the complex intertwining of cause and effect in urban intensification. Human population is the common measure of urban size, but growth typically is not achieved by reproduction among the existing population. Cities expand economically, by attracting (or forcing) people from rural areas and other cities to migrate. And then, as Glaeser and others have shown, increased population intensifies innovation and economic activity within the city, accelerating the growth in wealth and providing productive opportunities for more people. Once a population achieves some critical threshold of wealth, its biological rates of reproduction typically begin to decline, even as the city continues to intensify. Fertility rates in Brazil have plummeted over the last 40 years, while the gross domestic product (GDP) and populations of Rio and São Paolo have continued to grow. A more comprehensive measure of city size would be the total power they command. This measure would further highlight the contrast in wealth and configuration between an agricultural city based on the control of land (and sea) and the contemporary fuel-based megalopolis, whose much greater power derives from the extraction and efficient conversion of concentrated resources.

I keep returning to the pre-modern agricultural city, because all cities prior to the late eighteenth century were primarily supported by the capture and concentration of renewable energies. Except for mining and other forms of extraction, they offer a model of what is possible with renewable resource flows and pose the design question of the next century: What different urban arrangements for tapping renewable flows can we develop using the knowledge and technologies developed over the last 200 years? That has certainly been the point of reference for many of the strategies commonly recommended today, from urban farming to walkable cities. But as the 19.20.21 project noted, "in

1800, less than 3% of the population lived in cities," while more than half of today's 7 billion are urban dwellers (www.19.20.21.org 2014). The largest pre-modern cities, such as Rome, Beijing, or Cordoba, were the centers of military empires whose power came from organizing, storing, and transporting agricultural yields from vast territories. Roman grain came from across the Mediterranean basin, and literally fueled an economy based on the muscle power of animals and slaves, most of whom worked in the countryside (Hall and Klitgaard 2012).

A more comprehensive analysis shows that the wealth currently concentrated in contemporary megacities cannot simply be replaced by exchanging photovoltaics for coal-fired power plants and biofuels for gasoline. As the competition between corn for food and for biofuels makes evident, it quickly becomes a matter of land use, of the tradeoffs between land used to concentrate environmental energies into food, fuels, or electricity. This kind of transition between energy regimes is unprecedented—although populations and civilizations have collapsed throughout history—so we need to better understand its dynamics (Tainter 1988; Diamond 2004).

For over a decade, Shu Li Huang has studied and modeled the interaction between energy and urban development in Taiwan, documenting the evolution of different spatial patterns, temporal rhythms, and varieties of intensification that emerged with the increasing levels of available power (Huang and Chen 2005). His careful analysis documents the transition from rural to urban, and the emergence of land use hierarchies as Taipei grew through the twentieth century. Using data from 1,178 administrative units, Huang et al. identified six land use zones around Taipei, from natural and agricultural land to suburban, service and manufacturing, high-density residential, and mixed-use urban core (Huang et al. 2001). He developed many different metrics to detect the spatial and temporal hierarchies within the region, but the one that best describes the challenge of the transition to a renewable energy regime is the areal e[m]ergy density. The mixed-use core has an areal density of 52 ($\times 10^{13}$ sej/m^2), high-density residential is even higher at 94, with suburban areas at about 5, compared with a density of 0.19 for the natural areas. In other words, the urbanized land uses 25 to 500 times more total energy and resources than the environmental energies that arrive within their boundaries. Of course, each kind of land use has different population densities, but the e[m]ergy per capita follows an even stricter core to periphery hierarchy, from 3.84 ($\times 10^{16}$ sej/pop) in the dense core to .98 in suburban districts. Urban sprawl is a lower intensity use of land, wasteful in its displacement of natural ecosystems, but wastefulness at the periphery does not make the core of the contemporary metropolis inherently efficient.

The data needed for these kinds of study can be difficult to obtain, and come in a variety of forms and levels of uncertainty. But similar results have been elaborated in studies of West Virginia, Rome, Macao, San Juan (PR), and Beijing, with urban residents using from 50 to 700 times the renewable e[m]ergy base of their immediate urban regions to sustain contemporary lifestyles. Dense urban cores like Manhattan only exist as the concentrated centers of integrated urban systems, which are themselves part of regional, national, and international production hierarchies for distributing wealth. Much of the massive throughput is concentrated in economic products and services that did not exist in pre-modern cities, so a different kind of work is required to imagine how the renewable city of the future will differ from its predecessors (Odum et al. 1995; Campbell et al. 2005; Lei et al. 2008; Ascione et al. 2009; Liu et al. 2011).

To visualize the kinds of change involved in such a transition, Luke Butcher and Jill Kurtz recently prepared an energy and e[m]ergy evaluation of Chautauqua County in western New York, a largely rural county with a modest manufacturing base and a population of about 150,000 (Buter and Kurtz 2014). They examined the stages by which a renewable economy could be achieved, documenting a sequence of scenarios for the current population—from a more efficient county to one using available renewable resources to a radically changed county (see Figure 5.6). For each scenario, they determined the amounts of primary energy used and the total e[m]ergy required for all the resources, products, and services, including energy. They translated those scenarios to the areas of land that would be needed to gather and concentrate enough environmental energies, describing the total "footprint" of each economy. In every scenario, except the radically changed county, the amount of land needed exceeds the actual area of the county, meaning that, like all modern economies, Chautauqua County has to import energy and resources to maintain its levels of consumption. The existing county would require over 10 times as much land, the efficient county about 6.5, and the renewable county about 4.6. The final step to the all-renewable, changed county combines increased production efficiencies, renewable energies, and reduced levels of consumption, establishing a dense urban core in a largely agricultural county (see Figure 5.7).

Balancing the production and consumption of a county (or city or country) in this way is an extreme limit case, which assumes no extracted resources (fuels

Building-as-site in urban/economic locations

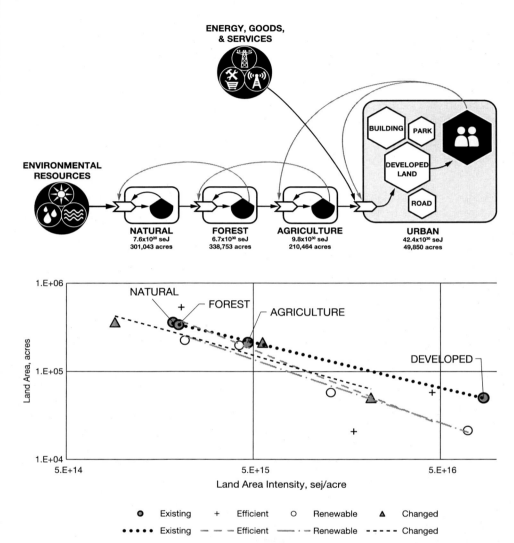

Figure 5.6: (a) Thermodynamic land use diagram of Chautauqua County, showing existing land use and e[m]ergy intensities; (b) Chart of land use and e[m]ergy intensity for four scenarios: existing, efficient, renewable, and changed county

Butcher and Kurtz (2014)

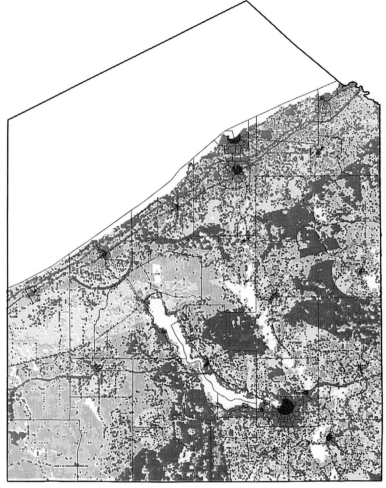

Figure 5.7: "A changed county," showing land use distribution in Chautauqua County after the redistribution of land uses to accommodate a renewable economy

Butcher & Kurtz (2014)

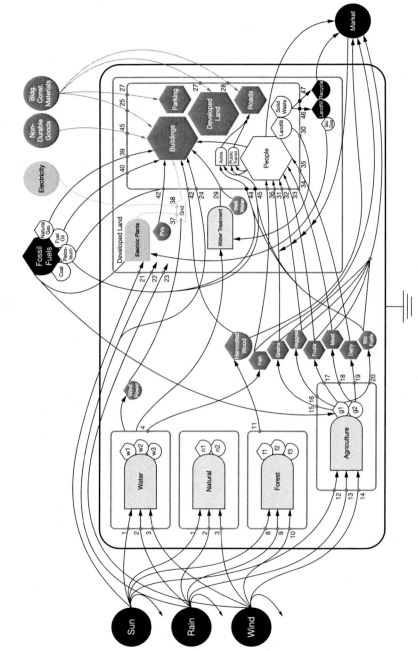

Figure 5.7 (continued) Thermodynamic diagram of Chautauqua County, showing resources flows for each land use

or minerals), no combined land uses (photovoltaics on parking lots, for example), and it uses every bit of work provided by the environment. There is none of the surplus that would be required for trade with the larger economy or consideration of the effect of competition for jobs and people with other counties and cities. As Garret Hardin argued (quoting Darwin's grandson), any community that voluntarily renounces growth will be outgrown by the communities that continue to enhance their power (Hardin 1968). New city forms will only succeed by finding ways to enhance both their own power and the prosperity of the larger ecological and economic systems in which they operate. Conducting e[m]ergy analysis at this scale puts contemporary urban design ambitions in context, making evident the potentials and limitations of efficiency improvements and the many interacting dimensions of change. With that dynamic picture in mind, we return to the Ellis House to understand how urban hierarchies set the value of specific locations in the urban landscape and provide constraints for the design of individual buildings.

Evaluating location

The real estate section of the *New York Times* often publishes cost comparisons to tantalize apartment dwellers, reporting the size of house that individuals could purchase for the same amount of money in different locations around the country. You could trade your one-bedroom apartment in Manhattan for a rowhouse in many other cities, a bigger house with a lawn in the suburbs, or (in a comparison the newspaper does not advertise) for a whole block of abandoned houses in some declining cities. Of course, the purchase price of a house is only part of the total cost of living in a different location, which includes available jobs and salaries, transportation modes and distances, the local cost of goods and services, and even the severity of the climate. Households regularly make calculations about these competing costs, and a host of social and cultural factors as well, when they decide to relocate within an urban area or to move to another city altogether.

As demonstrated in the studies of Taipei or Chautauqua, the thermodynamic value of land can be determined by evaluating the many forms of work and resources invested in building and maintaining urban configurations over time. But lacking such detailed studies, economists use the "market value of real estate minus the replacement cost of structures" (Nichols et al. 2010). As we know, real estate values fluctuate with business cycles. But when economists at the Federal

Reserve evaluated the rise and fall of real estate prices in the US through the 2008 economic crisis, shifting land values accounted for most of the variation, while the cost of the buildings themselves barely changed. Speculation in a variety of forms drove most of the swing in prices, and highlights the difference between what Frederick Soddy called virtual and real wealth (Soddy 1912). Currency is a powerful mechanism for transferring value from one location to another, but it can also disappear without a trace, even though the actual work of constructing and maintaining buildings and urban infrastructures remains the same.

In the economic downturn, land values changed more in some metropolitan regions than others, and more for residential than commercial buildings, but the relative value within regions barely changed. The real estate-driven crisis of 2008 may have accelerated population shifts within and between cities, but the underlying fundamentals of established locations remained. As the Federal Reserve economists observed, those are "transportation corridors and satellite commercial hubs, differences in the quality of services ... and the influence of topography and coast lines" (Nichols et al. 2010, 18). In other words, once a spatial hierarchy emerges on the landscape, larger populations, concentrated markets, and trade routes reinforce each other to enhance and preserve that pattern. These locational differences are situated on top of the natural geography and resources distribution, which together contribute the work and resources that give differential value to location.

A more convenient approach to evaluating location is through property taxes, which combine the market assessment of the location with the costs of maintaining municipal infrastructures that support it. Property assessments are often resented as inaccurate, but they fluctuate less quickly than market prices and largely reflect the organization of the urban area in which the site is located and the economy in which it operates. Using the thermodynamic value of currency (sej/$) for the same year as the tax assessment filters out some of the effects of the business cycle, and provides a provisional value of the location. In many locations, the cost of local infrastructures and institutions is spread among a variety of taxes connected to income and spending, but since property tax is directly connected to location, it has been used in the Ellis House example for clarity.

For the Ellis House, the annual thermodynamic cost of the location based on property tax is 22.5×10^{15} sej/yr, which in the normative version of the house is more than the annual cost of the utilities and represents about 18% of the total e[m]ergy cost of the household. If the building were located in center city

Philadelphia, the annual real estate tax could range from half of that to three or four times that amount, depending on the specific neighborhood. In the much more efficient *Passivhaus* version, the same property tax is over two and a half times larger than the photovoltaic and solar thermal energy costs and represents about 28% of the total. If the goal of a household is minimum total cost, then it would make sense to move that more efficient building to an area with lower property taxes, further away from the city or into its poorer, neglected neighborhoods.

The other readily determined cost of location is transportation. The fundamental criticism of low-density suburban development is the cost of automobile travel, which includes the depreciated cost of the car itself, the distances of travel, and the fuel to power it. In the normative version of the Ellis House, with two car-based commuters traveling average distances, the annual e[m]ergy cost is about 4.9×10^{15} sej/yr, which is a quarter of the property tax and about 4% of the total household expenses. This is an imperfect estimate—since many of the transportation infrastructure costs are concealed in federal and state taxes, which are nearly as large as the annual cost of the household—but it illustrates one of the principal pressures toward increased density. As fuels require more work and expense to extract, the costs of transportation and location increase. Consider, again, the Ellis House and its owners' transportation needs. The house is actually located along a commuting train line built in the nineteenth century, and the local density is higher than suburbs built for automobiles. In the more efficient *Passivhaus* version both residents commute to work by train, and so are able to reduce their annual transportation costs by over half.

To complete the analysis of location, the size of the land (or roof) area determines how much sun, wind, and rain can be collected and concentrated on the site (see Table B.2 in Appendix B). For the Ellis House, which sits in the middle of a modest suburban plot (1,207 m² or .33 acres), the annual amount of environmental potential used is only about 0.1% of the total e[m]ergy cost of the household (see Figure 5.8). Even more dramatically than the Chautauqua country example, it would take over 1,000 times as much land to make the household self-sufficient. If we omit the economic costs of non-durable goods and property taxes, it would still require over 500 times as much land to provide all the work and resources currently being used by the household. Taken together, the value of the location balances the intensity of the surrounding development and the potential for harvesting environmental resources against the costs of living and transportation.

Building-as-site in urban/economic locations

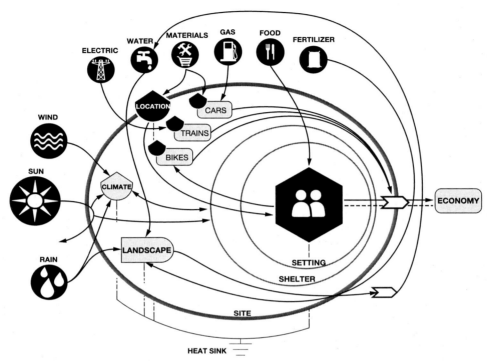

Figure 5.8: Thermodynamic diagram of the building-as-site, the Ellis House, original, normative version

Part of the evaluation of the building-as-shelter was the effect of the local climate, which could also be viewed as a differential cost of location and compared using relative measures of the climate, like total degree days. Glaeser noted that the average winter temperature of different cities correlates almost directly with the energy usage of buildings—the lower the temperature, the higher the heating bills—but we have included it as the primary task of building design (2011). For our purposes, the costs of modifying the climate are integral to the configuration of the envelope, but the choice to move to a milder location has been part of demographic shifts in the US for decades, so it cannot be ignored. Glaeser speculated about the energy savings of moving the entire US population to denser settlements in the milder climate of California, but this proposal overlooks exactly the kinds of systemic effect reviewed throughout this chapter. Not only should real estate dynamics discount colder regions to compete with warmer climates, but the current urban intensification of the California coast has already produced some of the most expensive land in the country. The total energy costs of the land on which buildings are built involve the structures, infrastructures, institutions, and economies that are built (and maintained) around them, where the pursuit of maximum power restlessly seeks advantage.

Design for location

Considering the value of location highlights the common-sense perspective provided by a systems view of design. Buildings not only have to fit their location within the spatial concentration of wealth in cities, but their presence alters those patterns and must adapt to its changes over time. Urban hierarchies not only emerge from individual household decisions about least cost or efficiency, but from the selection and reinforcement of indirect strategies for maximizing the power of the overall urban system. As with natural food webs, individual buildings and programs can succeed in specific locations and niches within an urban hierarchy, but can prove to be too specialized to exist without it or survive its changes. It requires a certain population and social complexity to support highly specialized stores, just as it requires a larger base of people, work, and resources to maintain high-rise construction.

We began this chapter with two goals. The first was to develop a thermodynamic accounting of the value of location, and the second was to understand how the dynamics of urban self-organization alter the assumptions of environmental building design. The two are strongly interconnected. The spatial organization of cities constitutes a form of high-quality information, which amplifies the concentration of energetic potential and limits the range of possibilities for any individual project. The promise of the contemporary metropolis is the highly refined information with which it is regulated and adapts to changes in its environment. As the scale of analysis expands, environmental building design increasingly becomes a matter of the social and economic activities of its household.

Social and economic hierarchies

Not long after he produced *An Inconvenient Truth*, a movie advocating energy conservation to minimize climate change, Al Gore was criticized for the amount of energy used every year by his family home in Nashville. According to factcheck.org, the "Associated Press reviewed the Gores' energy bills and reported that the family consumed 191,000 kilowatt-hours in 2006" which "was considerably more than the amount of electricity used by the typical house in Nashville, about 15,600 kilowatt-hours a year" (Karter 2009). The irony was evident and the emails quickly went viral in the partisan dispute about climate change. Since then, the Gores' house and its systems have been substantially upgraded, including the addition of 33 solar panels, which have become the symbol of the building's improved energy efficiency. The more balanced coverage noted that at 10,000 sf, the Nashville house was roughly four times larger than average (2,469 sf in 2006), so energy use comparisons should be based on the actual size of the house. Even with that factor, the building was still something of an energy hog, but the relentless focus on energy efficiency misses a more fundamental point. In our economy, different households control radically different amounts of wealth; wealthier, more mobile families can not only afford bigger houses but houses become symbols of that wealth and position.

Energy efficiency measurements are simply inadequate for discussing the appropriate size (or use) of a building. Why would a powerful politician such as Al Gore not have a larger house (or many houses, in fact)? As anthropology has taught us, every society since the first nomadic clans has relied on some specialization of labor, and the differentiation of power among people and classes only increases with the size and complexity of the society. Of course, the degrees of inequity are a constant source of dispute. Deciding on the appropriate size or quality of a building involves social and economic determinations about the household's contribution to society. By considering the question at this scale, we invert the question, from a matter of personal restraint to a society's collective decision about where to spend its wealth. Any decision to reduce consumption in one place, demanding that Al Gore move to a smaller house, for example, leads to a second decision about where to spend the resources that are saved (and about who should live in the big house). Stockpiling them only defers the decision, and increases the pressure to spend them.

Wealthy societies are currently enjoying a period of unprecedented abundance, largely derived from the increasingly efficient extraction of the potential stored in hydrocarbon fuels. Through technical ingenuity, fuels have been converted into every form of work and resource, from fresh food and disposable pens to cool, dry air. They have fueled the exponential growth in human population and the complexity of its societies for the last two centuries. Once a certain level of prosperity is achieved, however, the rates of population growth in wealthy societies typically decline, allowing the accumulation of abundance to continue. George Bataille called that accumulation the "accursed share," meaning that the resources that remain after all possible forms of growth have occurred still somehow have to be spent. In the neutral language of thermodynamics, human societies are open, "dissipative structures," like tornadoes, living organisms, or ecosystems, which need power to exist and exist to dissipate power. The greater the amount of available energy, the more the system selects structures that increase the rate of dissipation, altering and even destroying the arrangements developed in conditions of lower power. The appealingly productive climax forest, for example, only exists within a narrow range of rainfall, temperature, sunlight, and nutrients. Change the resource flows too much and different structures emerge: grasslands, wetlands, desert.

Bataille's *Essay on General Economy* begins with the basic premise of ecological economics, that "the origin and essence of our wealth are given in the radiation of the sun." Within that premise, he finds a moral lesson almost directly opposed to the contemporary fixation on efficiency and productivity: the sun "dispenses energy—wealth—without any return. The sun gives without ever receiving" (Bataille 1988, 28). Bataille's ideas about the sun and the "pressure" of accumulated wealth were drawn directly from the work of Vladimir Vernadsky, who described the biosphere as the "region of transformers that convert cosmic radiations into active energy in electrical, chemical, mechanical, thermal, and other forms" (Vernadsky 1926, loc 400). Vernadsky explained how biological life used the steady flow of solar energy to transform the materials of the geosphere, create the unstable gas mixture of the atmosphere, and expand under the pressure of the solar flow to the limits of available space:

> Living matter—organisms taken as a whole—is spread over the entire surface of the Earth in a manner analogous to a gas; it produces a specific pressure in the surrounding environment, either avoiding the obstacles on its upward path, or overcoming them. In the course of time, living matter clothes the whole terrestrial globe with a continuous envelope, which is absent only when some external force interferes with its encompassing movement.
> (Vernadsky 1926, loc 564)

The recognition that excess wealth moved around the globe under a kind of pressure had also inspired the economist Irving Fisher in his formulation of the quantity theory of money. While walking in Switzerland in 1894, where he watched water flowing into and out of mountain pools, he instantly recognized the behavior of currency (Economist 2009). The flowing stream was income, the water accumulating in the pool was capital, and, according to the basic calculations of hydraulics, the greater the amount of water in the pool (specifically, its depth) the greater the pressure on the outflowing stream. Fisher even built a hydraulic machine to simulate the flows and pools of money in the economy. By the early decades of the twentieth century, the economy Fisher was modeling derived increasingly from the release of the "pools" of solar energy that had accumulated in hydrocarbon fuels (mostly coal at that point). As the stored fuels were uncovered, the pressure to use them increased. Following the principle of maximum power, the pressure of accumulated resources is a system effect, a blind force, which leaves open the form of its expression. Bataille was fascinated by the ways in which different societies had handled the pressure, from the ritual destruction of wealth in the potlatch ceremonies of Native Americans to the often senseless levels of destruction in war.

The pressure of hydrocarbon fuels has driven the growth of human societies in both size and complexity, as well as experiments with many different forms of growth. However, there is no reason to assume that those forms are optimal. With the increased extraction of fuels, economists have identified another paradoxical condition called the "resource curse," in which national economies dominated by the extraction of a particularly valuable resource, usually oil, are less economically successful than more diversified economies. Countries that exhibit the resource curse have greater degrees of social inequity and tend to be dominated by oppressive political regimes. Like the results of other selection processes, the resource curse is not inevitable—Norway is the best counterexample—but theories about the connections between energy and cultural evolution struggle with the question of determinism.

Cultural evolution

In Leslie White's provocative formulation of 1959, the degrees of cultural development were a simple function of the energy that could be harnessed and the efficiency of the tools with which it was used, from human and animal labor to wind and water, and now concentrated fuels. He even expressed it as a formula: energy x technology yields culture, "$E \times T \rightarrow C$" (White 1959, 47).

The bald determinism of White's proposition alienated many anthropologists and the dominant model of cultural evolution that developed over the following decades incorporated multiple driving factors. In their classic text on the subject, Alan Johnson and Timothy Earle described the "primary engine" of cultural evolution as "population growth and technological development under environmental constraints," which lead to novel social solutions that are further intensified and institutionalized, producing further growth, development, and encounters with more constraints (Johnson and Earle 2000, 30). Environmental limits figure as constraints in many accounts of cultural evolution, but the underlying premise of systems ecology is that the capacity to do real work at a useful rate (power) remains the primary force driving selection processes at all levels. Like food, there are no substitutions for available energy.

Anthropologist Thomas Abel adapted the thermodynamic premise of systems ecology to chart the flows of work and resources in social and economic systems, revealing the hierarchies of wealth that emerge through cultural evolution in different societies. As his starting point, Abel disassembled the artificial distinction that economists make between production by businesses and consumption by households, and argued that "the term 'business firms' has no physical reality, but is rather an abstract nexus of interactions between 'households'" (Abel 2004, 190). In his view, households are the primary social units, whose members control different kinds of asset. Simpler households provide labor to receive wages, while more powerful households that control businesses contribute labor, land, capital, and the use of other assets. The anthropological diagram focuses on people and their interactions, tracing the physical flows through the economy that support and amplify their productivity (see Figure 5.9). In other words, economic and political power derive directly from the hierarchical concentration of energetic resources, although their economic values constantly change. Tracking e[m]ergy at this level reveals the social and economic forms of inequity that can develop over time, and the tremendous exchange and production hierarchies on which contemporary society depends to operate.

Abel's first study focused on the Caribbean nation of Bonaire, which rapidly developed from a near subsistence economy in 1950 to a modern tourist economy in the 1990s, with oil, investments, infrastructure, and expertise imported from the Netherlands. In the diagrams of the development over time, each unit represents a class of similar households positioned left-to-right according their different e[m]ergy intensities, with the wealthiest, most powerful

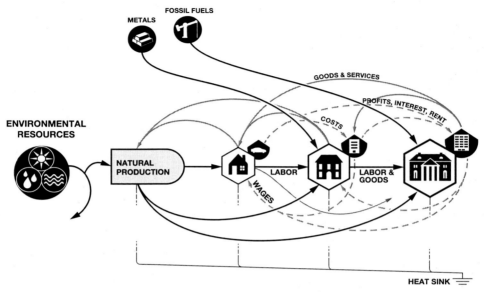

Figure 5.9: Socioeconomic hierarchy of households

After Abel

households located at the right (see Figure 5.10). The sequence shows the growth of the population, along with the proliferation and specialization of households, as new economic niches appear in the growing economy. In Abel's view, the transformations "are both a consequence and a cause within the self-organizing process that has rippled through the island" (Abel 2003, 16). The sequence illustrates the effect of the "pressure" of abundance described by Bataille, with the arrival of new, more powerful resources on Bonaire finding expression in new buildings, enterprises, and social arrangements. This scale of analysis provides a better context for discussing the appropriate size and use of buildings, and for thinking more critically about sustainability. The "curse" of excess resources is the pressure to dissipate them, so the challenge of environmental design is to spend them well, to enhance the prosperity of the whole economy in its ecosystem and to manage the effect of its wastes.

In a more recent study of the larger, more integrated island economy of Taiwan, Abel simplified the thermodynamic diagram: he showed the numbers of similar households by the size of the symbol, allowing him to chart the distribution of populations among regions of the island (Abel 2013)

Building-as-site in urban/economic locations

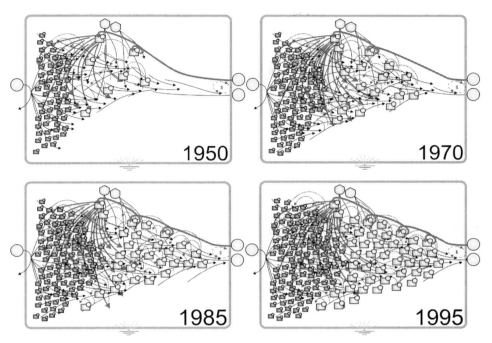

Figure 5.10: Socioeconomic web, Bonaire, 1950–1995. In 1950, Bonaire's future changed as the result of a new constitution, which redefined its relationship with the Kingdom of the Netherlands. Dutch financial aid began to flow in and was invested in building infrastructure such as a port, an airport, and roads. By the 1970s, several export industries had moved to Bonaire. Construction industries were emerging in support. A new water and electric plant was built. From 1950 to 1985, Bonaire's population doubled, and much of the population was working for wages. Tourism was about to take off, encouraged from within and without

Abel (2003)

(see Figure 5.11). Not surprisingly, the capital and financial center of Taipei had the largest concentration of upper middle-class and elite households involved in high-tech industries and government, but the rural regions only had a small population of agricultural households. The explanation for this is quite simple. Taiwan imports much of its food from Southeast Asia and South America, effectively exporting the population of lower income farm workers to those regions. In turn, it exports its high-quality products to the wealthier "core" countries of the US, EU, and Japan, locating it within the evolving global economic hierarchy. Similarly, as the US grew in wealth, it successfully reduced its immediate air and water pollution by exporting dirtier industries to other,

Building-as-site in urban/economic locations

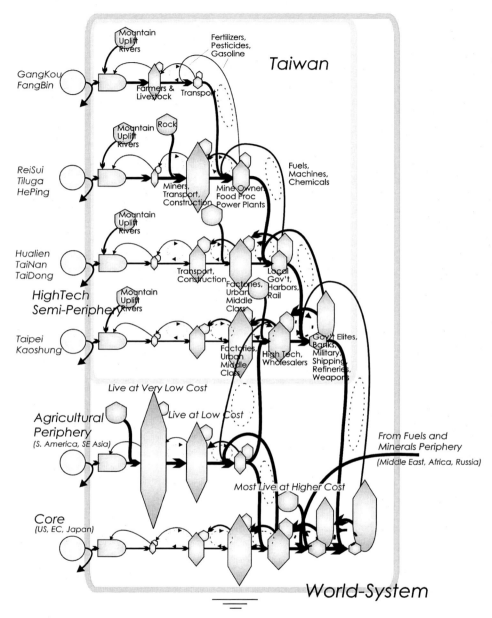

Figure 5.11: Spatial hierarchy of Taiwan within its world-system context, showing regional spatial hierarchies. Flows differ at each location in this spatial hierarchy of convergence and feedback. Each area has its unique environmental inputs, which are represented by the four distinct "production" symbols, and flows from sun, wind, rain, tide, and uplift to each. Only some areas receive direct inputs from international markets, which are selectively fed back as needed. Households (and the businesses they may control) attract different resources related to their different roles in the production

Image credit: Abel 2013

less wealthy countries, but that process has both biophysical and economic limits. Global climate change has no national boundaries, while the exporting of lower wage jobs eventually increases wealth in those locations.

The effect of high-quality fuels is visible in the restless redistribution of work and population at this scale, making evident the degree to which no household, city, region, or even country can remain isolated for long from the pressures of abundance. One of the fundamental premises of the book *Ecotopia* is that the Northwest region had not only seceded politically from the US, but had remained culturally and economically isolated while it developed an economy wholly based on renewable resources (Callenbach 1977). The isolation of households or countries in order to survive future social and environmental disruptions, a concept we can call "survivalism," can be tempting, and appears at many scales, from net zero energy buildings to plans for regional autonomy. But the principle of selection for maximum power suggests that the low-powered economy of ecotopia would eventually be reterritorialized by its higher powered neighbors in one way or another—by the direct military action hinted at in the novel, or by the many other paths by which the temptations of greater power would likely infiltrate the society and economy. The closest real-life approximation is probably the communities of Amish farmers spread throughout the Americas, which have largely retained pre-industrial agricultural practices. Those communities have persevered by remaining small and adaptable and by participating selectively in adjacent wealthier economies. They trade their labor and excess goods for industrial products from their neighbors, but they do not build cities.

The pressure of abundance can be discerned in the surplus e[m]ergy enjoyed by the Ellis household, in our case study of normative consumption in the early twenty-first century. The Ellis House was built at a moment of such wealth that the original driveway and entry walk had electric heaters embedded to melt the snow in the winter, saving the human labor of shoveling. That particular luxury has been omitted from this study, which uses data from around 2005, but the economy to which it belongs still delivers tremendous power to the household. If we use the e[m]ergy intensity of US currency (sej/$) and the average household income for the location, the Ellis household brings in over twice as much e[m]ergy as it spends to maintain the household. Even after deducting nominal values for state and national taxes, it has a generous surplus. Different households will make different choices about what to do with the excess, but it will eventually be expended somewhere, whether on entertainment, education, or charity, helping the household to prosper or not.

The common good

Considering environmental building design at the scale of the city and economy highlights the enduring tension between the desires of individuals and the good of the society as a whole. Individual households, institutions, and societies naturally approach such choices from their own perspective, while the behavior of the whole remains abstract and distant. As the authors of *Limits to Growth* (Meadows et al. 2004) observed, "The global social system is horrendously and wonderfully complex, and many of its crucial parameters remain unmeasured. Some are probably unmeasurable." Social and economic arrangements are equally complex, and so "the capacity for humans to observe, adapt and learn, to choose, and to change their goals makes the system inherently unpredictable." The World3 model developed by Forrester and the authors could only describe "the broad sweeps, the behavioral tendencies of the system" as it approaches the many different levels of limits in the geo-biosphere (Meadows et al. 2004, 140). Achieving the common good remains an ethical dilemma that cannot be resolved by systems theory alone, although it clarifies the choices we make about obeying the pressures of abundance.

We started this section with the question about Al Gore's house, and its place in the social and economic hierarchies of wealth. The emails that circulated at the time compared it to the smaller, more energy-efficient ranch owned at that time by then President George Walker Bush (who later bought a larger house when his term ended), and this partisan example makes evident the symbolic value of buildings. Public debates and private discussions about social excesses and degrees of inequity are vital forms of feedback that help regulate society and appear in almost every scale of architecture. We debate the inappropriateness of a "Class A" lobby in a "Class C" building with as much precision as we debate the efficiency of a furnace or a light fixture, and we can use the ecological concept of e[m]ergy and resource quality to help compare them.

The slow and the fast of location

In this fifth chapter, we explored the thermodynamics of location, placing the subject of environmental building design in an urban and economic context. The growth of urban areas and the increases in collective wealth of the last 200 years directly reflect the infusion of high-quality fuels. Cities and economies have evolved into ever more complex, hierarchical networks of production, driven both by the quantities of available energy and their enhanced quality. The long geological preparation and refinement of hydrocarbon fuels has made them especially concentrated, transportable, and readily transformed into products and services, but it has also made them nearly impossible to replace. With each degree of concentration, from simple fuels to electricity and currency, power can be transferred and implemented more quickly. The greater the concentration and dematerialization, the greater the contrast with the slow pace of building construction. Even the rapidly shifting economic value of land is constrained by the slower pace of adapting structures, infrastructures, and social institutions. Today's highways, suburbs, and malls form the "valley section" of the renewable metropolis.

Bibliography

Abel, Tom. 2003. "Understanding Complex Human Ecosystems: The Case of Ecotourism on Bonaire." *Conservation Ecology* 7 (3):art 10.

Abel, Thomas. 2004. "Systems Diagrams for Visualizing Macroeconomics." *Ecological Modelling* 178(1–2): 189–194.

Abel, Thomas. 2013. "Energy and the Social Hierarchy of Households (and Buildings)." In *Architecture and Energy: Performance and Style*, edited by William W. Braham and Daniel Willis. London and New York: Routledge.

Ascione, Marco, Luigi Campanella, Francesco Cherubini, & Sergio Ulgiati. 2009. "Environmental Driving Forces of Urban Growth and Development. An Emergy-based Assessment of the City of Rome, Italy." *Landscape and Urban Planning* 93: 238–249.

Bataille, Georges. 1988. *The Accursed Share: An Essay on General Economy*. New York: Zone Books.

Berry, Brian J. L., & Adam Okulicz-Kozaryn. 2012. "The City Size Distribution Debate: Resolution for US Urban Regions and Megalopolitan Areas." *Cities* 29: S17–S23.

Bettencourt, Luis, & Geoffrey West. 2010. "A Unified Theory of Urban Living." *Nature* 467 (October 21): 912–913.

Brown, Mark T. 1980. "Energy Basis for Hierarchies in Urban and Regional Landscapes." PhD, Department of Environmental Sciences, University of Florida, Gainsville.

Butcher, Luke, & Jill Sornson Kurtz. 2014. "Geographies of Emergy: Maximizing Environmental Settlement in Chautauqua." *Unpublished Final Project*. Master of Environmental Building Design, University of Pennsylvania.

Callenbach, Ernest. 1977. *Ecotopia: The Notebooks and Reports of William Weston*. New York: Bantam Books.

Calthorpe, Peter, & Suzan Benson. 1979. "The Solar Shadow: A Discussion of Issues Eclipsed." *Second National Passive Solar Conference*, Philadelphia, PA.

Calthorpe Associates. 2011. *Vision California: Charting Our Future: Statewide Scenarios Report*. Calthorpe Associates.

Campbell, Daniel E., Sherry L. Brandt-Williams, & Maria E. A. Meisch. 2005. "Environmental Accounting Using Emergy: Evaluation of the State of West Virginia." Narragansett, RI: US Environmental Protection Agency, Office of Research and Development.

Carroll, Glenn R. 1982. "National City-size Distributions: What do we Know after 67 Years of Research?" *Progress in Human Geography* 6(1): 1–43.

Christaller, Walter. 1933. *Die zentralen Orte in Süddeutschland: Eine ökonomisch-geographische Untersuchung über die Gesetzmässigkeit der Verbreitung und Entwicklung der Siedlungen mit städtischen Funktionen*. Jena: Gustav Fischer.

Christaller, Walter, & Carlisle Whiteford Baskin. 1966. *Central Places in Southern Germany*. Englewood Cliffs, NJ: Prentice-Hall.

Cristelli, Matthieu, Michael Batty, & Luciano Pietronero. 2012. "There is More than a Power Law in Zipf." *Scientific Reports* 2(812): 1–7.

Daly, Herman E., & Joshua Farley. 2011. *Ecological Economics: Principles and Applications*, 2nd ed. New York: Island Press.

Diamond, Jared. 2004. *Collapse: How Societies Choose to Fail or Succeed*. New York: Viking.

Economist. 2009. "Irving Fisher: Out of Keynes's Shadow: Today's Crisis has Given new Relevance to the Ideas of Another Great Economist of the Depression Era." *The Economist*, February 12.

Fujita, Masahisa, Paul R. Krugman, & Anthony Venables. 1999. *The Spatial Economy: Cities, Regions and International Trade*. Cambridge, MA: MIT Press.

Garreau, Joel. 1991. *Edge City: Life on the New Frontier*. New York: Doubleday.

Geddes, Patrick. 1949. *Cities in Evolution: An Introduction to the Town Planning Movement and to the Study of Civics*. London: Williams & Norgate.

Glaeser, Edward L. 2011. *Triumph of the City: How our Greatest Invention makes us Richer, Smarter, Greener, Healthier, and Happier*. New York: Penguin Press.

Hall, Charles A. S., & Kent A. Klitgaard. 2012. *Energy and the Wealth of Nations: Understanding the Biophysical Economy*. New York: Springer.

Hardin, Garret. 1968. "The Tragedy of the Commons." *Science* 162: 1243–1248.

Huang, Shu-Li, & Chia-Wen Chen. 2005. "Theory of Urban Energetics and Mechanisms of Urban Development." *Ecological Modelling* 189: 49–71.

Huang, Shu-Li, Hsiao-Yin Lai, & Chia-Lun Lee. 2001. "Energy Hierarchy and Urban Landscape System." *Landscape and Urban Planning* 53: 145–161.

Johnson, Alan W., & Timothy Earle. 2000. *The Evolution of Human Societies: From Foraging Group to Agrarian State*, 2nd ed. Stanford, CA: Stanford University Press.

Jorgensen, Sven Erik. 2007. *A New Ecology: Systems Perspective*. Amsterdam and Oxford: Elsevier.

Karter, Andrew. 2009. "Al Gore's Mansion." *Factcheck.org*, October 10.

Krugman, Paul. 1991. "Increasing Returns and Economic Geography." *Journal of Political Economy* 99(3): 483–499.

Lei, Kampeng, Zhishi Wang, & ShanShin Ton. 2008. "Holistic Emergy Analysis of Macao." *Ecological Engineering* 32: 30–43.

Light, Jennifer S. 2009. *The Nature of Cities: Ecological Visions and the American Urban Professions, 1920–1960*. Baltimore, MD: Johns Hopkins University Press.

Liu, Gengyuan, Zhifeng Yang, Bin Chen, & Lixiao Zhang. 2011. "Analysis of Resource and Emission Impacts: An Emergy-Based Multiple Spatial Scale Framework for Urban Ecological and Economic Evaluation." *Entropy* 13: 720–743.

Lösch, August. 1954. *The Economics of Location*. New Haven, CT: Yale University Press.

Meadows, Donella H., Jorgen Randers, & Dennis L. Meadows. 2004. *Limits to Growth: The 30-Year Update*, 3rd ed. White River Junction, VT: Chelsea Green.

Mumford, Lewis. 1956. "The Natural History of Urbanization." In *Man's Role in the Changing the Face of the Earth*, edited by William L. Thomas. Chicago, IL, and London: University of Chicago Press.

Nichols, Joseph B., Stephen D. Oliner, & Michael R. Mulhall. 2010. *Commercial and Residential Land Prices Across the United States*. Divisions of Research & Statistics and Monetary Affairs, Federal Reserve Board, Washington, DC.

Odum, Howard T. 1983. *Systems Ecology: An Introduction*. New York: John Wiley & Sons, Inc.

Odum, Howard T. 2007. *Environment, Power, and Society for the Twenty-First Century: The Hierarchy of Energy*. New York: Columbia University Press.

Odum, Howard T., Mark T. Brown, L. S. Whitefield, R. Woithe, & S. Doherty. 1995. "Zonal Organization of Cities and Environment: A Study of Energy System Basis for Urban Society." In a *Report to the Chiang Ching-Kuo Foundation for International Scholarly Exchange*. Center for Environmental Policy, University of Florida, Gainsville.

Owen, David. 2010. *Green Metropolis: Why Living Smaller, Living Closer, and Driving Less are Keys to Sustainability*. New York: Riverhead Books.

Smithson, Alison, & Peter Smithson. 1954. *Team 10: The Doorn Manifesto*. Cambridge, MA: MIT Press.

Soddy, Frederick. 1912. *Matter and Energy*. New York: H. Holt & Co.

Tainter, Joseph A. 1988. *The Collapse of Complex Societies, New Studies in Archaeology*. Cambridge and New York: Cambridge University Press.

Thünen, Johann Heinrich von, & Peter Geoffrey Hall. 1966. *Isolated State* [English edition of Der isolierte Staat (1826)]. New York: Pergamon Press.

Vernadsky, Vladimir. 1926. *The Biosphere*. New York: Springer.

Weber, Alfred, & Carl J. Friedrich. 1929. *Alfred Weber's Theory of the Location of Industries, Materials for the Study of Business*. Chicago, IL: University of Chicago Press.

White, Leslie A. 1959. *The Evolution of Culture: The Development of Civilization to the Fall of Rome*. New York: McGraw-Hill.

Zipf, George Kingsley. 1949. *Human Behavior and the Principle of Least Effort: An Introduction to Human Ecology*. Cambridge, MA: Addison-Wesley.

Figure 6.1: The Ark, Prince Edward Island, New Alchemy Institute

© 1977, John Todd

Chapter Six

Design of thermodynamic narratives

> [B]ut my point is really that dystopian and post-apocalyptic narratives are narratives, that is, stories: things that are inherently invented or collated ex post facto. Narratives are static. Real life is, is—Kinetic?
>
> (Row 2014)

Architecture is a process of discovery, of deciding what to work on before it ever becomes a matter of design (*disegno*, drawing). Discovery means identifying the narratives that make projects intelligible, but architectural narratives are more than marketing descriptions. They are interpretations we use to make sense of the "kinetics" of everyday life, which explain a building's purpose and expense. The argument presented in this book is that meaningful narratives about buildings are ultimately thermodynamic. The biophysical limitations of the planet and the inexorable second law provide the conditions of scarcity necessary for economic and biological competition, and buildings serve as both tools and symbols of the wealth that accumulates from that competition. Narratives are a form of concentrated power that helps fit buildings into social and economic hierarchies of production. Contemporary narratives used to explain environmental projects include wealth, power (or loss-of-power), survivalism, consumption, luxury, pollution, waste, resilience, and health.

For common forms of building, architectural narratives compress multiple aspects of building type, style, use, construction, and location into compact accounts—the all-glass high-rise or suburban mall, for instance—although more elaborate narratives are necessary for unusual or novel kinds of building. Many different architectural narratives were tried to explain the active glass wall as it was being developed, which ultimately settled into a more stable account about fresh air and energy efficiency as the numbers of active glass walls increased (see Introduction). Abstract performance achievements, like net zero energy or LEED Platinum, have proved difficult to convey, so environmentally ambitious buildings frequently adopt more visible elements such as green roofs and photovoltaic panels, even if they are not particularly effective. But once a technique like insulated windows or recycled plastic lumber becomes more common, it stops being considered particularly environmental. Much of the problem centers around the fact that the term "environmental" mostly describes buildings or practices that are not yet *economical*. Environmentally ambitious buildings are rarely built in poorer regions or declining cities, even when their long-term costs are lower. Put the other way around, buildings specifically identified as environmental are currently a kind of luxury, a sign of greater wealth and a means to reinforce it. We certainly need better narratives.

The thermodynamic principles of maximum power, energy concentration hierarchies, and the co-cycling of materials expand the kinds of narrative available for environmental building design. Situating a project in its urban, economic, and natural hierarchies provides more comprehensive terms to explain its environmental costs and evaluate its contribution to the production of wealth. The all-glass high-rise office building sits at the pinnacle of the contemporary metropolitan enterprise, concentrating materials, energy, and information of all kinds. The Freedom Tower in New York or the Burj Khalifa in Dubai require a full account of their intensification of land values and channeling of economic activity, which vastly outweighs the costs of the building itself. The thermodynamic narrative of the contemporary high-rise office must include the landscape of residences that house their occupants and the vast infrastructures for transportation, water, and food deployed to support them. The high-rise ultimately tells a story about the power of cities and the environmental footprint of that power.

In contrast, the survivalist retreat throws the all-glass building into the highest relief and provides a shadow narrative for much of sustainable design—situated off-the-grid, built from local materials, and outfitted to produce its own food and power. There are survivalists from every political persuasion, hedging against the risks of societal collapse and building some of the most extreme forms of net zero, autonomous compounds. Survivalist narratives can also be discerned in the photovoltaic panels, fuel cells, and rooftop gardens of environmental projects in cities and suburbs alike, which are conceived as much to mitigate risk and keep-the-lights-on, as to reduce environmental impact. Anxieties about the loss of power form an understandable response to the dire warnings about natural disaster and environmental collapse, amplified in dystopic and post-apocalyptic fiction. Like the images of power conveyed by the all-glass high-rise, environmental designers need to understand the competing narratives that are used to explain even the greenest buildings.

The paradoxes of the survivalist narrative are exemplified by the Ark, an elegant "bioshelter" built by the New Alchemists in the mid-1970s that illustrates the promise and limitations of their autonomous operation. The Ark was designed to support a single family, whose members could grow crops, raise fish, and process waste within almost completely closed resource cycles (Todd 1977). It is a model of ecological management and the experiments with aquaculture eventually led to "living machines," the now commercially available, biological sewage treatment facilities. But even the most ecological survivalist camp is ultimately a private farm without a market town or trade network, and this highlights the dangerous temptation for environmental design. For the long-term survivalist, a full thermodynamic accounting would reveal the many other concentrated resources, like tools and information, which are needed to maintain current lifestyles. The survivalist camp actually mirrors the appeals of the all-glass building, on a reduced scale, according to the fears of imminent scarcity that lurk within the wealthy abundance of contemporary civilization.

To fully transcend the marginal narratives available to environmental design, we need to embrace the world of consumption that is regularly indicted as the root of environmental problems, considering the full dimensions of the restaurant, shopping center, or luxury spa. In their book *Ecological Design*, Sim Van der Ryn and Stuart Cowan reviewed a host of commonly cited causes for the environmental problems driven by consumption—"capitalism, Christianity, colonialism, development, the population explosion, science and technology, and patriarchal culture" (Van der Ryn and Cowan 2005, 19)—and dismiss each as insufficient. In short: there are no single causes or solutions to the basic appetites of life. Systems ecology helps explain the many forms of feedback and amplification that occur between production and consumption, which interact to enhance the power flowing through the human economy. Only by understanding the environmental pressure to maximize power and expend available resources can we formulate a more complete narrative about consumption, which begins by exploring the link between consumption and waste.

Among the most positive environmental narratives is the elimination of local and global pollution, which sets absolute limits for design and ultimately means arranging for the consumption of waste by some other entity or process. As previous chapters have demonstrated, waste occurs at every scale in the construction and use of buildings, from construction debris to wastewater to the whole-scale replacement of buildings. A net zero waste imperative opens up many more design possibilities than net zero energy, because materials can actually be recycled and material waste involves the management of such substantial stuff. However, not every waste material can be efficiently contained within a building while it is consumed and transformed. Like the mitigation of indoor air pollutants, it is necessary to find the right site(s) and scale(s) for their consumption. Providing the additional space, work, and resources to neutralize wastes can be expensive, but it is the technique that natural ecosystems use to offset lower efficiencies. The less efficient, no-waste building offers a narrative of maximum power with minimum environmental impact.

Waste also occurs at different rates and scales. The cycles of change in land values and business opportunities create multiple forms of waste. The urban high-rise, the suburban shopping center, and the survivalist retreat are each designed for a specific near future scenario, accounting for a particular economy, infrastructure, climate, and society. If any of these elements change too much—if the economy falters, if a transit line is altered, if the climate warms up, if the government changes, or if social expectations shift—buildings must be adapted or abandoned. Many of these opportunities have already been embraced and form a large part of contemporary environmental design, from design-for-disassembly to the "long-life, loose-fit" approach coined by Alex Gordon in the 1970s and popularized in *Ten Shades of Green* (Buchanan and Architectural League of New York 2005). The virtues of adaptability can seem obvious after a natural disaster leaves buildings suddenly useless, but the same is true for the slower processes that empty downtown neighborhoods in American rustbelt cities or that replace Chinese courtyard houses with high-rises.

In a recent survey to determine which narratives would persuade more people to invest in energy-saving buildings, reviewers detected a strikingly partisan divide. Liberals responded much more strongly to explicitly environmental references, while conservatives were more persuaded by appeals to energy independence (Gromet 2013). Unlike buildings and their systems, which can be hard to change once they have been built, narratives can be adapted more freely. But they are not wholly fictional; they are a form of public information produced and refined by designers, clients, real estate advertisements, and the media as new forms and uses of buildings are tested. Historians later seek to identify and explain these collective interpretations, and this narrative information constitutes much of what is "selected" as buildings are copied and multiplied.

The dynamic interaction between buildings and their narratives is exemplified by the persistent question about the appropriate style of a sustainable (or green or efficient) building (Braham 2013). Discussions of the superficial, stylistic features of buildings compete with descriptions based on typology, which remain the source of most methods of building design, classification, and regulation. In the common understanding, type describes the deeper characteristics of buildings that styles make visible (more or less well). For example, net zero energy is a type of building explained by the formula limiting energy consumption to the amount of onsite renewable energies available. The large, mostly flat roofs of photovoltaic panels then become the distinctive result of that formulation, but does it really constitute a style? As Charles Jencks, the careful documenter of architectural styles observed in his review of twentieth-century architecture: "One would have thought the ecological imperative might have been monopolized by the Activist tradition, but it has been taken up by all of them in different ways [...] the point is that green architectures, in the plural, are coming from everywhere while we might have thought the ecological issue would be taken over by just one or two movements" (Jencks 2000, 78).

As Jencks' work illustrates, styles (or traditions or trends or movements) are now mostly used for positioning among the top 20% of architects, with the competitive pressures making environmental features useful to all of them to some degree. In contrast, most explicit design methods are based on some form of building typology. Zoning and energy codes, for example, are largely based on typologies of use or occupancy—residential, retail, manufacturing, office, etc.—because the activities housed in a building mostly produce the effects the agencies are trying to regulate, such as noise, traffic, and pollution. Conversely, the typologies employed in construction codes are based on classes of materials and methods of assembly—steel frame, bearing wall—while designers and architectural historians are more likely to talk about typologies of form, of bar buildings or high-rise towers. The thermodynamic nature of typological descriptions becomes clear when we ask how new types develop over time, what makes them persist, and why they disappear. Using Alfred Lotka's charming term, typology seeks to provide "the principle of the persistence of stable forms" (Lotka 1922, 151).

Framing the question in thermodynamic terms reveals the shortcomings of the concept of type and its use as a method of design, especially in periods of rapid growth (or decline). The many specialized building types that characterize the modern architectural era directly reflect the specialization of work (and play), along with the growing size and complexity of the economy. Typologies are descriptions of the forms that stabilize and persist long enough to be identified, but they can only be explained by the selection processes that produce them, not as immutable categories. Even the descriptive aspect of the energy systems language can get caught up with the idea of fixed building types, so it is important to remember Lotka's caution: "Mechanism is all important." For architecture, the translation of narratives into designs is realized with specific methods, tools, and goals.

Design methods at multiple (or at least three) scales

Even the most ambitious environmental buildings have to fit the current economies of production if they are to persist. However efficient their configuration, they are constrained by the social expectations and supply chains of the high-powered, networked society for which they are built (or to which they aspire). This situation largely dictates the current methods of performance design. Beginning with the energy supply crisis of the 1970s (which actually had its roots in the early 1950s), design for energy performance has been framed as an incremental improvement over current practices. To wit: A reference building is identified, usually some form of average based on the typology of use and floor area, and projected designs are evaluated against the reference. That pragmatic, incremental, and typological approach is embodied in the building codes and standards that determine the performance of the fourth energy generation buildings, and the methods used to design them.

The amount of improvement established in energy codes increased slowly at first. But in the last decade, standards have been pushed to 30%, and even 50%, below current norms, responding to the urgency of climate change and improvements in construction and operation. However, performance strategies all have limits beyond which their effect on consumption diminishes or even "rebounds," and the principle of maximum power suggests that they will be circumvented if possible. For example, the practice of normalizing energy performance standards to floor area makes it possible to compare the efficiency of buildings of different sizes; but it also means that codes do not regulate the size or numbers of buildings, which have continued to increase. LEED and the other suites of environmental standards have successfully expanded the categories of performance evaluated, but have only been able to penetrate the market by adopting the method of incremental improvement over norms.

In contrast, net zero (site) energy strategies have an absolute formulation: determine the maximum amount of power that can be captured and concentrated on site (usually with photovoltaics) and design the building to match that target. The use of absolute limits linked to the capacity of sites or ecosystems—net zero energy, net zero waste, and prohibited materials—demands more comprehensive design methods and provides more narratives connecting environmental work to buildings of all kinds. The contribution of systems ecology to such design methods is twofold: First, the use of e[m]ergy accounting to assess the total environmental costs of different materials and resources provides a more systemic measure of projects and an objective method of comparing the many different categories of work and resources involved in buildings. For example, it facilitates the comparison between the materials invested in the building envelope and the fuels used for environmental conditioning. And second, and more importantly, the thermodynamic principles of maximum power, energy concentration hierarchies, and the co-cycling of materials provide richer design narratives that reach beyond the marginal definitions of environmental, efficient, or sustainable design.

Using the diagrams of the energy systems language, we identified the hierarchical interactions among the different spatial and temporal scales at which buildings operate, connecting building design and operation to the self-organization of natural, technical, social, and economic systems. Of course, architects rarely engage projects at more than one scale at a time. Like the buildings themselves, the profession has divided into an array of subdisciplines that specialize in the different scales of building explored in this book—from city and regional planning to interior and product design. Like other trades and industries, specialization has deepened design expertise and made project delivery more efficient, but environmental building design demands a comprehensive view, if only to frame the limits of design at each scale. Students are often surprised when they first use e[m]ergy accounting to evaluate the effect of a high-performance skin or a net zero photovoltaic configuration, and learn that the cost of structures and infrastructures rivals the costs of more efficient building operations. Even more confounding is the recognition that the reduced costs of an efficient building can be dramatically overshadowed by the work and resources consumed by the activities it houses or the costs of its location. Changing the size, use, or location of buildings or "engineering" the occupants is not a regular service of the architecture profession, but the extent of change required by the transition to a renewable economy simply demands new narratives, methods, and paradigms of design at all three scales: shelter, setting, and site.

Shelter

The discussion of buildings began with the intermediate scale—the building as shelter—because it is the disciplinary focus of architecture and the scale around which explicitly architectural narratives develop. Let us return for a moment to Banham. After his parable about the tribe in the woods, he described the two traditional thermodynamic narratives of shelter that have developed over time in different climates: the massive "conservative mode" that absorbs and releases heat as needed, and the lighter, "selective mode" that filters and discriminates among climate conditions. But he was actually fascinated by the newer, power-operated, "regenerative mode," which converts high-quality fuels and electricity into total control over temperature and humidity (Banham 1969). A few decades later, Dean Hawkes re-designated it the "exclusive mode," because by that time, high-powered building envelopes were almost entirely sealed (Hawkes 1996). By the early twenty-first century, Rem Koolhaas had rechristened the result "junkspace . . . the product of the encounter between escalator and air conditioning, conceived in an incubator of sheetrock" (Koolhaas et al. 2002). Junkspace marks the globalization of the power-operated solution and the increasing dematerialization of buildings, although Banham's enthusiasm lurks in the many efforts to reterritorialize the envelope.

The building envelope has become the great hope and most visible expression of an architecture that resists the regenerative, exclusive mode of junkspace. The many narratives explored over the last few decades demonstrate the depth of the envelope's possibilities, and the steady testing and refinement these narratives undergo. The active glass walls, discussed in the Introduction, are concretely tied to a technical configuration of the building envelope, while the narrative of "living" buildings succeeds by being more metaphorical than typological. With the integration of photovoltaic panels in building envelopes, the many different formal explorations seem to be converging on the strict definition of net zero energy (Torcellini et al. 2006), although the more comprehensive requirements of super-insulated construction (balancing losses and gains) dramatically broadened its reach when it was rebranded as *Passivhaus* (Shurcliff 1980; Passive House 2014). The original daylighting function of the conditioned atrium has coevolved with the biofilter and biophilia in a uniquely broad narrative. As designers have sought to identify more fundamentally architectural narratives, a number of recent experiments have reversed the formula, exploring the energy and environmental narratives latent in generic building forms. Iñaki Ábalos has explored the thermodynamics of mixed use and high-rise buildings (Ábalos 2012), while Kiel Moe has been fascinated by the thermal properties of weighty materials themselves (Moe 2010, 2014). And for over 30 years, Ken Yeang has refined the narrative of the green skyscraper, with the argument that it has been the dominant form of building in the megacities of the Pacific Rim (Yeang 1997, 2002).

The interaction of climate and envelope remains a source of tremendous thermodynamic invention, a fact attributed to the temporal variations of temperature, humidity, wind, and sunlight, as well as the different aspects of the envelope that influence heat exchange: lossiness, thermal mass, time constant, transparency, and shading. The building-as-shelter is also the most constrained by the rigid typological concepts and methods regulated by codes and standards. The internal load-dominated condition of junkspace that emerged in the post-war period is too readily accepted as a normal or natural typology, rather than a symptom of excess power and of buildings out of balance. Thermodynamic narratives of the envelope are deepened and extended by considering the scales above and below the building-as-shelter.

Setting

As Koolhass remarked in his critique, junkspace "is always interior." It is the building-as-setting that imposes the most intimate consequences and provokes the deepest criticisms of that homogenized, power-mediated experience. It is in the interior where the excesses of available energy collide with the experiences of everyday life, through the specialization of work, increased productivity, and increased time for leisure. Buildings have become engines of power concentration and dissipation, increasingly compressed into the "three screens" of the early twenty-first century (handheld, desktop, and TV). The narratives of the building-as-setting are almost wholly bound up with the collective enthusiasm for the value of information, whether for production or entertainment. But those are still narratives about what people do with their time.

The exciting stories about the enhanced productivity of networked living and working are captured by the contrast between two common screen-based images. In the first, a person at leisure sits in a picturesque setting—a beach, lawn, or veranda—working on a networked laptop or mobile device, turning leisure time into work. In the second, people in trains, planes, waiting areas, or even offices, who are bound to the situation by obligations of work, watch TV on a similarly networked device, releasing precious moments from working. These convey powerful stories about work, leisure, and productivity, and the thermodynamic diagram of production and consumption (see Figure 4.4) unites those two images in the relentless concentration of energy and maximization of power.

Current environmental narratives of the building-as-setting revolve around the tradeoff between labor and information, exemplified in the responsive version of the Ellis House. The adaptations of the building envelope were either accomplished through the physical labor and intelligence of the occupant (with or without a PhD) walking around to adjust windows or by the deployment of sophisticated devices that use concentrated power (and software) to perform that work automatically. Any transition to a renewable economy will require new forms of working, as the costs of concentrated power increase. The transition from the house-of-more-work to the smart house characterizes the current range of approaches with which we are experimenting, from lighting (occupancy sensors), plumbing (autoflush), and conditioning (learning thermostats) to food (anticipatory delivery), but the real tradeoffs remain nearly invisible. We need a full e[m]ergy accounting of the interaction between work and information in buildings.

Site

Every building is designed for a particular location in the landscape (and economy), regardless of whether it is actually located in that place. Design narratives of the building-as-site combine an assessment of the actual location and an argument about the role of the project. As we noted in Chapter 5, the value of location is established by its relation to urban and economic concentrations. At the scale of the city and region, design becomes an intervention into powerful processes of self-organization, which then determine the kinds of building that will or will not be built.

As we noted in the opening provocation of the book, the design challenge over the next century is to return to the renewable resource base of the eighteenth-century city using the technologies and expectations of the twenty-first-century metropolis. The changing spatial organization of cities and their economies will alter the conditions for which buildings are designed, from their size and purpose to appropriate levels of quality, while technical innovations such as information technology continue to disrupt current patterns of settlement. Ecologists confront this kind of complexity as a matter of course, and the thermodynamic principles of systems ecology provide tools to help environmental building design overcome the tension between apocalyptic, Malthusian environmentalists and cornucopian, technological optimists, between the calls for reduced consumption and more power.

If systems ecology teaches us anything, we have learned that the future is indeterminate. Peak oil (or gas or coal) and climate change can be predicted with confidence, but the timing and specifics of how and when these changes will unfold can only be imagined. That is the terrain of design. The darker implication of the principle of maximum power is that the powerful fuels still in the ground will likely be extracted, and that any country or population that simply renounces their use will be outcompeted by those that continue to use them. But the rates at which these fuels are extracted, how they are used, and how their wastes are handled is a matter for design (and policy) at multiple scales. Focusing that project on the century of transition helps overcome the incremental calculations that dominate economic planning and better fits the characteristic cycles of construction and renewal in buildings and cities. The fuel-powered civilization of the last 200 years has altered everything from the ways we build and organize cities to the ways we live together, and there is no reason to assume that the pace of change will slow as the fuels that powered that growth become more difficult to obtain and more costly to use.

New thermodynamic narratives for the urban transition have emerged in recent decades, from ecotopia to smart cities, which combine new forms of power production, agriculture, transportation, and patterns of settlement. Masdar in Abu Dhabi captured the collective imagination with a net zero infrastructure arranged in the form of a walled desert city. But visionary narratives for new urban arrangements, from eco-cities such as Dongtan and Tianjin to the European Union's Roadmap 2050, largely fall into the category that David Orr calls "technological" sustainability. He contrasts that to an "ecological" mode of rethinking the premises and "practices that got us into trouble in the first place" (Orr 1991, 24). The technological mode is exemplified by "smart-city" techniques, which use the massive quantities of information available in networked systems to streamline urban operations. In its current formulation, smart information improves efficiencies to enhance power, but the paradoxical first principle of systems ecology is that maximum power occurs at intermediate efficiencies. The ecological interpretation can help locate the critical leverage points in urban metabolisms as the power supply changes.

The opening pages of the novel *Ecotopia* describe the quieter, greener streets of a city forced to use slower means of travel, but everything about the premise of that ecological utopia is based on the political and economic "forces" required to restrict the pursuit of speed. Traffic jams and the individual desire for speed illustrate the complexity of intervening in collective processes of self-organization. Why? Because everyone sitting in a traffic jam actually chose to be there. They all collaborated to produce a condition that no one actually sought, by individually pushing for maximum speed and distance of travel. Each new expansion and refinement of the highway system provides new opportunities for individuals to test the limits, while the average speeds of travel remain surprisingly low as the overall system trades individual speed for the power of the whole.

Thermodynamic principles for environmental building design: a conclusion

Architects are natural systems thinkers, trained to see parts and wholes together and to imagine multiple possible futures. But that training is rooted in spatial arrangements and Euclidian geometry, so their approach to energy, growth, and transformation remains largely descriptive and typological. In her book *Thinking in Systems*, Donella Meadows observed that "although people deeply involved in a system often know intuitively where to find leverage points, more often than not they push the change in the wrong direction" (Meadows 2008, 145).

Architects have been deeply engaged in the radical transformations of the last few decades, developing new forms of building, patterns of settlement, and methods of design, but they have too often been pushing in the wrong direction. The profession has too readily accepted the formula of technological sustainability based solely on more efficient buildings.

The energy systems language helps designers better understand the behavior of the leverage points they have already identified, and to develop more meaningful narratives and methods to translate them into design. Following the three system principles of thermodynamics, we can identify three points of leverage for environmental building design, which can each be elaborated at multiple scales.

Three points of leverage

The first leverage point is efficiency, whose effectiveness for buildings and their systems has profound limits. More efficient conversions reduce waste, but maximum power occurs at intermediate efficiencies, so we have to embrace waste in all its forms. This applies to spatial and temporal efficiencies, as well as efficiencies of converting explicit fuels, from urban densities to the way people spend their time.

Design for the total consumption of wastes at all scales

The second leverage point is the use of concentrated, environmentally expensive resources in buildings. Reducing or eliminating costly resources seems sensible, but the judicious use of high-intensity resources, such as plastics, electricity, and information, can enhance the prosperity of the whole.

*Design for the full hierarchy of resource concentration,
intensity, and quality in buildings*

The third leverage point is the durability of materials, buildings, and locations. The longer the life of a building or component, the more services it can deliver, but landfills are full of durable granite counter tops tossed out in the five-year cycle of US household relocation. Disposable products and short-lived events are as important as long-lived constructions for faster paced activities.

Design the durability and longevity of buildings to match characteristic cycles of change

All three points are a matter of balance, scale, and proportion in complex self-organizing systems, which require designers attuned to the dynamic patterns with which the built environment unfolds over time.

Building well

An environmental method of design considers buildings in their full context, recognizing that they are tools used by people in social and cultural enterprises, whose economies are ultimately constrained by the ecology of the biosphere. This approach involves three things: a clearer account of the "environment" using the principles of systems ecology and ecological economics; an expanded understanding of buildings at three scales of activity; and finally, an expanded concept of design and its narratives. Architects have been "recalled to order" so many times over the years that it can seem like so much posturing, but architecture succeeds best when it helps shape and accommodate new ways of living. The final principle of environmental building design is to build well so we can live well (Frascari 1991).

Bibliography

Ábalos, Iñaki. 2012. "Thermodynamic Somatisms Verticalscapes. In *Thermodynamics Applied to Highrise and Mixed Use Prototypes*, edited by Iñaki Ábalos and Daniel Ibáñez. Cambridge, MA: Harvard Graduate School of Design.

Banham, Reyner. 1969. *The Architecture of the Well-Tempered Environment*. Chicago, IL: University of Chicago Press.

Braham, William W. 2013. "Architecture, Style, and Power: The Work of Civilization." In *Architecture and Energy: Performance and Style*, edited by William W. Braham and Daniel Willis. New York: Routledge.

Buchanan, Peter, & Architectural League of New York. 2005. *Ten Shades of Green: Architecture and the Natural World*. Architectural League of New York. New York: Distributed by W. W. Norton.

Frascari, Marco. 1991. *Monsters of Architecture: Anthropromorphism in Architectural Theory*. Savage, MD: Rowman & Littlefield.

Gromet, Dena. 2013. "Political Ideology Affects Energy-efficiency Attitudes and Choices." *Proceedings of the National Academy of Sciences* 110(23): 9314–9319.

Hawkes, Dean. 1996. *The Environmental Tradition: Studies in the Architecture of Environment*. London and New York: E. & F. N. Spon/Chapman & Hall.

Jencks, Charles. 2000. "Jencks's Theory of Evolution: An Overview of Twentieth-century Architecture." *Architectural Review* 208(1241): 76–79.

Koolhaas, Remment, Chuihua Judy Chung, Jeffrey Inaba, & Sze Tsung Leong, Eds. 2002. *Harvard Design School Guide to Shopping. Harvard Design School Project on the City*. Cambridge, MA: Harvard University Graduate School of Design.

Living Machine Systems. 2014. www.livingmachines.com.

Lotka, Alfred J. 1922. "Natural Selection as a Physical Principle." *Proceedings of the National Academy of Sciences* 8: 151–154.

Meadows, Donella. 2008. *Thinking in Systems: A Primer*. White River Junction, VT: Chelsea Green.

Moe, Kiel. 2010. *Thermally Active Surfaces in Architecture*. New York: Princeton Architectural Press.

Moe, Kiel. 2014. *Insulating Modernism: Isolated and Non-Isolated Thermodynamics in Architecture*. Basel: Birkhäuser.

Orr, David W. 1991. *Ecological Literacy: Education and the Transition to a Postmodern World*, SUNY Series in Constructive Postmodern Thought. Albany, NY: State University of New York Press.

Passive House Institute. 2014. *Active for More Comfort: Passive House. Information for Property Developers, Contractors, and Clients*. Darmstadt, Germany: International Passive House Institute.

Row, Jess. 2014. "The Empties." *New Yorker*, November 3.

Shurcliff, William. 1980. *Superinsulated Houses and Double-Envelope Houses: A Preliminary Survey of Principles and Practice*, 2nd ed. Cambridge, MA: William A. Shurcliff.

Todd, John. 1977. "Tomorrow is Our Permanent Address." *Journal of the New Alchemists* 4: 85–113.

Torcellini, Paul, Shanti Pless, Michael Deru, & Drury Crawley. 2006. "Zero Energy Buildings: A Critical Look at the Definition." ACEEE Summer Study, Pacific Grove, CA.

Van der Ryn, Sim, & Stuart Cowen. 2005. *Ecological Design*, 10th anniversary ed. Washington, DC: Island Press.

Yeang, Ken. 1997. *Skyscraper, Bioclimatically Considered: A Design Primer*. London: Wiley-Academy.

Yeang, Ken. 2002. *Reinventing the Skyscraper: A Vertical Theory of Urban Design*. Chichester: Wiley-Academy.

Appendix A: Energy systems language

This appendix describes the basic symbols and diagrams used throughout the book. The energy systems language is a method of describing complex systems by tracking the exchanges of energy, materials, and information. Inspired by Lindeman's trophic-dynamic method, H. T. Odum and his colleagues expanded the approach to describe the structure and organization of almost any system (see Chapter 1). He drew heavily on existing systems for diagraming electrical circuits, and conceptually the diagrams resemble electrical diagrams, with wires being replaced by energy circuits, showing the movement of energy from one point to another. However, Odum developed many new symbols for the processes common to ecosystems, and specifically for the many different forms in which energetic potential is conveyed and concentrated. The language is grounded in thermodynamics and the principles of self-organizing systems.

The starting point for any environmental assessment is the identification of the scope or boundary of analysis, which begins by preparing a diagram of all the stocks, flows, funds, and services of work and resources in the building. This book argues that there are three natural boundaries of analysis for buildings—site, shelter, and setting—but the scope of analysis will ultimately depend on the purpose of the analysis. Diagrams of buildings can be organized by function, according to spatial relationships, by materials or resources. In many ways, the drawing of the diagrams is the most important step in the method, and typically begins as a messy process of discovery, identifying the subject of the analysis and determining the different resources and interactions involved. It can

Appendix A

be constrained by the kinds of data available, but begins by identifying all the forms of work and exchanges of resources through the project.

The energy systems language is typically used to track two interrelated quantities—energy and cumulative, dissipated energy or e[m]ergy—which are present in the storages and flows of nutrients, materials, fuels, and anything capable of accomplishing some kind of work. By normalizing e[m]ergy to common units of solar energy, many different kinds of input and process can be compared and evaluated. The results are simple diagrams that compress a great deal of information in a description of a system's critical relationships.

The following symbols are those used within this text to describe the Ellis House. While this list is sufficient to understand all the examples provided here, it is not comprehensive, and many additional terms and symbols exist that may be encountered in the description of other systems. The specific symbol chosen will also depend on the scope and purpose of the diagram. For example, a building can be a storage of potential in a diagram focused on building operations or a consumer of resources in a diagram of a regional economy. More details on the energy systems language and the "algebra" for tracking e[m]ergy can be found in the research literature (Odum 1983, 1996, 2007; Brown 2004; Brown and Ulgiati 2004).

Consumer. This unit stores and transforms energy before returning it to the system. Humans are the consumers most commonly included in this book, but in diagrams of larger urban and economic arrangements, buildings could also be viewed as consumers.

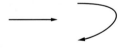

Energy circuit. The energy circuit symbol forms the basis of energy systems diagrams. Each arrow represents a transfer of some energetic capacity as conveyed by different materials and mechanisms.

General process. This unit represents a complex subsystem, simplified to make the diagram legible and intelligible. It includes everything from furnaces and air-conditioners to spatial units like a kitchen. The activities within any general process can be expanded in a separate, detailed diagram.

Appendix A

Heat sink. This represents the dispersion of useful energy out of the system as low-level heat that cannot be further utilized. All transactions and flows of energy involve the loss of energy to friction and entropy, so that it can no longer perform useful work.

Interaction. This represents the interaction of two or more flows of energy to produce one or more outflows of energy. The interaction can be simply proportional to the inputs or complexly determined by multiple factors.

Producer. This unit collects and transforms low-quality energy and returns it as a usable outflow of energy to the system. Green plants are the classic example of producers in an ecosystem, but in certain contexts, solar collectors or wind-turbines could be represented this way as well.

Self-organizing entity. This can be any system that has the capacity to store energetic potential and to use some of that potential to regulate or enhance its capture of available energy. Internally, the more complex units like consumers and producers are self-organizing, and their internal mechanisms can be represented as needed.

Source. This symbol represents the result of a complex chain of production outside the system being analyzed, which is simplified to make the diagram more legible. Explicit energy sources, such as the sun or electrical supply, are represented as sources, as is anything that carries energetic potential into the system being considered, from minerals to information.

Storage. This symbol represent elements within a system that are capable of capturing and storing incoming energetic potential and releasing it according to a predefined rule set. This can represent the physical storage of goods, the concentrated storage of energy, or the e[m]ergy embodied in the building envelope.

Appendix A

 *Transaction.* This represents an economic transaction, when money is exchanged for energy, goods, or services. Currency moves in the opposite direction to the flows of energy or e[m]ergy. Prices fluctuate according to market (receiver) valuation.

Figure A.1: Symbols of the energy systems language

Bibliography

Brown, Mark T. 2004. "A Picture is Worth a Thousand Words: Energy Systems Language and Simulation." *Ecological Modelling* 178: 83–100.

Brown, Mark T., & Sergio Ulgiati. 2004. "Emergy Analysis and Environmental Accounting." In *Encyclopedia of Energy*, edited by Cutler J. Cleveland. Amsterdam: Elsevier.

Odum, Howard T. 1983. *Systems Ecology: An Introduction.* New York: John Wiley & Sons, Inc.

Odum, Howard T. 1996. *Environmental Accounting: EMERGY and Environmental Decision Making.* New York: John Wiley & Sons, Inc.

Odum, Howard T. 2007. *Environment, Power, and Society for the Twenty-First Century: The Hierarchy of Energy.* New York: Columbia University Press.

Appendix B: E[m]ergy synthesis of the Ellis House

This appendix summarizes the e[m]ergy synthesis of the three versions of the Ellis House used as a case study throughout the book. Each of the following subsections describes a table of results, followed by a section explaining the sources of data and calculations for each table. Table B.1 presents the materials of the building and its contents; Table B.2 presents a concise summary of all the work and resources used by the building; while Table B.3 presents the same material broken down into the three scales of use and individual activities.

A full environmental account includes the total cost of construction materials—from site work to furniture—to the purchased power and of the various forms of renewable resources. We use the Ellis House to illustrate the full range of factors that might be included. The format of the calculation depends on the units in which the particular item is typically tracked, whether by weight (kg), by energy content (J), or by dollar ($). One of the great attractions of the energy systems language explored in this book is the ability to directly compare the environmental cost of items tracked in different units.

Comparing environmental costs

Materials tracked by weight (kg)

Construction materials and water are the primary items tracked by weight. The construction data for the Ellis House were based on a detailed building information model that was used to generate estimates of every assembly and material. The basic method of accounting for the total work and resources is to use unit e[m]ergy values (UEV) reported in the research literature or developed from primary sources. For building materials, the estimate of the total work and resources invested in specific material is based on the weight:

Total e[m]ergy, material A (sej) = Weight, material A (kg) x UEV, material A (sej/kg)

As explained in Chapter 3, the total annual cost is based on a simple depreciation calculation, dividing the total environmental cost by the anticipated useful life of the material or assembly.

$$\text{Annual e[m]ergy cost, material A (sej/yr)} = \frac{\text{Total environmental cost, material A (sej)}}{\text{Average useful life, material A (yr)}}$$

Materials tracked by energy content (J)

The items tracked by energy content are conceptually the easiest to document. Renewable energy resources and purchased utility energy are readily available in this form, as is any other process directly tracked in terms of work. For the Ellis House, there were no utility data available from before the renovation, and the house is not sub-metered, so normative data derived from surveys were used to estimate the energy consumption before renovation as well as the allocation of energies among different uses. As with the calculation based on weight, the method of accounting relies on the unit e[m]ergy values (UEV), which have been well explored in the literature. Since these are reported as annual flows of resources, no depreciation accounting is needed:

Annual e[m]ergy cost, source A (sej/yr) = Energy, source A (J/yr) x UEV, source A (sej/J)

Materials tracked by economic cost ($)

For those products or services for which explicit weight or energy data are not available, their environmental cost is estimated by using the average UEV of the economy in which the building is built and operated. For the Ellis House, this approach was used to estimate the annual cost of the "non-durable" supplies that are consumed by the household in a year, the annual cost of the location, and the value of labor:

Annual e[m]ergy cost, source A (sej/yr) = Cost, source A ($/yr) x UEV economy (sej/$)

Summary tables

Three summary tables were prepared for the Ellis House. Table B.1 itemizes the materials of construction, detailing the weight of each element, its UEV, and average lifespan, to yield a total annual e[m]ergy cost. Table B.2 summarizes all the household costs and is organized by the different types of input or cost, including renewable resources, depreciated assets, material services, concentrated power, and costs directly associated with the location. This format is useful in order to understand the relative cost of different sources and to determine relative costs and impacts in ratios such as the environmental loading ratio, ELR, which indicates the proportion of purchased to renewable inputs. Table B.3 presents the same material as B.2, divided into sections based on the categories of site, shelter, and setting, and making explicit the different activities for which the resources are used. This is particularly useful for evaluating the different design tasks of buildings, and for evaluating the costs of modifying the climate as opposed to the costs of providing food or water.

Table B.1: Materials of construction

Item	Specification	UEV (sej/kg)	Life (yr)	Base Raw data (kg)	Base Em[ergy (sej)	Base Annual em[ergy (sej/yr)	Improved Raw data (kg)	Improved Annual em[ergy (sej/yr)	Passivhaus NZE Raw data (kg)	Passivhaus NZE Annual em[ergy (sej/yr)
Sitework										
Land use	Excavated ground	1.13E+11	80	258,505.7	2.9E+16	3.65E+14	258,505.7	3.65E+14	258,505.7	3.65E+14
Exterior pavements	Concrete, cast-in-place gray	1.81.E+12	40	5,361.4	9.70E+15	2.43E+14	5,361.4	2.43E+14	5,361.4	2.43E+14
	Concrete, cast-in-place gray	1.81.E+12	40	2,027.5	3.67E+15	9.17E+13	2,027.5	9.17E+13	2,027.5	9.17E+13
	Concrete, cast-in-place gray	1.81.E+12	40	904.9	1.64E+15	4.09E+13	904.9	4.09E+13	904.9	4.09E+13
	Wood plank, 2" oak	8.80.E+11	40	7,142.5	6.29E+15	1.57E+14	7,142.5	1.57E+14	7,142.5	1.57E+14
Driveway	4" asphalt	4.74.E+11	40	13,331.8	6.32E+15	1.58E+14	13,331.8	1.58E+14	13,331.8	1.58E+14
	2" gravel	1.06.E+10	80	35,552.6	3.77E+14	4.71E+12	35,552.6	4.71E+12	35,552.6	4.71E+12
	Sitework totals		54	**3.23E+05**	**5.72E+16**	**1.06E+15**	**3.23E+05**	**1.06E+15**	**3.23E+05**	**1.06E+15**
Structure										
Structure column	Steel	6.97.E+12	80	560.1	3.90E+15	4.88E+13	560.1	4.88E+13	560.1	4.88E+13
Structure beam	Steel(ASTM A992)	6.97.E+12	80	1,373.6	9.57E+15	1.20E+14	1,373.6	1.20E+14	1,373.6	1.20E+14
Lumber frame	2X4, 16" OC	8.80.E+11	80	724.1	6.37E+14	7.96E+12	724.1	7.96E+12	724.1	7.96E+12
Sheathing	1/2" plywood—OSB	2.66.E+12	80	638.9	1.70E+15	2.12E+13	638.9	2.12E+13	638.9	2.12E+13
Exterior block wall	Concrete masonry units	1.81.E+12	80	29,564.4	5.35E+16	6.69E+14	29,564.4	6.69E+14	29,564.4	6.69E+14
Roof rafter	2X10, 24" OC	8.80.E+11	80	1,794.1	1.58E+15	1.97E+13	1,794.1	1.97E+13	1,794.1	1.97E+13
Roof sheathing	1/2" plywood—OSB	2.66.E+12	80	1,416.4	3.77E+15	4.71E+13	1,416.4	4.71E+13	1,416.4	4.71E+13
	Structure totals		80	**3.61E+04**	**7.47E+16**	**9.33E+14**	**3.61E+04**	**9.33E+14**	**3.61E+04**	**9.33E+14**
External envelope										
Groundwork	4" granular fill	1.06.E+10	80	35,500.3	3.76E+14	4.70E+12	35,500.3	4.70E+12	35,500.3	4.70E+12
	0.23" HDPE	8.85.E+12	80	31.9	2.82E+14	3.52E+12	31.9	3.52E+12	31.9	3.52E+12
	4" reinforced concrete	1.81.E+12	80	44,374.5	8.03E+16	1.00E+15	44,374.5	1.00E+15	44,374.5	1.00E+15
	5.4% of concrete	6.97.E+12	80	7,823.6	5.45E+16	6.82E+14	7,823.6	6.82E+14	7,823.6	6.82E+14
	1" exp. polystyrene	7.87.E+12	80	175.0	1.38E+15	1.72E+13	350.1	3.44E+13	507.6	4.99E+13
External brick wall	Brick—common	8.38.E+11	80	15,444.4	1.29E+16	1.62E+14	15,444.4	1.62E+14	15,444.4	1.62E+14

Category	Material									
	HDPE	8.85.E+12	80	15.3	1.35E+14	1.69E+12	15.3	1.69E+12	15.3	1.69E+12
	Fiberglass fiber batt (R-11)	7.87.E+12	80	61.1	4.81E+14	6.01E+12	122.1	1.20E+13	287.9	2.83E+13
	1/2" gypsum wallboard	1.68.E+13	80	1,866.8	3.14E+16	3.92E+14	1,866.8	3.92E+14	1,866.8	3.92E+14
	Acrylic paint	1.50.E+13	80	23.4	3.51E+14	4.39E+12	23.4	4.39E+12	23.4	4.39E+12
External block wall	Cement base stucco	4.50.E+09	40	5,603.6	2.52E+13	6.30E+11	5,603.6	6.30E+11	5,603.6	6.30E+11
	0.1" mortar	3.30.E+12	80	481.2	1.59E+15	1.99E+13	481.2	1.99E+13	481.2	1.99E+13
	HDPE	8.85.E+12	80	20.1	1.78E+14	2.23E+12	20.1	2.23E+12	20.1	2.23E+12
	2" exp. polystyrene	7.87.E+12	80	229.7	1.81E+15	2.26E+13	459.3	4.52E+13	1,102.3	1.08E+14
	1/2" gypsum wallboard	1.68.E+13	80	2,457.3	4.13E+16	5.16E+14	2,457.3	5.16E+14	2,457.3	5.16E+14
	Acrylic paint	1.50.E+13	10	30.8	4.62E+14	4.62E+13	30.8	4.62E+13	30.8	4.62E+13
Roof	Asphalt shingle 1/4"	3.26.E+12	25	1,895.3	6.18E+15	2.47E+14	1,895.3	2.47E+14	1,895.3	2.47E+14
	Fiberglass fiber batt, 2" batt	7.87.E+12	25	34.3	2.70E+14	1.08E+13	68.6	2.16E+13	188.6	5.94E+13
	15lb felt paper	5.20.E+12	25	193.4	1.01E+15	4.02E+13	193.4	4.02E+13	193.4	4.02E+13
Chimney	Brick—common(6lb/unit)	8.38.E+11	80	7,505.0	6.29E+15	7.86E+13	7,505.0	7.86E+13	7,505.0	7.86E+13
	Binder—mortar	3.30.E+12	40	1,468.4	4.85E+15	1.21E+14	1,468.4	1.21E+14	1,468.4	1.21E+14
Windows	Wood	2.40.E+12	80	1,366.4	3.28E+15	4.10E+13	1,366.4	4.10E+13	1,366.4	4.10E+13
	Glass	1.41.E+12	40	1,679.6	2.37E+15	5.92E+13	3,359.3	1.18E+14	5,028.9	1.77E+14
	Acrylic paint	1.50.E+13	10	34.1	5.11E+14	5.11E+13	34.1	5.11E+13	34.1	5.11E+13
Doors	Wood	2.40.E+12	80	848.7	2.04E+15	2.55E+13	848.7	2.55E+13	848.7	2.55E+13
	Glass	1.41.E+12	40	51.1	7.21E+13	1.80E+12	102.2	3.60E+12	154.7	5.45E+12
	AL sash	2.13.E+12	40	689.5	1.47E+15	3.67E+13	689.5	3.67E+13	689.5	3.67E+13
	Acrylic paint	1.50.E+13	10	22.4	3.35E+14	3.35E+13	22.4	3.35E+13	22.4	3.35E+13
	AL	2.13.E+12	40	1,861.5	3.97E+15	9.91E+13	1,861.5	9.91E+13	1,861.5	9.91E+13
	Envelope totals		70	1.32E+05	2.60E+17	3.73E+15	1.34E+05	3.85E+15	1.37E+05	4.04E+15

(Continued)

Item	Specification	UEV (sej/kg)	Life (yr)	Base Raw data (kg)	Base E[m]ergy (sej)	Base Annual e[m]ergy (sej/yr)	Improved Raw data (kg)	Improved Annual e[m]ergy (sej/yr)	Passivhaus NZE Raw data (kg)	Passivhaus NZE Annual e[m]ergy (sej/yr)
Systems: HVAC, electric, plumbing										
Drainage systems	0.03" aluminum alloy	2.13.E+12	20	47.3	1.01E+14	5.04E+12	47.3	5.04E+12	47.3	5.04E+12
	Bathtub, porcelain	3.06.E+12	40	35.4	1.08E+14	2.71E+12	35.4	2.71E+12	35.4	2.71E+12
	Bathtub, porcelain on steel	5.03.E+12	40	42.6	2.14E+14	5.36E+12	42.6	5.36E+12	42.6	5.36E+12
	Shower base, terrazzo	5.40.E+12	40	68.0	3.67E+14	9.19E+12	68.0	9.19E+12	68.0	9.19E+12
	Toilets, TOTO CST764SG	3.06.E+12	30	148.3	4.54E+14	1.51E+13	148.3	1.51E+13	148.3	1.51E+13
	Lavatories	3.06.E+12	30	63.5	1.94E+14	6.48E+12	63.5	6.48E+12	63.5	6.48E+12
Mech. systems	Furnace, Bryant 355AAV	7.76.E+12	25	92.1	7.15E+14	2.86E+13	92.1	2.86E+13	92.1	2.86E+13
	Air-conditioner, Bryant 552A	7.76.E+12	25	76.2	5.91E+14	2.37E+13	76.2	2.37E+13	76.2	2.37E+13
	Hot water heater	7.76.E+12	25	95.3	7.40E+14	2.96E+13	95.3	2.96E+13	95.3	2.96E+13
	Sink	6.97.E+12	25	7.3	5.06E+13	2.02E+12	7.3	2.02E+12	7.3	2.02E+12
Ducts, wire, pipes	Galvanized steel	2.27.E+12	80	672.7	1.53E+15	1.91E+13	672.7	1.91E+13	672.7	1.91E+13
	PVC insulated copper wire	9.90.E+13	80	183.0	1.81E+16	2.26E+14	183.0	2.26E+14	183.0	2.26E+14
	Light bulbs	2.87.E+12	0.33	1.7	4.88E+12	1.48E+13	1.7	1.48E+13	1.7	1.61E+13
	Carbon steel (supply)	3.38.E+12	80	362.6	1.23E+15	1.53E+13	362.6	1.53E+13	362.6	1.53E+13
	PVC (drainage)	5.84.E+12	80	119.1	6.96E+14	8.70E+12	119.1	8.70E+12	119.1	8.70E+12
	Systems totals		61	2.02E+03	2.51E+16	4.12E+14	2.02E+03	4.12E+14	2.02E+03	4.13E+14
Interior and finishes										
Roof ceiling	Ceiling joist 2X10, 24" OC	8.80.E+11	80	1,713.2	1.51E+15	1.88E+13	1,713.2	1.88E+13	1,713.2	1.88E+13
	Gypsum board 5/8"	3.68.E+12	40	2,253.1	8.29E+15	2.07E+14	2,253.1	2.07E+14	2,253.1	2.07E+14
	Acrylic paint	1.50.E+13	10	49.6	7.43E+14	7.43E+13	49.6	7.43E+13	49.6	7.43E+13
Floor ceiling	Ceiling joist 2X10, 24" OC	8.80.E+11	80	1,536.7	1.35E+15	1.69E+13	1,536.7	1.69E+13	1,536.7	1.69E+13
	Gypsum board 5/8"	3.68.E+12	40	2,021.0	7.44E+15	1.86E+14	2,021.0	1.86E+14	2,021.0	1.86E+14
	Acrylic paint	1.50.E+13	10	44.4	6.67E+14	6.67E+13	44.4	6.67E+13	44.4	6.67E+13
Floors	Hardwood flooring 7/8"	2.40.E+12	40	3,230.3	7.75E+15	1.94E+14	3,230.3	1.94E+14	3,230.3	1.94E+14
	Floor truss 24" OC	8.80.E+11	80	1,536.7	1.35E+15	1.69E+13	1,536.7	1.69E+13	1,536.7	1.69E+13

Ground floor	Hardwood flooring 7/8"	2.40.E+12	40	3,413.1	8.19E+15	2.05E+14	3,413.1	2.05E+14	3,413.1	2.05E+14
Interior stair	2X6, wood joist	8.80.E+11	80	22.4	1.97E+13	2.46E+11	22.4	2.46E+11	22.4	2.46E+11
	Hardwood flooring 7/8"	2.40.E+12	40	81.2	1.95E+14	4.87E+12	81.2	4.87E+12	81.2	4.87E+12
	Acrylic paint	1.50.E+13	10	1.1	1.68E+13	1.68E+12	1.1	1.68E+12	1.1	1.68E+12
Walls	2X4, 16" OC	8.80.E+11	80	4,165.5	3.67E+15	4.58E+13	4,165.5	4.58E+13	4,165.5	4.58E+13
	1/2" gypsum wallboard	1.68.E+13	40	10,739.8	1.80E+17	4.51E+15	10,739.8	4.51E+15	10,739.8	4.51E+15
	Acrylic paint	1.50.E+13	10	269.3	4.04E+15	4.04E+14	269.3	4.04E+14	269.3	4.04E+14
	Interior totals		38	**3.11E+04**	**2.26E+17**	**5.95E+15**	**3.11E+04**	**5.95E+15**	**3.11E+04**	**5.95E+15**
Furniture, fixtures, equipment										
Equipment	Washing machine, Frigidaire	4.55.E+12	25	99.8	4.54E+14	1.82E+13	99.8	1.82E+13	99.8	1.82E+13
	Dryer, Frigidaire	4.97.E+12	25	58.5	2.91E+14	1.16E+13	58.5	1.16E+13	58.5	1.16E+13
	Dishwasher, Frigidaire	4.97.E+12	25	35.8	1.78E+14	7.12E+12	35.8	7.12E+12	35.8	7.12E+12
	Wall oven, electric	4.97.E+12	25	63.5	3.16E+14	1.26E+13	63.5	1.26E+13	63.5	1.26E+13
	Cooktop range, gas	4.97.E+12	25	17.7	8.80E+13	3.52E+12	17.7	3.52E+12	17.7	3.52E+12
	Refrigerator, LG LRFC21755	4.97.E+12	25	126.1	6.27E+14	2.51E+13	126.1	2.51E+13	126.1	2.51E+13
	Microwave oven	4.97.E+12	25	13.6	6.76E+13	2.70E+12	13.6	2.70E+12	13.6	2.70E+12
	Computer	7.48.E+13	5	9.1	6.81E+14	1.36E+14	9.1	1.36E+14	9.1	1.36E+14
Fixtures	Kitchen cabinets	1.35.E+12	40	428.4	5.78E+14	1.45E+13	428.4	1.45E+13	428.4	1.45E+13
House contents	Wood	2.40.E+12	25	4,558.7	1.09E+16	4.38E+14	4,558.7	4.38E+14	4,558.7	4.38E+14
	Steel	6.97.E+12	25	1,098.6	7.66E+15	3.06E+14	1,098.6	3.06E+14	1,098.6	3.06E+14
	Plastic	5.84.E+12	25	620.7	3.63E+15	1.45E+14	620.7	1.45E+14	620.7	1.45E+14
	Paper	3.69.E+12	25	3,191.0	1.18E+16	4.71E+14	3,191.0	4.71E+14	3,191.0	4.71E+14
	Textile	5.85.E+12	25	377.8	2.21E+15	8.84E+13	377.8	8.84E+13	377.8	8.84E+13
	Ceramic	3.06.E+12	25	127.0	3.89E+14	1.55E+13	127.0	1.55E+13	127.0	1.55E+13
	Aluminum	2.13.E+12	25	237.3	5.06E+14	2.02E+13	237.3	2.02E+13	237.3	2.02E+13
	FF&E totals		24	**1.11E+04**	**4.04E+16**	**1.72E+15**	**1.11E+04**	**1.72E+15**	**1.11E+04**	**1.72E+15**
	Entire structure			**5.35E+05**	**6.83E+17**	**1.38E+16**	**5.37E+05**	**1.39E+16**	**5.40E+05**	**1.41E+16**

Table B.2: E[m]ergy synthesis summary

Item	Ellis House, base				Ellis House, improved				Ellis House, Passivhaus NZE			
	Data (units/yr)	Unit	UEV (sej/unit)	Solar e[m]ergy (E12 sej/yr)	Data (units/yr)	Unit	UEV (sej/unit)	Solar e[m]ergy (E12 sej/yr)	Data (units/yr)	Unit	UEV (sej/unit)	Solar e[m]ergy (E12 sej/yr)
RENEWABLE INPUTS (R)												
Sunlight	6.70E+12	J	1	7	6.70E+12	J	1	7	6.70E+12	J	1	7
Rain (chemical potential)	2.55E+09	J	3.02E+04	77	2.55E+09	J	3.02E+04	77	2.55E+09	J	3.02E+04	77
Rain (geopotential)	3.66E+06	J	4.70E+04	0.17	3.66E+06	J	4.70E+04	0.17	3.66E+06	J	4.70E+04	0.17
Wind (kinetic energy)	3.30E+10	J	9.83E+02	32	3.30E+10	J	9.83E+02	32	3.30E+10	J	9.83E+02	32
Subtotal				*116*				*116*				*116*
PURCHASED INPUTS (F)												
Depreciated assets			(yrs)				(yrs)				(yrs)	
Building construction	6.83E+17	sej	n/a	13,804	6.90E+17	sej	n/a	13,922	7.01E+17	sej	n/a	14,117
Cars	1.46E+16	sej	14	1,045	1.46E+16	sej	14	1,045	0.00E+00	sej	14	0
Subtotal				*14,850*				*14,967*				*14,117*
Material services												
Water	5.57E+05	L	1.22E+09	680	1.53E+05	L	1.22E+09	187	1.53E+05	L	1.22E+09	187
Wastewater	3.83E+05	L	3.54E+09	1,356	1.05E+05	L	3.54E+09	373	1.05E+05	L	3.54E+09	373
Food	1.53E+10	J	7.50E+05	11,462	1.53E+10	J	7.50E+05	11,462	1.53E+10	J	1.60E+05	2,445
Non-durable supplies	1.78E+04	$	2.50E+12	44,429	1.78E+04	$	2.50E+12	44,429	8.89E+03	$	2.50E+12	22,214
Solid waste	2.93E+03	kg	2.97E+11	871	1.47E+03	kg	2.97E+11	436	1.47E+03	kg	2.97E+11	436
Fertilizer, P	3.92E+03	g	3.70E+10	145	0.00E+00	g	3.70E+10	0	0.00E+00	g	3.70E+10	0
Fertilizer, N	1.16E+04	g	4.05E+10	470	0.00E+00	g	4.05E+10	0	0.00E+00	g	4.05E+10	0
Subtotal				*59,413*				*56,886*				*25,655*

Concentrated power—utilities									
Natural gas	1.28E+11	J	1.78E+05	22,855	4.97E+10	J	1.78E+05	8,855	0.00E+00	J	1.78E+05	0
Electricity	6.81E+10	J	3.97E+05	27,045	2.64E+10	J	3.97E+05	10,479	5.65E+10	J	1.45E+05	8,193
Solar thermal									1.25E+10	J	3.62E+04	451
Subtotal				*49,900*				*19,334*				*8,193*
Location and transportation												
Location (annual property tax)	9.00E+03	$	2.50E+12	22,500	9.00E+03	$	2.50E+12	22,500	9.00E+03	$	2.50E+12	22,500
Commuting, car (fuel)	6.16E+10	J	1.87E+05	11,515	3.08E+10	J	1.87E+05	5,758	0.00E+00	J	1.87E+05	0
Commuting, train (electricity)	0.00E+00	J	3.97E+05	0	3.44E+09	J	3.97E+05	1364.6061	7.33E+09	J	3.97E+05	2,908
Subtotal				*34,015*				*29,622*				*25,408*
Labor												
Labor, homeowner	8.57E+07	J	3.92E+07	3,362	1.12E+08	J	3.92E+07	4,403	1.12E+08	J	3.92E+07	4,403
Subtotal				*3,362*				*4,403*				*4,403*
Subtotal purchased inputs, F				*161,540*				*125,212*				*77,776*
		Total e(m)ergy, U		161,656		Total e(m)ergy, U		125,329		Total e(m)ergy, U		77,892
IMPORTS												
Household income	1.18E+05	$	2.50E+12	293,990	1.18E+05	$	2.50E+12	293,990	1.18E+05	$	2.50E+12	293,990
Subtotal imports				*293,990*				*293,990*				*293,990*
EXPORTS												
Federal tax	3.29E+04	$	2.50E+12	82,317	3.29E+04	$	2.50E+12	82,317	3.29E+04	$	2.50E+12	82,317
State tax	3.65E+03	$	2.50E+12	9,114	3.65E+03	$	2.50E+12	9,114	3.65E+03	$	2.50E+12	9,114
Subtotal exports				*91,431*				*91,431*		*Subtotal exports*		*91,431*
NET INCOME		Imports − exports		202,559		Imports − exports		202,559		Imports − exports		202,559

Table B.3: E[m]ergy synthesis summary, organized by site, shelter, and setting

	Ellis House, base				Ellis House, improved				Ellis House, Passivhaus NZE			
Item	Data (units/yr)	Unit	UEV (sej/unit)	Solar e[m]ergy (E12 sej/yr)	Data (units/yr)	Unit	UEV (sej/unit)	Solar e[m]ergy (E12 sej/yr)	Data (units/yr)	Unit	UEV (sej/unit)	Solar e[m]ergy (E12 sej/yr)
Site												
Renewable inputs												
Sunlight	6.70E+12	J	1	7	6.70E+12	J	1	7	6.70E+12	J	1	7
Rain (chemical potential)	2.55E+09	J	3.02E+04	77	2.55E+09	J	3.02E+04	77	2.55E+09	J	3.02E+04	77
Rain (geopotential)	3.66E+06	J	4.70E+04	0.17	3.66E+06	J	4.70E+04	0.17	3.66E+06	J	4.70E+04	0.17
Wind (kinetic energy)	3.30E+10	J	9.83E+02	32	3.30E+10	J	9.83E+02	32	3.30E+10	J	9.83E+02	32
Subtotal				*116*				*116*				*116*
Landscape												
Sitework (depreciated)	5.98E+03	kg	1.77E+11	1,060	5.98E+03	kg	1.77E+11	1,060	5.98E+03	kg	1.77E+11	1,060
Water, outdoor	1.74E+05	L	1.22E+09	212	4.79E+04	L	1.22E+09	58	4.79E+04	L	1.22E+09	58
Fertilizer, P	3.92E+03	g	3.70E+10	145	0.00E+00	g	3.70E+10	0	0.00E+00	g	3.70E+10	0
Fertilizer, N	1.16E+04	g	4.05E+10	470	0.00E+00	g	4.05E+10	0	0.00E+00	g	4.05E+10	0
Labor, homeowner	8.57E+07	J	3.92E+07	3,362	8.57E+07	J	3.92E+07	3,362	8.57E+07	J	3.92E+07	3,362
Subtotal				*5,250*				*4,481*				*4,481*
Location and transportation												
Location (property tax)	9.00E+03	$	2.50E+12	22,500	9.00E+03	$	2.50E+12	22,500	9.00E+03	$	2.50E+12	22,500
Commuting, car (fuel)	6.16E+10	J	1.87E+05	11,515	3.08E+10	J	1.87E+05	5,758	0.00E+00	J	1.87E+05	0
Commuting, train (electric)	0.00E+00	J	4.81E+05	0	3.44E+09	J	3.97E+05	1,365	7.33E+09	J	3.97E+05	2,908
Cars (depreciated)	1.46E+16	sej	14	1,045	1.46E+16	sej	14	1,045	0.00E+00	sej	14	0
Subtotal				*35,060*				*30,667*				*25,408*
Subtotal, site				*40,427*				*35,265*				*30,006*
Shelter												
Building construction, shelter			Life (yrs)				Life (yrs)				Life (yrs)	
Structure (deprec.)	7.47E+16	sej	80	933	7.47E+16	sej	80	933	7.47E+16	sej	80	933
External envelope (deprec.)	2.60E+17	sej	70	3,730	2.67E+17	sej	69	3,848	2.77E+17	sej	69	4,042
Systems (prorated, deprec.)	1.26E+16	sej	61	206	1.26E+16	sej	61	206	1.26E+16	sej	61	206
Labor, homeowner	0.00E+00	J	3.92E+07	0	2.65E+07	J	3.92E+07	1,041	2.65E+07	J	3.92E+07	1,041
Subtotal				*4,870*				*6,028*				*6,222*
Building conditioning—utilities												
Heating	9.12E+10	J	1.78E+05	16,228	3.53E+10	J	1.78E+05	6,288	2.94E+10	J	1.45E+05	4,265
Cooling	1.88E+10	J	3.97E+05	7,465	7.29E+09	J	3.97E+05	2,892	6.07E+09	J	1.45E+05	880

Item	Value	Unit	Transformity	Life (yrs)	Result	Value	Unit	Transformity	Life (yrs)	Result	Value	Unit	Transformity	Life (yrs)	Result
Ventilation	0.00E+00	J	3.97E+05		0	0.00E+00	J	3.97E+05		0	1.26E+09	J	1.45E+05		183
Illumination	1.20E+10	J	3.97E+05		4,767	4.65E+09	J	3.97E+05		1,847	4.47E+09	J	1.45E+05		648
Subtotal					**4,767**					**1,847**					
Subtotal, shelter					**28,460**					**11,027**					**5,976**
					33,330					**17,055**					**12,198**
Setting															
Building construction, setting															
Interiors and finishes (deprec.)	2.26E+17	sej		38	5,953	2.26E+17	sej		38	5,953	2.26E+17	sej		38	5,953
Furniture, fixt., equip. (deprec.)	4.04E+16	sej		24	1,716	4.04E+16	sej		24	1,716	4.04E+16	sej		24	1,716
Systems (prorated deprec.)	1.26E+16	sej		61	206	1.26E+16	sej		61	206	1.26E+16	sej		61	206
Subtotal					**7,874**					**7,874**					**7,874**
Kitchen, material services															
Water	4.22E+04	L	1.22E+09		51	1.16E+04	L	1.22E+09		14	1.16E+04	L	1.22E+09		14
Wastewater	4.22E+04	L	3.54E+09		149	1.16E+04	L	3.54E+09		41	1.16E+04	L	3.54E+09		41
Water—heating	3.69E+09	J	1.78E+05		656	1.43E+09	J	1.78E+05		254	1.37E+09	J	3.62E+04		50
Food	1.53E+10	J	7.50E+05		11,462	1.53E+10	J	7.50E+05		11,462	1.53E+10	J	1.60E+05		2,445
Food—refrigeration	7.93E+09	J	3.97E+05		3,146	3.07E+09	J	3.97E+05		1,219	2.95E+09	J	1.45E+05		428
Food—cooking, gas	3.74E+09	J	1.78E+05		665	1.45E+09	J	1.78E+05		258	0.00E+00	J	1.78E+05		0
Food—cooking, electricity	3.74E+09	J	3.97E+05		1,484	1.45E+09	J	3.97E+05		575	2.78E+09	J	1.45E+05		404
Solid waste	1.47E+03	kg	2.97E+11		436	7.33E+02	kg	2.97E+11		218	7.33E+02	kg	2.97E+11		218
Subtotal					**18,050**					**14,041**					**3,599**
Bathroom, material services															
Water	2.42E+05	L	1.22E+09		295	6.65E+04	L	1.22E+09		81	6.65E+04	L	1.22E+09		81
Wastewater	2.42E+05	L	3.54E+09		856	6.65E+04	L	3.54E+09		235	6.65E+04	L	3.54E+09		235
Water—heating	2.12E+10	J	1.78E+05		3,765	8.20E+09	J	1.78E+05		1,459	7.88E+09	J	3.62E+04		285
Subtotal					**4,917**					**1,775**					**602**
Laundry, material services															
Water	9.89E+04	L	1.22E+09		121	2.72E+04	L	1.22E+09		33	2.72E+04	L	1.22E+09		33
Wastewater	9.89E+04	L	3.54E+09		350	2.72E+04	L	3.54E+09		96	2.72E+04	L	3.54E+09		96
Water—heating	8.65E+09	J	1.78E+05		1,540	3.35E+09	J	1.78E+05		597	3.22E+09	J	3.62E+04		117
Electricity—wet cleaning	6.65E+09	J	3.97E+05		2,638	2.58E+09	J	3.97E+05		1,022	2.47E+09	J	1.45E+05		359
Subtotal					**4,649**					**1,748**					**605**
Work and entertainment, material services															
Non-durable supplies	1.78E+04	$	2.50E+12		44,429	1.78E+04	$	2.50E+12		44,429	8.89E+03	$	2.50E+12		22,214
Solid waste	1.47E+03	kg	2.97E+11		436	7.33E+02	kg	2.97E+11		218	7.33E+02	kg	2.97E+11		218
Electricity—electronics	1.90E+10	J	3.97E+05		7,546	7.37E+09	J	3.97E+05		2,924	7.08E+09	J	1.45E+05		1,026
Subtotal					**52,410**					**47,570**					**23,459**
Subtotal, setting					**87,900**					**73,009**					**36,140**
Total emlergy					**161,656**					**125,329**					**78,344**

Appendix B

Inputs, sources, and data for e[m]ergy synthesis

1. Sunlight

Equations

> Annual energy = (Average total annual insolation) ⋆ (Site area)
> Annual energy (J/yr) = (Wh/yr/m^2) ⋆ (3600 J/Wh) ⋆ (m^2)

Definitions

Average total annual insolation (Wh/yr/m^2): a user input, obtained from TMY3 weather data. This should be determined for the specific location of the structure. 5.29E+9 J/m^2/yr used for the Ellis House location.
Site area (m^2): the area of the property in square meters (B.19).

Transformity

1 Joule = 1 sej

(By definition 1 Joule from sunlight equals 1 solar equivalent Joule.)
[Source: GHI (global horizontal irradiance) – TMY3 data sets, NREL 2005]

2. Rain (chemical)

Equations

> Chemical potential energy of rain = (Annual rainfall rate) ⋆ (Site area) ⋆ (Gibbs' free energy of water) ⋆ (Runoff coefficient)
>
> Chemical potential energy of rain (J/yr) = (m/yr) ⋆ (m^2) ⋆ (10^6 g/m^3) ⋆ (4.72 J/g) ⋆ (1-Runoff coefficient)

Definitions

Annual rainfall rate (m/yr): a user input obtained from TMY3 weather data. This should be determined for the specific location of the structure. 1.0667 m/yr used for the Ellis House location.

Site area (m^2): the area of the property in square meters. (B.19).

Gibbs' free energy of water (J/g): the chemical energy associated with water that can be used to do useful work, given in Joules per gram. Calculated as 4.72 J/g using the equation:

(8.314 J/mole/degree K) ★ (287K) ★ (18g/mole) ★ ln(999990ppm/965000ppm)

Runoff coefficient, %: A user input; the percentage of rainfall that leaves the site as runoff

Transformity

1 J = 3.02E+4 sej

[Source: Formula for Gibbs' free energy of rain – Lu et al. 2007]

3. Rain (geopotential)

Equations

Geopotential energy of rain = (Annual rainfall rate) ★ (Footprint) ★ (Runoff rate) ★ (Density of water) ★ (Average elevation) ★ (Gravity)

Geopotential energy of rain (J/yr) = (m/yr) ★ (m^2) ★ (%) ★ (1000 kg/m^3) ★ (m) ★ (9.8 m/s^2)

Definitions

Annual rainfall rate (m/yr): a user input obtained from TMY3 weather data. This should be determined for the specific location of the structure. 1.0668 m/yr used for the Ellis House.

Footprint (m^2): the area of the roof in square meters (B.19).

Runoff rate (%): a user input; the percentage of rainfall that leaves the roof as runoff. This is typically 100% for rooftops without rain storage.

Density of water (1000 kg/m^3): a constant; the weight of a cubic meter of water in kilograms.

Average elevation (m): a user input; the average height of the roof at gutters. 2m used for the Ellis House.

Appendix B

Gravity (9.8 m/s²): a constant; the acceleration due to the force of Earth's gravity near its surface.

Transformity

1 J = 4.70E+4 sej

[Source: Odum 2000, Folio #1]

4. Wind (kinetic energy)

Equations

> Kinetic energy of wind = (Site area) ★ (Air density) ★ (Drag coefficient) ★ (Geostrophic velocity)³ ★ (Seconds per year)
> Kinetic energy of wind (J/yr) = (m²) ★ (1.25 kg/m³) ★ (Drag coefficient) ★ (m/s)³ ★ (31,700,000 s/yr)

Definitions

Site area (m²): the area of the property in square meters (B.19).
Air density (1.25 kg/m³): a constant, for most elevations, should only be revised for higher altitudes.
Drag coefficient: a unit-less constant dependent on the vegetation and structures present on the site that would impede wind flow. This value should be determined by the user for each site based on existing conditions. 1.87E-3 used for the Ellis House site, 1.00E-3 for open water (Garrat 1977).
Geostrophic velocity (m/s): a user input; the average theoretical wind speed resulting from atmospheric conditions without drag and other real-world conditions that interfere.
Seconds per year (31,700,000 s/yr): a constant to convert to annual values.

Transformity

1 J = 9.83E+2 sej

[Source: Formula for kinetic energy of wind, Transformity for kinetic energy of wind – Odum 2000, Folio #1]

Appendix B

5. Building construction (depreciated)

Equations

> Building annual depreciation = (Weight of material) * (UEV) / (Lifespan)
>
> Building annual depreciation (sej/yr) = (kg) * (sej/kg) / (yrs)

The equation is used for each material in the structure and the results summed to produce an sej/yr value for the entire building. This calculation occurs entirely on the building construction worksheet, described in Table B.1 of this appendix, and this result is automatically updated on the inputs worksheet.

Definitions

Weight of material (kg): calculated from user inputs about the building construction.
Useful life (yrs): calculated from user inputs about the building construction.

Transformity

$1 \text{ J} = X \text{ sej}$

(There is no single transformity value, instead this equation is used for each material, all of which have their own calculated weights and referenced UEV.)
[Source: See Table B.1]

6. Car (depreciated)

Equations

> Car annual depreciation = (Weight per car) * (UEV) / (Lifespan)
>
> Car annual depreciation (sej/yr) = (kg/car) * (sej/kg) / (yrs)

The calculation used assumes that all cars used are relatively similar and have the same weight and transformity. This is not necessarily the case and this equation should be performed separately for any significantly different vehicles and the results summed to provide the total sej/yr for the group of vehicles.

Appendix B

Definitions

Weight per car (kg): a user input describing the weight of the car(s) in kilograms. This should be looked up by the user for the specific make and model of vehicles at the property or average values from statistical databases may be used for theoretical simulations. 1361 kg used for the Ellis House cars.

UEV (sej/kg): this value is calculated by combining averaging the UEV of each of the major materials used in the construction of the car (steel, aluminum, plastic, rubber, and glass). This average is weighted by the percentage of the car that is made up of each material type, described in Table B.4.

Lifespan (yrs): a user input describing the number of years the vehicle is expected to operate.

Transformity

$1 J = X$ sej

(There is no single transformity value; instead this is calculated for each vehicle type based on the transformities of the major materials used in the vehicle, weighted by the percentage of the car they account for. This calculation occurs on the house contents worksheet of this calculator and is summarized in Table B.4.)

[Source: Percent of car, by material – Consumer Reports 2014. See Table B.4]

Table B.4: Automobile composition, weight, and sej

		sej/kg	%*sej/kg
Steel	62.10%	4.13E+12	2.56E+12
Aluminum	11.50%	1.25E+13	1.44E+12
Plastic	15.50%	5.85E+12	9.07E+11
Rubber	9.60%	4.3E+12	4.13E+11
Glass	2.30%	2.16E+12	4.97E+10
		Total sej/kg	5.37E+12

7. Water

The water input is fairly simple but the breakdown among uses is used to derive a number of different figures used to determine what sections or purposes of a

Appendix B

structure are accountable for the e[m]ergy of the entire structure. This breakdown is used heavily on the summary charts and the details can be found there for all three versions of the Ellis House.

Equations

Annual consumption of water = (Number of people) * (Days per year) * (Liters of water per person each day)

Annual consumption of water (L/yr) = (# people) * (365 days/yr) * (L/day per capita)

Definitions

of people (#): user input, the number of people occupying the structure. Four people assumed for the Ellis House.

Days/year (#): a constant.

L/day per capita (L/day): a user input describing how much water a person uses in the structure each day. In the US residential sector, the value of 381.6 L/day may be used, as it was derived from a US EPA residential water use survey, but for other regions or structures the L/day per capita of water usage should be determined.

Transformity

1 J = 1.22E+9 sej

(This value will vary depending on the regional water source.)
[Source: Annual consumption of water – AWWARF 1999. Transformity of potable water – Buenfil 2000]

8. Wastewater

Equations

Volume wastewater = (Annual consumption of water) * (Percent of water used indoors)

Volume wastewater (L/yr) = (L/yr) * (%)

Appendix B

Definitions

Annual consumption of water (L/Yr): calculated on the inputs worksheet under water, described in section B1.7. This value automatically updates here.

% of water used indoors (%): for residences in the US the rate of 68.7% may be used in most instances. Rates for other regions or structure types will need to be determined by the user.

Transformity

1 J = 3.54E+9 sej

(This value may vary depending on how the wastewater is treated.)
[Source: % of water used that becomes wastewater – US EPA Residential Water Use Survey 1999. Transformity of wastewater – Bjorklund 2001]

9. Food

Equations

> Food consumption = (Number of people) ★ (Calories consumed each day per capita) ★ (Days per year) ★ (Joules per calorie)
>
> Food consumption (J) = (# people) ★ (2,500 Cal/day/person) ★(365 days/yr) ★ (4,187 J/Cal)

Definitions

# of people (#): a user input, the number of people eating in the structure. Four people assumed for the Ellis House.

Calories/day per capita (Cal): a user input, the average daily caloric intake of an individual within the structure. For residences in the US, 2,500 cal is typical.

Days per year (365 days/yr): a constant.

Joules per calorie (4,187 J/Cal): a constant.

Transformity

1 J = 7.50E+5 sej

[Source: Transformity of food – Emergydatabase.com, Johansson et al. 2000]

Appendix B

10. Supplies

Equations

Annual consumption = (0.96 ★ Household income) ★ (Percent of income for non-durables)

Annual consumption ($) = (0.96 ★ $) ★ (%)

Definitions

Household income ($): this is a user input entered into a different section of this worksheet and it is referenced here. See Section B.17.

Percent of income for non-durables (%): a user input, this value should represent the actual, or estimated, percentage of the household income that is expended on non-durable household goods, excluding food and beverage items, as these are accounted for under B.9. For the typical US family, the Bureau of Labor Statistics reports that this value is 15.74%, although this value should be updated to reflect any information pertinent to a specific property.

Transformity

1 $ = 2.50E+12 sej

(This is the typical transformity assigned to capital.)
[Source: Average % income spent on non-durable goods – Bureau of Labor Statistics 2013. Transformity of money – NEAD, 2012]

11. Solid waste

Equations

Solid waste = (Number of people) ★ (Annual waste per capita)
Solid waste (kg) = (# people) ★ (kg/person/yr)

Definitions

Number of people (#): a user input, the number of people producing waste at the property. Four people assumed to be producing solid waste in the Ellis House.

Appendix B

Annual waste per capita (kg/person/yr): a user input, the estimated solid waste produced by an individual using the property over a year.

Kitchen proportion (%): a user input, represents the proportion of the solid waste that is produced in the kitchen as compared to elsewhere in the house. While this variable is not referenced in the above equation, it is used in the summary hierarchy worksheet when dividing emergy between different household functions.

Transformity

1 kg = 2.97E+11 sej

[Source: Transformity of solid waste – Brown 2001]

12. Utilities

The usage of utilities and the resultant e[m]ergy associated with a structure is simple on the surface but becomes more nuanced when trying to analyze the components and purposes of the structure and how that emergy is divided between them for analysis on the summary pages.

The comparison of the summary charts shows how the total natural gas, electricity, and solar thermal energy were distributed in each version of the house.

Equations

None

Definitions

Annual consumption, natural gas (J): this value is based on the end use survey.

Annual consumption, electricity (J): this value is based on the end use survey.

Annual consumption, heating oil (J): this value is based on the end use survey.

Annual consumption, solar thermal (J): this value is based on the end use survey.

Appendix B

Transformity

1 J natural gas = 1.78E+5 sej
1 J electricity = 3.97E+5 sej
1 J heating oil = 1.81E+5 sej
1 J solar thermal = 3.63E+4 sej
1 J photovoltaic = 1.45E+5 sej

[Source: Transformities of Natural Gas and Heating Oil – Brown et al. 2011. Transformity for Solar Thermal – Paoli 2008. Transformity of photovoltaic, Brown et al. 2012. Transformity of Electricity – derived from EIA 2010 Annual Energy Report, which lists % breakdown of energy sources for electricity and the transformities for electricity from these sources. These are listed in Table B.5.]

Table B.5: Transformity of electricity based on 2010 EIA Annual Energy Report

Generation	% mix	sej/J	(%)*(sej/J)	Source
Coal	47.42	3.73E+05	1.77E+05	Brown 2012
Natural gas	19.40	6.58E+05	1.28E+05	Hayha 2011; Brown 2012
Oil	0.95	5.69E+05	5.41E+03	Brown 2012
Nuclear	20.83	3.36E+05	7.00E+04	Odum 1996; Hayha 2011
Hydro	6.27	1.12E+05	7.02E+03	Brown 2004; Hayha 2011
Wind	2.28	1.10E+05	2.51E+03	Brown 2004; Hayha 2011
Wood	0.86	1.91E+05	1.64E+03	Odum 1996
Geothermal	0.37	1.47E+05	5.44E+02	Brown 2002
Biomass	0.69	4.86E+05	3.36E+03	Odum 1996
Solar PV	0.03	1.45E+05	4.35E+01	Brown 2012
Other	0.90	1.90E+05	1.71E+03	
	Weighted average		**3.97E+05**	sej/j

13. Labor, homeowner

Equations

Labor, site = (Hours worked by occupants per year) * (Calories consumed per day) * (Joules per calorie)/(Hours per workday)

Appendix B

Labor, site (J) = (hr/yr) ∗ (2,500 Cal/day) ∗ (4,186 J/Cal)/(8 hr/day)
Labor, shelter = (Hours worked by occupants per year) ∗ (Calories consumed per day) ∗ (Joules per calorie)/(Hours per workday)
Labor, shelter (J) = (hr/yr) ∗ (2,500 Cal/day) ∗ (4,186 J/Cal)/(8 hr/day)

Definitions

Hours worked by occupants per year (hr/yr): a user input, this value represents the hours worked by the occupants each year on the property on aspects of the property relating to site or shelter. Assumes 65.5 hrs worked by the owner for site labor in all three versions. Assumes 0 hrs of labor for shelter in the base version, but 20.3 hrs of labor for shelter in the improved and Passivhaus versions.

Calories consumed per day (Cal/day): a constant, represents the average caloric intake of an individual in the US. This value should be modified for regions or cultures where this is not representative for that population.

Joules per calorie (J/Cal): a constant.

Hours per workday (hr/day): a constant, this value should be modified for regions or cultures where this is not representative for that population.

Transformity

1 J = 3.92E+7 sej

This is derived from the equation:

[(Income per adult ∗ sej/$) + (sej of food)]/(Joules of food)

[Source: Transformity of labor – Brandt-Williams 2002]

14. Location

Equations

None

Definitions

Annual property tax ($): a user input, the annual taxes that are collected on the property.

Appendix B

Transformity

1 $ = 2.50E+12 sej

[Source: Transformity of money – NEAD 2012]

15. Commuting

Equations

Commuting, car = [(Number of commuters) * (Length of commute) * (Day per year commuting) / (Miles per gallon)] * (Btus per gallon) * (Joules per Btu)

Commuting, car (J) = [(# commuters) * (mi/day) * (days/yr) / (mi/gal)] * (114,000 Btu/gal) * (1,055 J/Btu)

Commuting, train = (Number of commuters) * (Length of commute) * (Day per year commuting) * (Kilowatt hours per mile) * (Joules per kilowatt hour)

Commuting, train (J) = (# commuters) * (mi/day) * (days/yr) * (0.1447 kWh/mi) * (3,600,000 J/kWh)

If multiple people are commuting in either cars or trains then they should be grouped together in the same equation only if the commutes are similar in miles, days/year, and fuel efficiency. However, if, for example, two people from a property commute by car but one travels 30 miles each day in an SUV 200 days a year and the other travels 10 miles each day in a hybrid compact 240 days a year, then the equation should be used separately for each single commuter and the results summed.

Definitions

Number of commuters (#): a user input, the number of people who commute from the property on a regular basis by either car or train, or both. Enter the appropriate value for each type of commuting. In the base version of the Ellis House, two people commute by car; in the improved version, one person

Appendix B

commutes by car and one by train; and in the *Passivhaus* version, two people commute by train.

Length of commute (mi/day): a user input, the round trip miles traveled by a commuter each day for either car or train; 32 mi used as commute length for the Ellis House.

Days per year commuting (days/yr): a user input, the number of days this means of commuting is utilized each year; 220 days/yr used for all three versions of the Ellis House.

Miles per gallon (mi/gal): a user input, the fuel economy of the vehicle used to commute. If the specific MPG of a vehicle is know then this should be used; otherwise the default value of 27.5 may be used.

Btus per gallon (Btu/gal): a constant.

Joules per Btu (J/Btu): a constant.

Kilowatt hours per mile (kWh/mi): a constant based on regional rail efficiency. If specific values are known for the region of the property being evaluated then these should be used.

Joules per kilowatt hour (J/kWh): a constant.

Transformity

1 J, Gasoline = 1.87E+5 sej
1 J, Electric = 3.97E+5 sej

[Source: Transformity of electricity, see Table B.5. Transformity of gasoline – Brown et al., 2011]

16. Fertilizer

Equations

Phosphate = (Grams of phosphate used per square meter) ★ (Site area − footprint)

Phosphate (g) = (g/m^2, P) ★ (m^2, prop − m^2, struc)

Nitrogen = (Grams of nitrogen used per square meter) ★ (Site area − footprint)

Nitrogen (g) = (g/m^2, N) ★ (m^2, prop − m^2, struc)

Appendix B

Definitions

Grams used per square meter (g/m²): a used input, the amount of active ingredient (phosphate or nitrogen) that is applied per square meter of outdoor area. It is important to determine the grams of active ingredient, rather than total weight of fertilizer used. 3.59 g/m² used for the base version of the Ellis House for both phosphate and nitrogen. Use of compost in the improved and *Passivhaus* versions of the Ellis House cause this to drop to 0 g/m².

Site area (m²): a user input, see B.19.

Footprint (m²): a user input, see B.19.

Transformity

1 g, Phosphate = 3.7E+10 sej
1 g, Nitrogen = 4.05E+10 sej

[Source: Transformity of phosphate and nitrogen – Odum 2000, Folio #1]

17. Annual household income

Equations

None

Definitions

Household income ($): a user input, the annual income earned by the residents of the property. Median income for location, $118,000 used as the household income for all three versions of the Ellis House.

Transformity

$1 = 2.50E+12 sej

[Source: Median income - U.S. Census Bureau 2010. Transformity of money – NEAD 2012]

Appendix B

18. Annual income taxes

Equations

    Federal tax = Household income ⋆ Federal tax rate

    Federal tax ($) = ($) ⋆ (%)

    State tax = Household income ⋆ State tax rate

    State tax ($) = ($) ⋆(%)

Definitions

Household income ($): the income earned by the household inhabitants. Taken from B.17.

Federal tax rate (%): the overall tax rate on the earned income levied by the federal government. Assumed to be 28% for all three versions of the Ellis House.

State tax rate (%): the overall tax rate on the earned income levied by the state government. Assumed to be 3% for all three versions of the Ellis House.

Transformity

$1 = 2.50E+12 sej

[Source: Transformity of money – NEAD 2012]

19. Dimensions

Site area (m^2): the total area of the property.
Floor area (m^2): the total internal area of any structures. Includes multiple floors.
Footprint (m^2): the total area of the property covered by a structure.

Bibliography

AWWARF, American Water Works Associations Research Foundation. 1999. *Residential End Uses of Water*. Denver, CO: AWWARF.

Bjorklund, Johanna, Ulrika Geber, and Torbjorn Rydberg. 2001. "Emergy analysis of municipal wastewater treatment and generation of electricity by digestion of sewage sludge." *Resources Conservation & Recycling* 31: 293–316.

Brandt-Williams, Sherry L. 2002. *Handbook of Emergy Evaluation, Folio #4, Emergy of Florida Agriculture*. Gainesville, FL: Center for Environmental Policy, University of Florida.

Brown, Mark T., and Vorasun Buranakarn. 2001. "Emergy evaluation of material cycles and recycle options." *EMERGY SYNTHESIS 1: Theory and Applications of the Emergy Methodology*, Gainesville, FL: University of Florida.

Brown, Mark T., Gaetano Protano, and Sergio Ulgiati. 2011. "Assessing geobiosphere work of generating global reserves of coal, crude oil, and natural gas." *Ecological Modelling* 222:879–887.

Brown, Mark T., Marco Raugei, and Sergio Ulgiati. 2012. "On boundaries and 'investments' in Emergy Synthesis and LCA: A case study on thermal vs. photovoltaic electricity." *Ecological Indicators* 15:227–235.

Brown, Mark T, and Sherry L. Brandt-Williams. 2001. *Handbook of Emergy Evaluation, Folio #3, Emergy of Ecosystems*. Gainesville, FL: Center for Environmental Policy, University of Florida.

Bureau of Labor Statistics. 2013. *Consumer Expenditures in 2012*. In *BLS Reports*. Washington, DC: U. S. Bureau of Labor Statistics.

Consumer Reports. 2014. *Cars*. www.consumerreports.org (accessed July, 2014).

Garrat, J.R. 1977. "Review of drag coefficients over oceans and continents." *Monthly Weather Review* 105:915–929.

Johansson, Susanne, Steven Doherty, and Torbjorn Rydberg. 2000. "Sweden Food System Analysis." *EMERGY SYNTHESIS 1: Theory and Applications of the Emergy Methodology*, Gainesville, FL: University of Florida.

Lu, Hongfang, Daniel E. Campbell, Jie Chen, Pei Qin, and Hai Ren. 2007. "Conservation and Economic Vitality of Nature Reserves: An Emergy Evaluation of the Yancheng Biosphere Reserve." *Biological Conservation* 139:415–438.

NEAD, *National Environmental Accounting Database*. 2012. Gainesville, FL: Center for Environmental Policy, University of Florida. www.cep.ees.ufl.edu/nead/.

NREL, National Renewable Energy Laboratory. 2005. *National Solar Radiation Data Base, 1991–2005 Update: Typical Meteorological Year 3*. rredc.nrel.gov/tmy3/.

Odum, H. T., Mark T. Brown, and Sherry L. Brandt-Williams. 2000. *Handbook of Emergy Evaluation, Folio #1, Introduction and Global Budget*. Gainesville, FL: Center for Environmental Policy, University of Florida.

Paoli, Chiara, and Paolo Vassallo. 2008. "Solar power: an approach to transformity evaluation." *Ecological Engineering* 34:191–206.

U.S. Census Bureau. *Median Income, 2010*. Prepared by Social Explorer (accessed July 27 2014).

Buenfil, Andres. 2001. "Emergy Evaluation of Water." PhD Dissertation. Environmental Engineering Sciences, University of Florida.

Index

Ábalos, I. 207
Abel, T. 127, 187–8
Abu Dhabi 210
abundance 21, 40, 108, 162, 184–5, 188, 191–2, 201
accounting systems 5, 7, 22, 27, 66–7; e[m]ergy synthesis 220; maximum power 31, 41, 43, 54; narratives 201, 205–6, 208; setting 133, 137, 139–40, 142, 144, 150, 154; shelter 70, 72–6, 102; site 162, 171, 183
active glass walls 9, 81, 200
activists 8, 40, 203
Adams, R.N. 17–18, 48
adaptation 22, 48, 50–2, 75, 78–9, 162, 191, 202–3, 208
agriculture 4, 21, 33–5, 118, 135; narratives 209; setting 142; site 161–4, 166, 172–5, 189, 191
air gaps 129
air-conditioning 10, 12, 14, 65, 81; narratives 206; shelter 88, 91, 95–7, 99–100, 108, 111
all-glass walls 91, 110, 201, 206
American Society of Heating Refrigerating and Air-Conditioning Engineers (ASHRAE) 22
American Woman's Home 73
Americas 9, 191
Amish 191

anthropologists 127, 139, 187
aquaculture 201
aquifers 130, 133
architects 49, 61, 66, 73, 81; narratives 203, 205; shelter 95; thermodynamic principles 210, 212
architectural theory 62
Architecture and Energy 29
Architecture of the Well-tempered Environment 14
Ark 201
ascendency index 47
Athena Institute 30
Auerbach, F. 170
avant-garde 72
average mutual information 51
Ayres, R. 40, 152

balance point temperature 113
Banham, R. 14, 69–70, 81–2, 89–90, 95, 98, 110, 206
Bataille, G. 21, 31, 52, 135, 185–6
bathing 126–7, 129, 132, 155
Beecher, C. 73
Beijing 8, 164, 174–5
Bell Labs 32
bioclimatic charts 81–6
biodegradability 132
bioenergetics 31–4
biofilters 102, 207

Index

biofuels 142, 174
biologists 62, 72
biomass 51–2, 142
biophilia 12, 207
bioshelters 201
biosphere 5, 21, 27, 44, 62; maximum power 53; setting 130, 137, 143, 151; shelter 100–2, 117; site 185, 192; thermodynamic principles 212
Biosphere II 100
black water 132
Boltzmann, L. 32, 34, 46–7
Bonaire 187–8
bottled water 130, 132
Brand, S. 73
Braungart, M. 78, 137, 139
Brazil 173
Brown, M.T. 45, 76, 78, 171
Buenfil, A. 130
building style 3, 6–7, 15, 18, 26–7; aspects 61–8; maximum power 24, 36, 48–9, 53–5; narratives 199–200, 203–5; setting 155; shelter 69, 71; site 162; thermodynamic principles 212
built environment 54–5, 61–2, 64, 73, 78, 82
Buranakarn, V. 30, 78
Burj Khalifa 200
Bürolandschaft 73
Bush, G.W. 192
Butcher, L. 175
Butler, S. 73

California 182
Calthorpe, P. 171–2
Campbell, D. 149
Campbell, E.T. 102
carbon cycle 100, 137, 172
Caribbean 187
Carnot, S. 25, 27, 31, 34, 36, 54, 95, 145
Carrier, W. 81, 95, 97
Carroll, G. 170
cars 233–4
Cedar Creek Bog 37
Center for Advanced Computation (CAC) 30
central heating 82, 88, 106, 117
central place theory 166

Chautauqua 175, 179, 181
Chicago 8
China 202
Christaller, W. 166
Clausius, R. 25, 34, 36, 54
Clean Water Act 132
cleaning 126–7
Clements, F. 17
climate 4, 6, 11, 62–3, 65; change 183–4, 191, 204, 209; glass walls 13; maximum power 21, 41, 44; modification 70, 75, 80–115, 117, 140, 182; narratives 202, 207; shelter 69, 72, 93, 95, 111, 113–14, 206; site 162–3, 179
climax forest 16–17, 42, 50, 53, 185
co-cycling 18, 200, 205
coal 24–5, 40, 70, 78, 83; narratives 209; setting 128, 141, 145; shelter 98; site 164, 174, 186
coefficient of performance (COP) 27
cogeneration 146
The Collapse of Complex Societies 47
combined heat and power (CHP) 146
comfort 80–2, 86–90, 98, 100, 104, 111, 113, 117
commercial buildings 4, 72–3, 80, 95, 99; setting 126, 149–50; shelter 106–8, 111, 113, 115; site 180
Commerzbank 13
common good 192
commuters 172, 181, 241–2
complex systems 6
composting 134, 138–9
concentrated power 126, 139–52, 154, 199, 208
Congress 108
Connecticut 172
construction 14, 70–80, 106, 118, 166, 180, 232–3
consumers, definition 216
consumption 14, 22–3, 28, 31, 66; e[m]ergy synthesis 220; maximum power 40–1; narratives 199, 201–3, 205, 208–9, 211, 220; setting 125–8, 133, 135, 138, 140–1, 152, 154; shelter 79, 90, 96, 100, 109, 118; site 161, 175, 184, 187, 191
The Conundrum 41, 173
Cook, R.E. 37

Index

cooking 126–7, 145, 155
cooling *see* heating and cooling
core-periphery model 166, 168, 171, 174–5
correalism 5–8, 62
corrosion 125, 137
Costanza, R. 171
Cowan, S. 201
Cowles, H. 17
Cradle to Cradle 137
cradle-to-cradle assessment 22, 30–1
Cristelli, M. 170–1
cultural evolution 186–92
currency 150–2, 180, 186, 191, 193
cybernetics 5, 17, 32, 46, 82
Cybernetics or Control and Communication in the Animal and the Machine 32

Daly, H. 151
damage-oriented protocol 31
Darwin, C. 31–3, 35, 73, 179
daylight 13, 27, 91, 105–7, 109–10, 207
decomposition 137
demand 4, 96, 102, 111, 127–8, 140, 148, 168
dematerialization 125–6, 140, 151, 162, 193, 206
Department of Defense 102
depreciation 49, 52, 72, 75–6, 181; e[m]ergy synthesis 232–3; setting 148; shelter 79, 88, 97
desertification 21, 185
design methods 204–10
design-for-disassembly 202
designers 6, 13, 16, 21, 63; maximum power 29, 31, 40; narratives 201, 203, 207, 211–12; setting 148, 154; shelter 69, 73; site 163
determinism 17, 186–7
deterritorialization 162
Detroit 163
diagramming language 43–4
Dickens, C. 127–8
dimensions 244
disposal 76–8
dissipative systems 32
DNA 22
Dongtan 210

Doorn Manifesto 164
Douglas, M. 139
downcycling 78
Drinker, E. 129
Drinker, H. 129
Dubai 8, 200
Duffy, F. 73
dynamic building behavior 86–8

Earle, T. 187
Eco-Indicator 99 31
ecocities 210
Ecological Design 201
ecological succession 47–8
ecologists 46, 171, 209
econometrics 150
economic crises 180, 204
economic hierarchies 183–92
economic locations 161–98
economic production 4–5
economies of scale 132, 166, 168
economists 5, 40–1, 63, 70, 140; setting 150–1; site 165, 179–80, 185, 187
ecosystems ecology 3
Ecotopia 191, 210
ecotopias 16–18, 162, 209
Edison, T. 105–6
education 148–50
efficiency 4, 8–10, 13, 18, 25; limitations 26–7; maximum power 27–8, 31–2, 34–7, 40–2, 44–5, 54; narratives 200, 202, 205–6; setting 125, 134–5, 144–6, 149–52, 154; shelter 69, 79, 83–4, 90–1, 93, 95–6, 99–100, 105, 108–10, 113, 117–18; site 161–2, 169, 172–3, 175, 179, 181, 183–6, 192; thermodynamic principles 211
Eighth Day 17
electricity 41–2, 145–7, 184, 193
elevation 163
elites 189
Ellis House 66–7, 73, 79–80, 86–7, 89; e[m]ergy synthesis 219–45; setting 134–5, 137–9, 145, 147–9, 152, 154–5, 208; shelter 95–7, 99, 102, 109–11, 113, 115, 117; site 165, 179–81, 191; systems language 216

Index

e[m]ergy 41–5, 53–4, 66, 71, 76; narratives 205–6, 208; setting 126–7, 134–5, 137–41, 144–9, 152, 154; shelter 79–80, 82–3, 88–90, 93, 96, 108–10, 114–15, 117–18; site 162, 174–5, 179–81, 187, 191–2; synthesis 219–45; systems language 216
e[m]ergy yield ratio (EYR) 144–6, 152
energy 3–5, 7–8, 10–11, 21, 64–5; density 141–5; ecotopias 18; embodied 22, 24, 28–31, 43, 70, 137, 171; forms 48; glass walls 13–14; intensity 30; maximum power 21; production hierarchies 41–4; quality 27–31; shelter 79; supply crises 11, 29, 91, 99, 204; systems language 215–18; thermodynamics 24; transformation hierarchies 41–4
energy circuits, definition 216
Energy Information Agency (EIA) 139
energy recovery ventilators (ERVs) 100, 102
energy return on investment (EROI) 143–4
energy use intensities (EUI) 91
EnergyStar rating system 22
engineers 81, 130
entropy 24–6, 31–2, 36–8, 46–7, 53–4, 70, 93, 151–2
environment 6, 21–60
Environmental Accounting 43
environmental accounting 22–4, 27
environmental costs 27, 65, 83, 96–7, 109; comparison 219–21; narratives 205–6; setting 132, 147, 154; shelter 115
environmental design 3–5, 9, 16, 64, 67; ecotopias 18; maximum power 24, 31, 33, 35–6, 40, 53; narratives 199–214; setting 129, 146, 150, 155; site 162, 170, 173, 183, 188, 192; thermodynamic principles 210–12
environmental impact 22–3, 27–8, 31, 96, 161, 201–2, 215
environmental loading ratio (ELR) 221
Environmental Protection Agency (EPA) 22, 76
environmentalists 8, 40–1, 82, 138, 209
Erewhon 73
Essay on the Principle of Population 33
ethics 21–2, 61, 98, 192
Euclidean geometry 210

Europe 9, 13, 16, 142
European Union (EU) 189, 210
evaluation 5, 7, 14, 23, 27; building envelopes 88–90; location 179–83; maximum power 41, 45, 47, 51; narratives 204–6; setting 134, 142, 144, 147–8; shelter 75, 78–9, 108, 110, 118; site 162, 166, 171
evolution 6, 14, 16–18, 55, 61–2; maximum power 24, 32–3, 35, 42, 48; shelter 72–3, 117–18; site 164
exergy 26–8, 44, 46
explicit heat 93

factcheck.org 183
Fairmount Water Works 127–8
Farley, J. 151
Federal Reserve 180
Federal Water Pollution Control Act 132
feedback devices 45–6, 50, 81–3, 168, 192, 201
Fernández-Galiano, L. 29, 53, 150
fertilizer 242–3
first law of thermodynamics 5, 25–7, 31–2, 41, 43, 46, 76, 145–6, 171
first-order cities 168–9, 171
Fisher, I. 185–6
Fitch, J.M. 90
Florida 130, 171
food chain 22, 24, 37, 41–2, 45, 53, 135, 141
food supply 135–6, 140, 236
food web 64
Ford Foundation 101
Forrester, J.W. 43, 192
fossil fuels 141–2, 145, 162, 173
Four Books 49
fourth law of thermodynamics 36
France 135, 171
Frankfurt 13
Freedom Tower 200
fuels 141–5, 148–9, 151, 161–2, 164; narratives 205–6, 209; site 168, 172–4, 184, 186, 191, 193; thermodynamic principles 211
Fujita, M. 163
Fuller, R.B. 5–7
fund-of-services 70, 75
future research 67, 79

Index

gain-to-loss ratio 86–7
gain-to-mass ratio 86–7
Geddes, P. 117, 164
general processes, definition 216
Georgescu-Roegen, N. 151
Germany 66
Gibbs, J.W. 26, 46
Giedion, S. 16, 72, 129
Glaeser, E. 161–2, 172–3, 182
glare 8, 12
Glasarchitektur 8
glass walls 8–16, 18, 81, 91, 110, 200–1, 206
Gleason, H.A. 17
globalization 162, 206
Gordon, A. 202
Gore, A. 183–4, 192
gray water 132
green building design 22, 203
Green Globes 22
green high-rises 13
Green Metropolis 172
green roofs 14, 200
greenhouses 101
gross domestic product (GDP) 151, 173

Hall, C.A.S. 143
Hamburg 73
Hardin, G. 179
Hawkes, D. 90, 206
health 13
heat gain 8
heat loss 8
heat recovery ventilators (HRVs) 100
heat sinks, definition 217
heating and cooling 93–7, 140, 147
Helmholtz, H. von 25
hierarchical cascades 53, 114–15
historians 203
Holling, C.S. 50–1
homeowners 239–42
Honfang Lu 149
House of the Future 125
households 187, 189, 191–2
Howe, G. 95
human environments 6
humidity 10, 81, 90, 93, 97, 99–100, 206–7
Hutchinson, G.E. 37

identity 162
illumination 103–10
incinerators 138
income 243–4
An Inconvenient Truth 183
Industrial Dynamics and World Dynamics 43
Industrial Revolution 128, 148, 151
inequity 184, 186–7, 192
inertia 162
information society 49
information in systems 45–9, 69–70, 73, 75, 81, 147–50, 183, 208–10
information theory 32, 47–8
infrastructures 6–7, 16, 79, 103, 106; narratives 200, 202, 206, 210; setting 130, 134, 142–3; shelter 108, 115; site 162, 165, 171, 180–1, 183, 187
innovation 6, 16, 22–3, 26, 34; maximum power 41; narratives 209; setting 126, 128, 149, 151; shelter 82, 91, 97–8, 108; site 173
input-output (I-O) analysis 29–30, 43, 137
insulation 11, 66, 79–81, 83, 86–9, 113–14, 117, 200, 207
interactions, definition 217
International Living Future Institute 23
international space station 100
investment 25, 61, 72, 79–80, 88; setting 138, 142–3, 149, 152; shelter 106, 108–9, 111, 115, 118; site 162, 168, 171, 179, 187
invisible hand 5

Jablonka, E. 62
Jencks, C. 203
Jevon, W.S. 40, 127, 172
Jobard, J.-B. 8
Johnson, A. 187
Joule, J.P. 25–6, 34, 44, 54
junkspace 206–7

Kelly, K. 16
Khazzoom-Brookes postulate 40
Kiesler, F. 6, 62, 73, 106
Koolhaas, R. 110, 206–7

Index

Krugman, P. 168
Kurtz, J. 175

labor 239–42
lamps 103–10
land ethic 22
land use 53, 162, 172, 174, 179
land-rent theory 166
landfills 76, 78, 138, 211
Larkin Building 95
Lavoisier, A. 32
law 6, 82, 91, 108, 132
layers of construction 79–80
Le Corbusier 9, 11, 72
Leadership in Energy and Environmental Design (LEED) 22–3, 200, 205
least effort principle 169
LEDs 108–10
leisure time 125, 150, 154–5, 208
Leontief, W. 29–30
Leopold, A. 22
Lescaze, W. 10, 95
leverage points 210–11
life cycle assessment (LCA) 22, 28, 30, 76, 137, 148
life-cycle inventory (LCI) 30
Limits to Growth 43
Limits to Growth: The 30-Year Update 192
Lindeman, R. 37, 42, 54, 215
linguists 168
Lippincott, M. 66
livability index 61
Living Building Challenge (LBC) 23–4
living systems 24–53
location 4, 44, 63–5, 83, 161–98, 206, 208–11
logic types 6
long-life-loose-fit approach 118, 202
longevity 79–80, 107, 162, 212
longitude 163
Loomis, A. 10
Lösch, A. 166
lossiness 86–7, 111, 113, 207
Lotka, A. 32–6, 38, 41–2, 49, 54, 204
Lovins, A. 41
Luxfer glass 106–7
luxuries 6, 69, 82, 95, 134–5, 191, 199–201

Macao 175
McDonough, W. 78, 137, 139
maintenance 72, 102, 139, 147, 150, 152, 180
Maison Citrohan 9
Malthus, T. 33–4
Mandeville, B. 5
Manhattan 172, 175, 179
market system 5
Masdar 209
material selection 3–5, 8, 18, 65, 67; cycles 49–53; e[m]ergy synthesis 220–1; maximum power 22–3, 55; narratives 202–3, 207; setting 137–9; shelter 70–1, 76, 78–9, 118; thermodynamic principles 211
material services 126–39
maximum economy principles 72
maximum power environments 21–61, 111, 114, 117–18, 200–2; narratives 205, 208–9; setting 145, 150, 155; site 171, 183, 186, 191; thermodynamic principles 211
Maxwell, J.C. 46
Mayer, J. von 25–6, 32, 34, 44, 54
Meadows, D. 210
mechanical approach 90–3
mechanical selection 72–3
Mechanization Takes Command 129
media 125, 150, 155, 162, 203
megacities 173–4, 207
metering 128, 130
methane 138
metrics 5, 23, 31, 44, 142, 144, 150, 174
migration 170, 173
military 191
miners 24
Moe, K. 207
monetary flow 137
money 150–2, 186
multiple-scale design 204–10
Mumford, L. 117, 164
mur neutralisant 9

narratives 199–214
NASA 21, 100, 102
Nashville 183–4

National Renewable Energy Laboratory (NREL) 30
Native Americans 186
natural environments 6
natural selection 15, 17, 22, 34–7, 42, 62, 72–3
naturalists 17
net zero energy (NZE) 23, 66–7, 70, 79–80, 93; narratives 200, 202–3, 205–7; setting 146–7; shelter 118; site 161, 191
net zero waste 202, 205
Netherlands 31, 187
New Alchemists 201
new economic geography 168
New York 200
New York Times 179
Newcomen, T. 24
Niagara Falls 12
nomads 42, 184
North America 16
Norway 186
nostalgia 108, 164

Occidental Chemical Company 12
Odum, H.T. 3, 34, 37–8, 40–3, 45, 47, 49, 52–4, 62, 76, 96, 114, 149, 152, 170–1, 215
Oldfield, P. 90–1
Olgyay brothers 81
O'Neill, G. 100
operating costs 13
Operating Manual for Spaceship Earth 5, 7
orderliness 32
Origin of Species 73
Orr, D. 210
outcomes 117, 138
overcrowding 4
Owen, D. 41, 172–3
Ozenfant, A. 72

Pacific Rim 207
Palladio, A. 49
Passivhaus 66–7, 70, 79–80, 87–9, 93; narratives 207; setting 134, 147, 154; shelter 99–100, 109–11, 113, 115, 118; site 181
peak oil 209
Pennsylvania 172

people 93, 97–8, 127, 133, 149, 154, 162, 184, 187
performance design 18, 204
Philadelphia 66, 86–7, 89, 113, 127–9, 165, 172, 181
photosynthesis 100
photovoltaics 27, 93, 110, 118, 146–7; narratives 200–1, 203, 205–7; site 174, 179, 181
physics 32, 38, 80, 170
physiocrats 150
Pinkerton, R.C. 38, 40
planting 101–2
plate tectonics 163
pollution 4, 22, 33, 62, 96, 189; narratives 199, 202–3; setting 125–6, 132, 155; shelter 98–100, 102, 105
population growth 4, 14, 24, 33–4, 37; narratives 201; site 162–4, 166, 168–70, 173, 184, 187–8
potlach ceremonies 186
poverty 161, 166
power 4–5, 14, 16, 18, 126; concentrated 126, 139–52, 154, 199, 208; maximum 21–61, 111, 114, 117–18, 145, 150, 155, 171, 183, 186, 191, 200–2, 205, 208–9, 211; shelter 79, 90–1, 110–11, 114, 117–18; site 184–5, 187
power-operated solutions 69–70, 81–2, 90–1, 115, 118
predator-prey dynamic 23, 33, 36, 42, 46, 50
Prigogine, I. 32
Princeton 12
prismatic optics 106
probability theory 32
process analysis 30
producers, definition 217
production hierarchies 4, 41–5, 49, 53–4, 65, 187, 199
productivity 13, 34, 45, 82, 95; setting 125–6, 150–1, 154–5, 207–8; shelter 104, 108, 118; site 161–2, 166, 173, 185, 187
profit 52, 166
prosperity 161–2, 173, 179, 188, 192
Prudential Enerplex 12
PSFS Building 95
psychrometric charts 81

Index

public health 129
pulsing of systems 49–54
Purists 72

Quakers 129
quality measures 27, 42, 44–6, 64, 79; narratives 206, 209; setting 126, 136, 140–1, 145, 147, 152, 155; shelter 82–3, 90, 96–7, 105, 115; site 162–3, 171–3, 183, 189, 191–3; thermodynamic principles 211
Quickborner Team 73

rainfall 163, 165, 181, 185, 230–1
rates of change 72, 75, 86, 162, 209
Raugei, M. 76
real estate 15, 55, 61, 63, 89, 179–80, 203
rebound effect 40–1
recycling 17, 30, 37, 52–3, 76–8; narratives 200, 202; setting 132, 134, 137–9, 146
red lists 23
Reflections on the Motive Power of Fire 25
regions 161–2, 165–6, 168, 170, 175, 189, 191
renewable resources 5, 64, 82, 97, 118; narratives 203, 206, 209; setting 142–3, 147, 152; site 173–5, 191
reproduction rates 173
resilience 50, 53, 118, 199
Resilience and Stability 50
resource curse 185–6, 188
reterritorialization 191, 206
returns on investment (ROI) 143, 168
Ricardian land 165
Rio da Janeiro 173
Roadmap 2050 142, 210
Roman Empire 127
Rome 127, 174–5
Rumford, Count 26

St Gobain Glass Company 9
San Diego 132–3
San Juan 175
São Paulo 173
Saunders, H. 40
Savery, T. 24
scalarity 204–12
Scandinavia 11

scarcity 5, 21, 34, 36, 40, 54, 62, 130, 199
Scheerbart, P. 8
Schrodinger, E. 32, 46
scope of analysis 27–31
Scottish Enlightenment 5
screen-based activities 125, 154, 208
second law of thermodynamics 5, 25–7, 31–2, 34, 36; maximum power 38, 43–4, 46, 52; narratives 199; shelter 70, 83, 93
Second World War 135
second-order cities 168–9, 171
self-organization 4–5, 16–18, 21–4, 61–3, 65; definition 217; maximum power 34–5, 41–2, 44–5, 50, 52–5; narratives 205, 209–10; shelter 90, 96, 110, 114; site 170–1, 183, 188; systems language 215; thermodynamic principles 212; urban 163–83
services review 22
setting 4, 18, 62–7, 80, 125–60, 206–8, 215
sewage 127, 129, 132–3, 139, 201
Shannon, C.E. 32
shearing layers 73–5
shelter 4, 18, 61–7, 69–124, 134; maximum power 49; narratives 201, 206–7; setting 140, 152; site 182; systems language 215
Shu Li Huang 174
sick building syndrome 99, 102
simulations 5, 84, 86
site 4, 62–7, 73, 80, 161–98; ecotopias 18; narratives 206, 208–10; setting 140; systems language 215
slaves 161, 174
slums 172
Smart Architecture 73, 208–10
Smil, V. 142
Smith, A. 5
Smithson, A. 164
Smithson, P. 164
social hierarchies 183–92
Soddy, F. 180
software 31, 73, 75, 208
solar collectors 4, 12, 27, 142, 147, 181
Solar Decathlon buildings 27
solar emjoule (sej) 43–4
solar gain 12, 113
solar panels 14, 184
sources, definition 217

South America 189
Southeast Asia 189
space exploration 100
spatial hierarchies 163–83
spectrum of intensities 53, 115, 117–18, 125–6, 154
sprawl 163, 172, 174
Srinivasan, R. 76
standardization 72
steam power 24–5, 32, 40, 44–6, 50, 128
Stein, R. 29
storage, definition 217
Stowe, H.B. 73
structural solutions 69–70, 81, 115
Stuttgart 9
summary tables 221
sunlight 221
supplies 136–40, 237
survival of fittest 21, 35, 40
survivalists 18, 147, 150, 191, 199–200, 202
sustainability 5, 16, 23, 31, 33; maximum power 50; narratives 203, 205, 210; shelter 108; site 161, 188; thermodynamic principles 211
swamp coolers 95
Sweden 135, 144
Sweet's Catalog 72
Switzerland 9, 186
synergy 5–8, 17
Systems Ecology 43
systems ecology 18, 61–2, 65–7, 76, 79–80; narratives 201, 205, 209–10; site 187; thermodynamic principles 212
systems theory 5, 17, 34, 43, 46, 54–5, 192

Tainjin 210
Tainter, J. 47
Taipei 179, 189
Taiwan 174, 188–9
taxes 130, 180–1, 191
technocracy 6
technology 4–8, 18, 22, 26, 62; maximum power 34–5, 40, 47–9; narratives 201, 209–10; setting 127–9, 137, 140, 148–51, 155; shelter 81–2, 90–1, 95, 106, 108, 114, 117–18; site 162, 173, 186–7
technosphere 130, 137
television 125, 148, 150, 208

Ten Shades of Green 202
Ternoey, S. 90
territorialization 22
Theory of the Location of Industries 168
thermodynamics 3–5, 14, 18, 61–3, 66; building envelopes 88–9; maximum power 22, 24, 32–3, 46–7, 49, 53–4; minimum 115–18; narratives 199–214; natural selection 34–7; principles 210–12; setting 126, 133–5, 137–40, 149–52, 154; shelter 70–2, 75–6, 78–80, 82–4, 91, 95, 100, 102–3, 110, 113–14; site 161, 163, 179–80, 183, 185, 187–8, 192; statistical 32; systems language 215
thermostats 46, 50, 69, 82, 118, 208
Thinking in Systems 210
third law of thermodynamics 36
third-order cities 168–9
Thoreau, H.D. 17
Tilley, D. 102, 148
time constants 86–7, 110, 113, 207
toilets 126, 132–4
toplighting 105–6
topography 163, 165, 168, 180
tourism 187
trade 49, 161, 165, 170–1, 179–80, 191, 201
traffic jams 210
transactions, definition 218
transportation 6, 8, 14, 30, 66; maximum power 34; narratives 200, 209; setting 135, 154; shelter 70, 76; site 166, 168, 172, 174, 179–81, 193
trash 135, 137–8
Triumph of the City 172
trophic webs 42
"Trophic-Dynamic Aspect of Ecology" 37, 215
tropical rain forests 16

Ulanowicz, R. 25, 46–7, 51
Ulgiati, S. 76
underfloor air distribution systems (UFAD) 97
unit e[m]ergy values (UEV) 220
United Kingdom (UK) 171
United States Green Building Council (USGBC) 22–3

Index

United States (US) 12, 66, 72–3, 75–6, 93; maximum power 30, 41; narratives 202; setting 125, 132, 137, 139, 145, 148–9, 151–2; shelter 95, 108; site 163, 168, 172, 180, 182, 189, 191; thermodynamic principles 211
University of Chicago 17
University of Illinois 30
up-stream processes 29
upstream costs 71, 75, 83, 97, 140; setting 142; shelter 102, 104–5, 107–8, 114–15; site 173
urban agglomerations 4, 8, 64, 161–98
urbanization 168, 174
utilities 238–9

valley sections 164, 193
value theory 150, 165
Van der Ryn, S. 201
variations 35–6, 48, 79, 117, 168, 171, 180
ventilation 13, 98–102, 117, 140
Vernadsky, V. 185
Villa Rotunda 49
Villa Schwob 9
Vision California 172
Von Thünen, H. 166, 168, 172

Warr, B. 40, 152
wars 186
washing 127, 132, 134
waste 3–4, 8, 31, 62, 65; heat 110–15; maximum power 35–7, 44–5, 53; narratives 199, 201–2; processing 98–102; setting 126, 132, 135, 137, 139–41, 145–6, 154–5; shelter 70, 78, 93, 128; site 161, 174–5, 188; solid 136–9, 237–8; thermodynamic principles 211
wastewater treatment 132–4, 235–6
water 125, 127–9, 137, 140, 145; e[m]ergy synthesis 234–6; setting 147, 154; site 163–4, 186, 189; supply 130–2
Watt, J. 24, 44–5
wealth 4–8, 14, 18, 31, 62; maximum power 41, 52–3; narratives 199–200; setting 127–8, 132, 150–2, 154–5; shelter 65, 104; site 161–2, 166, 172–5, 180, 183–7, 189, 191–3
Weber, A. 168
Weissenhof Siedlung 9
West Virginia 175
White, L. 186–7
Wi-Fi 125, 155
Wiener, N. 32
wind 231–2
windows 103–10, 113–14
wood 24, 142, 144, 165
work 4–5, 7, 18, 21, 65–6; of living 125–60; maximum power 24–7, 29–32, 41, 44–6, 51, 53; narratives 204, 206; setting 130, 133–5, 137, 140, 144–5, 148–9, 151–2, 208; shelter 70–1, 75–6, 83, 89, 108, 110, 113; site 171, 175, 179, 184, 187
World3 model 192
Wright, F.L. 95

Yale University 37, 46
Yeang, K. 207

Zipf distribution 168, 170
Zipf, G.K. 168–70
zoning 203